Event History Analysis in Life Course Research

Life Course Studies
David L. Featherman
David I. Kertzer
  Series Editors

Nancy W. Denney
Thomas J. Espenshade
Dennis P. Hogan
Jennie Keith
Maris A. Vinovskis
  Associate Series Editors

Event History Analysis in Life Course Research

Edited by

Karl Ulrich Mayer and Nancy Brandon Tuma

The University of Wisconsin Press

The University of Wisconsin Press
114 North Murray Street
Madison, Wisconsin 53715

3 Henrietta Street
London WC2E 8LU, England

Library of Congress Cataloging-in-Publication Data
Event history analysis in life course research / edited by Karl Ulrich
   Mayer and Nancy Brandon Tuma.
      320 pp.   cm. —(Life course studies)
   Revised version of the papers presented at a conference held at
the Max Planck Institute for Human Development and Education in
Berlin on June 5–7, 1986.
   Includes bibliographical references.
   1. Event history analysis—Congresses.   2. Life cycle, Human—
Congresses.   I. Mayer, Karl Ulrich.   II. Tuma, Nancy Brandon.
III. Series.
H61.E94   1989
301—dc20   89–40261
ISBN 0–299–12200–X   CIP
ISBN 0–299–12204–2 (pbk.)

Contents

III. Methodological Issues

Contributors

Gerhard Arminger, Gesamthochschule Wuppertal
Hans-Peter Blossfeld, European University Institute, Florence
Glenn R. Carroll, University of California, Berkeley
Andreas Diekmann, Universität Mannheim
David L. Featherman, University of Wisconsin–Madison and Social
    Science Research Council
Heinz P. Galler, Universität Bielefeld
Alfred Hamerle, Universität Konstanz
Jan M. Hoem, University of Stockholm
Johannes Huinink, Max-Planck-Institut für Bildungsforschung, Berlin
Reinhard Hujer, Johann Wolfgang Goethe-Universität Frankfurt
Judah Matras, Brookdale Institute for Human Development, Jerusalem,
    Carleton University, Ottawa, and University of Haifa
Karl Ulrich Mayer, Max-Planck-Institut für Bildungsforschung, Berlin
Trond Petersen, University of California, Berkeley
Ulrich Poetter, Johann Wolfgang Goethe-Universität Frankfurt
Bo Rennermalm, Statistics Sweden, Stockholm
Hilmar Schneider, Johann Wolfgang Goethe-Universität Frankfurt
Randi Selmer, University of Oslo
Yossi Shavit, University of Haifa
Aage B. Sørensen, Harvard University
Seymour Spilerman, Columbia University
Nancy Brandon Tuma, Stanford University
Michael Wagner, Max-Planck-Institut für Bildungsforschung, Berlin
Lawrence L. Wu, University of Wisconsin–Madison

Preface

Event history analysis, the use of discrete-state, continuous-time stochastic models to investigate sample path data on discrete variables (i.e., event history data), has been a major innovation in the analysis of temporal data in recent years. To date, event history analysis has influenced research in demography, economics, and sociology alike. In fact, it is beginning to help break down century-old barriers between these disciplines. Initially the main effort was to develop and explicate methods of event history analysis (or its simpler relative, survival analysis). Paramount concerns at the early stage included sorting out various types of time dependencies, struggling with the problem of population heterogeneity (especially unobserved heterogeneity), and solving problems of estimation in the face of incomplete data. Other concerns, at least as important, have been overcoming stumbling blocks involved in obtaining event history data, in organizing and manipulating large complex data files, in interpreting new kinds of coefficients, and in developing useful software for managing and analyzing event history data. Naturally, an important, on-going concern is to bring mathematical models of the occurrence of transitions and events over time into agreement with substantive theories of social change.

In reflecting on these previous efforts, we concluded that the time had come to make a sober assessment of the contribution of event history analysis to substantive problems in an area of great interest to both of us—life course research. To this end, on June 5–7, 1985, we convened a conference on applications of event history analysis to life course research at the Max Planck Institute for Human Development and Education (Max-Planck-Institut für Bildungsforschung) in Berlin. Four major groups helped to bring this conference into being.

(1) For several years a research program on "Life Course and Social Change" has been underway at the Max Planck Institute. The major task of this program is to collect and analyze retrospective life history data on five cohorts of West Germans: those born in 1929–1931, 1939–1941, 1949–1951 (already collected), 1919–1921 (in the field), and 1959–1961 (planned for 1988–1989). Members of the research team of the German

Life History Study have a special interest in event history analysis because they regard it as the most appropriate methodology for using these data to study the processes underlying job trajectories, class mobility, family formation, fertility, and migration.

(2) Since 1980 the U.S. Social Science Research Council's Committee on Comparative Stratification, chaired by David L. Featherman (University of Wisconsin–Madison), has sponsored a subcommittee on life history research in a cross-national context, and this subcommittee has had a special interest in event history analysis. The SSRC, therefore, made a portion of a substantial grant from the National Science Foundation available to support the conference by funding the attendance of young scholars.

(3) The Special Research Unit of the Deutsche Forschungsgemeinschaft on "Micro-analytic Foundations of Social Policy" (Sonderforschungsbereich 3), based in Frankfurt, Mannheim, and Berlin, has initiated a large socioeconomic panel involving about 6,000 households and 12,000 individuals. The prospect of analyzing these new data has led this group to make a major investment in the methods of longitudinal data analysis, including event history analysis.

(4) Finally, there is an informal German working group on mathematical sociology called MASO, which has a long-term commitment to bringing together formal models and substantive sociological research. The conference was the 1985 annual meeting of MASO.

With the support of these groups, the conference was unusually rich and intense. It included almost all West German social scientists using event history analysis and a strong contingent of its international protagonists. The conference provided the participants with a clear sense of progress. Social mobility research, for instance, is now beginning to give up conventional static comparisons over very unequal time intervals (e.g., comparisons of father's and son's statuses at unspecified times). Moreover, time-varying explanatory variables are increasingly being introduced into analyses—although the implications of the results are not always well understood. A piece-wise constant model of transition rates was surely the winner of the day: More analysts at the conference reported favorably on the usage of this model than on any other because of this model's great flexibility in representing dependencies of transition rates on both time and covariates.

This volume comprises a selection of revised versions of the papers presented at the conference. We greatly appreciate the initiative and unrelenting support of the general editors of the Life Course Series of the University of Wisconsin Press, especially David L. Featherman. We are especially indebted to the colleagues who took upon themselves the time-consuming task of reviewing the manuscripts: Charles E. Denk, David L.

Featherman, Michael T. Hannan, Christof Helberger, Olaf Huebler, Lothar Krempel, Heiner Meulemann, Hillmar Schneider, Aage B. Sørensen, Annemette Sørensen, Douglas A. Wolf, and Rolf Ziegler.

We also gratefully acknowledge the permission of Oxford University Press to reproduce parts of Karl Ulrich Mayer and Glenn Carroll's, "Jobs and Classes: Structural Constraints on Career Mobility," which appeared in the *European Sociological Review.* In addition, we thank the publishers of the *Journal of Mathematical Sociology* for letting us reprint Andreas Diekmann's article, "Diffusion and Survival Models for the Process of Entry into Marriage."

May 1988

Karl Ulrich Mayer   Nancy Brandon Tuma
Berlin   Stanford, California

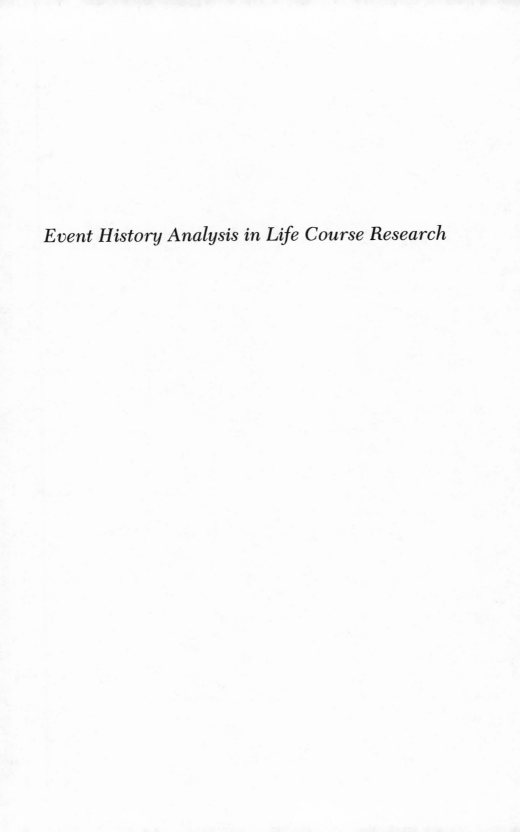

Event History Analysis in Life Course Research

1 *Karl Ulrich Mayer and Nancy Brandon Tuma*

Life Course Research and Event History Analysis: An Overview

In this collection we try to present exemplars of applications of event history analysis to life course research. The contributions deal with various substantive issues in life course research and with several unsolved methodological problems in event history analysis.

By life course research we mean the study of social processes extending over the individual life span or over significant portions of it, especially the family cycle (marriage and child-rearing), educational and training histories, and employment and occupational careers. The life course is shaped by, among other things, cultural beliefs about the individual biography, institutionalized sequences of roles and positions, legal age restrictions, and decisions of individual actors. The goal of life course research is not only to provide better descriptions and explanations of the processes shaping the life course, but also to link these together. Life course research is, we believe, an important—indeed, indispensable—instrument for studying societal change and differences between birth cohorts.

By event history analysis we mean various statistical methods for examining shifts between successive states (or categories) within some continuous interval of time on the basis of a complete temporal record for some sample. The states that can occur are discrete, and they are usually fairly small in number; in general the shifts (or transitions or events) may occur at any arbitrary point in time and are random (i.e., possibly predictable on the aggregate level but not for any individual). Thus, event history analysis involves statistical methods for analyzing what are called discrete-state, continuous-time stochastic processes in probability theory.

The relationship between event history analysis and life course research may be seen as the intersection of two lines of research. As a set of statistical models and methods, event history analysis is naturally applicable to many substantive problems other than the life course. Examples in sociology have included organizational dynamics (Hannan and Freeman 1988; Carroll 1987), class room processes (Felmlee and Eder 1983), political change (Hannan and Carroll 1981), and ethnic conflict and mobilization (Olzak 1986, 1987). Similarly, the life course has been studied with quite different methods (e.g., Hogan 1981; Oppenheimer 1981; Müller 1986). But we believe that event history analysis is especially congenial to research on life course dynamics. Indeed, event history analysis appears to have made a major breakthrough in life course research by providing an appropriate way of studying multiple time dependencies in social life—for example, aging in the individual life course, acquisition of experience and seniority rights with increasing duration in social positions, and changing societal conditions as history unfolds (Tuma and Hannan 1984; Featherman 1986).

We outline our views on both life course research and event history analysis in this introductory chapter. In the next section we discuss the life course as an emerging research program. Then we outline important features of event history analysis as a methodology and indicate a number of unresolved problems, giving special emphasis to those pertinent to chapters in this volume. The last section provides a guide to the various chapters in this volume and notes their contributions within the framework developed in the present chapter.

Life Course Research

Life course research is an interdisciplinary program of study that has been developing over the last decade or so. Though the individual is the unit of analysis in empirical research on the life course, the life course itself is an important element of social structure. The life events usually studied include leaving the parental home, marital formation and dissolution, births of children, job entry and exit, movement from one locale to another, and retirement. The states or role incumbencies that are typically examined include class and household membership, and educational, marital, and employment statuses. Still other role incumbencies could be studied— for example, political party membership, religious affiliation, participation in voluntary groups and activities—but as yet have received little attention by those employing event history methods. The "life course" includes *not only* the institutionalized sequences of events and activities in various life domains *but also* variations from the customary sequences.

Life course research has two main objectives: (1) to explain individual life events and social patterns of life trajectories within a common conceptual and empirical framework, and (2) to represent the social processes that generate these events and trajectories. It is innovative both in the particular substantive questions that it addresses and also in its potential for transcending long-held distinctions between micro- and macroanalyses of social life, and between theoretical schools and scientific disciplines. Due largely to common data and research designs, what was formerly separated into the fields of microeconomics, demography, sociology of the family, migration studies, and social mobility and status attainment research is being brought into common discourse, though it involves competing approaches and theories.

According to the life course paradigm, the life course of an individual is mainly a product of larger social forces and structures. But if the life course was *only* a product of existing social institutions, the details and variations in individuals' lives might be left for novelists and playwrights to consider. Social scientists could just look at the institutional rules. However, variations from the "standard" life course inevitably occur; often they reflect systematic social processes so that they are predictable on an aggregate level, if not for an individual. Moreover, variations from institutionalized patterns not only affect subsequent events in the life of any given individual but also can, when they occur in sufficient number at historically opportune times, generate new social structures and institutions. Social forces thus not only "trickle down" from social institutions to individuals' lives but also "percolate up" from individuals' actions to modify existing social patterns and institutions, and perhaps even create new ones.

Consider patterns of first marriage in industrialized societies. In the decade or so after World War II, first marriage rates for birth cohorts sharply rose and then fell with age; consequently, the timing of first marriage was concentrated within a relatively few years of the life span, especially for women. Social institutions strongly regulated the timing of what the participants themselves regarded as one of the most personal and individualistic aspects of the life course—choosing a life partner. But in recent decades the marked concentration in the timing of first marriage has eroded significantly for a variety of reasons, few of which concern preexisting institutional arrangements. Rather, it seems to have resulted partly from greater individual variation in the timing of other life events—leaving school, getting vocational training, entry into the work force, shifts among jobs, movement from region to region, and so forth. Another important factor is the gradually expanding number of individuals participating in nonmarital cohabitation, which is scarcely institutionally regulated at all. These variations from former social patterns pertaining to marriage and other major life events have helped to create new social patterns and/or to legitimate old ones—for example, the career woman, the grey-haired mother, the house husband, the permanently and intentionally childless couple, long-term cohabitation without an official marriage, and the marriagelike relationship between persons of the same sex.

What is the core of the life course perspective? The main assumptions can be expressed as a set of heuristic statements (see also Elder 1985; for basic tenets of life span psychology, see Baltes et al. 1986):

(1) Social structure is conceived as interrelated elements of varying duration, not as a cross-section of positions or persons with certain properties (Linton 1945; Blau 1984; Mayer 1986). A simple analogy might be a piece of rope that is composed of interwoven strands of fibers (interdependent social elements) of overlapping and different lengths (varying durations with different starting points). The system of elements can be explained as the product of individual action in specific but changing social contexts.

(2) The life course is an element of social structure that is a product of both individual action, organizational processes, and institutional and historical forces. It refers to socially patterned trajectories, not to individual biographies.

(3) Life courses emerge in particular historical settings. From a historical perspective, they have become an important part of the study of social structure only recently. This has happened because individuals have become more differentiated from one another and from the larger social groups to which they belong (e.g., their families, work organizations, churches, and towns) and because individual actions are increasingly governed by distinct institutional domains (e.g., schools and the labor market as contrasted with the family) (Mayer and Müller 1986) so that individuals move from one institutional domain to another over time (e.g., from school to the army to employment to a retirement community). An added impetus to the study of the life course in modern times (Elder 1985) is the increased instability of primary groups (families and households), which individuals pass through in ways that are loosely coupled to their moves through larger institutional domains.

(4) Individual life courses must be considered within the context of the collective life trajectories of birth cohorts. Competition between members of different birth cohorts and also of the same cohort (e.g., a job or

marriage squeeze) is a population-level process shaping the life course (Featherman 1986).

(5) Research on the life course needs to use both a multilevel and multitime framework. With regard to levels, it needs to relate individual development, formal organizations (e.g., schools, firms), cohorts, ethnic groups, localities, and nation states. With regard to time, it needs to relate individual time (e.g., age, duration in a social position), organizational time (e.g., age of a firm), historical eras (e.g., the "war" years), and point-in-time events (e.g., a change in national laws). Our point is not only that these distinctions *should* be made conceptually, but also that event history analysis *allows* them to be integrated into formal, testable models (Tuma and Hannan 1984; Mayer and Huinink 1989).

(6) The life course is not identical with aging. Age subcultures and patterns of age norms are secondary rather than primary determinants of the life course. From a life course perspective, duration in a position or situation is often more important than chronological age (for an example in this volume, see Petersen and Spilerman). Psychological development and biological aging are independent mechanisms that partly condition the life course.

(7) Events within single life domains (such as job shifts in a occupational career or the birth of children within a fertility history) usually cannot be explained without reference to events in other life domains.

(8) Life course research is based on the testable proposition that single events or life phases cannot be adequately understood in isolation (e.g., as in a "sociology of youth" or a "sociology of old age"). Rather, life events and phases must be studied as part of a life trajectory in which later outcomes are partly consequences of earlier conditions, events, and experiences. The life course constitutes an endogenous causal system.

(9) Timing of life events is highly contingent. "Early" or "late" events often have substantial impacts on subsequent outcomes because they affect the amount of exposure to critical experiences, the amount of time remaining for other life activities, and perceptions of relative social success or failure. The impacts are often both unintended and unforeseen.

These tenets of the life course perspective do not arise de novo, of course. Life course research has at least three main precursors: social mobility research, studies of aging, and social biography. It has, however, challenged each of these precursors in at least one main way that pertains to event history analysis.

Advocates of a life course approach have taken issue with conventional social mobility studies that represented mobility either through a single transition matrix (usually comparing social positions of members of two generations, such as fathers and sons, at two poorly specified times), or through a set of linear equations relating statuses at a few points in time (e.g., most status attainment studies). In contrast, life course advocates argue that social mobility can and should be conceived and modeled as event histories—sequences of moves and events unfolding over time (for the life course side, see Tuma 1976; Mayer and Carroll 1987; Sørensen 1987; for the mobility side of the controversy, see Erikson and Goldthorpe 1987).

A second challenge concerns the relation of theories of the life course to earlier theories of aging. Most aging theorists have stressed the primordial character of age distinctions and the primary, self-contained nature of social age differentiation and age norms (Riley et al. 1972; Neugarten et al. 1965; Foner and Kertzer 1978). In contrast, recent approaches to the life course emphasize its embeddedness in institutional domains. The latter greatly expands the scope of the issues addressed and calls for a more contingent, more historical perspective than was found in theories of aging. As noted earlier, event history analysis both raises the question of multiple time dimensions and offers an empirical solution to studying these. Age is one time dimension, perhaps a very important one. But its importance is an issue for empirical research, not a presupposition.

A third precursor to life course research is biographical studies (Bertaux and Kohli 1984). Around 1970 it was still the case that social demography and biography were poles apart in terms of number of variables versus number of cases. In Galtung's (1967) typology it seemed almost a necessity to distinguish research designs with many variables on a very few cases (biographies, case studies) from designs combining a few variables with many cases (social demography). Large-scale, over-time surveys and contemporary methodology (especially event history analysis) make this distinction partially obsolete when studying individuals' lives. Now the advantages of a large representative sample and comparability of measurement can be combined with many of the advantages provided by the multivariable richness of individual biographies. As a result, traditional biographical research has lost much of its claim to distinctiveness. In fairness, it must be said that biographical research retains a unique domain: subjective interpretation; biography as active, meaning producing self-reconstruction; and linguistic and phenomenological analysis of narratives.

In sum, what does event history analysis offer life course research? Most important, it helps social scientists to see patterns in variation over time—to detect order in apparent disorder. It also helps in disentangling forces occurring on different levels of aggregation (e.g., the individual, family, local neighborhood, class, ethnic group, birth cohort) and also in distinguishing between different time dimensions (e.g., age, duration in a given social status, exposure to a particular social situation, historical eras, and point-in-time events). Of course, other methods have similar goals. But event history analysis is especially well-suited to this task: It provides not only methodological tools but also concepts pertinent to the most subtle issues in life course research. Its inherent focus on the unfolding of interdependent events over time meshes well with the key themes of life course research itself.

Event History Analysis

Event history data provide information on the *times* during a specified interval (i.e., a continuous "observation period") when members of a sample change from one discrete state of the outcome to another, plus the *sequence of states* that they occupy. That is, for each member of the sample, it consists of the sequence of times of changes and of the discrete states occupied, $\{t_0, y_0, t_1, y_1, \ldots, t_n, y_n\}$, where n is the number of changes in state, and t_0 and y_0 are the starting time and starting state, respectively. Usually n varies across members of the sample; t_0 and y_0 often vary as well. There are often supplementary data on miscellaneous covariates thought to affect the timing and nature of changes. The covariates may describe attributes of the individuals experiencing the events, of some larger collectivity to which they belong, or of environmental conditions. Covariates may vary over time, or not.

Event history analysis refers to the methods that exploit all of the information in such data. Some methods of analyzing such data are primarily descriptive in nature; their purpose is to find summary statistics that give an overall picture of the change process. Others are oriented toward testing whether two or more groups differ in the change process and are not concerned with the nature of the differences, except perhaps their general direction. Still others are based on estimation of fully or partially parametric models; the goal is to estimate parameters and draw inferences about them and to assess the overall fit of the model. An additional step, which is still rare, is to predict the consequences of some model that has been estimated for a population, either with the same initial conditions as those in the sample analyzed or with a somewhat altered set of conditions (e.g., after some hypothetical environmental change). This step is useful in assessing model fit for cases with unusual combinations of attributes, as well as for drawing policy implications from well-specified models (i.e., for social forecasting).

Precursors to these methods can be found in life table analysis in demography, in biostatistics (especially in studies of mortality after various medical interventions), in quality control in engineering, and in operations research (where the typical problem has been to derive implications of a model rather than to estimate model parameters from empirical data). In recent years, methods for analysis of event history data have been extended rapidly within sociology (Tuma 1976; Tuma et al. 1979; Tuma and Hannan 1984) and in economics (various papers by Heckman and co-authors; Amemiya 1985). Several basic texts are now available (Kalbfleisch and Prentice 1980; Coleman 1981; Lawless 1982; Allison 1984; Blossfeld, Hamerle, and Mayer 1986 and 1989; Namboodiri and Suchindram 1987).

We do not give a formal statement of basic concepts and terms in event history analysis since such statements are readily available in texts like those mentioned above. Moreover, authors of most chapters in this volume define whatever terms they use. Instead we concentrate mainly on broad themes and key problems.

The first step in event history analysis is to specify the relevant *time domains* (e.g., age, duration in a state, historical time) and the *state space* of the outcome being studied (e.g., categories of occupational position in a study of occupational mobility). These seemingly prosaic tasks have critical consequences for the conclusions that are drawn.

It is possible, for example, that as *age* increases, change becomes less likely, but that as *duration* in a state increases, change becomes first more likely and then less likely, even though age and duration are positively correlated. For example, this seems to be the approximate pattern when the outcome is birth of the second child, where duration refers to the time since the first birth. Though such complex patterns of time dependence can be spurious (resulting from improper specification of the time domains, of the state space, or of factors promoting change), they can also be genuine. Moreover, they are often a key aspect of what one wants to study (see especially chapter 4 in this volume).

Proper specification of the state space is also crucial, though this fact is not always fully appreciated. Treating two distinct states as one (e.g., cohabitation as equivalent to unmarried, or alternatively, as equivalent to marriage) can lead to drastically different conclusions than those reached when the states are not combined but treated as distinct. It is obvious that combining two distinct states into one tends to lengthen the average time spent in the combined state. But, more important, it can alter the nature of the dependence of the change process on various dimensions of time and on various covariates. We admit that not much attention is given to this potential problem in the chapters that follow, except those by Mayer and Carroll (chapter 2) and Hoem et al. (chapter 11). We point to it primarily as an area for future work and as a possible difficulty that readers should keep in mind.

Proper specification of the dependence of the change process on time and on covariates is also very important, despite some evidence (e.g., Tuma and Michael 1986; Trussell and Richards 1985; chapter 12 in this volume) that qualitative conclusions about the effects of time and/or co-variates are often relatively insensitive to minor differences in the postulated relationships.[1] Concern with proper specification of parametric models used in event history analyses is a major theme of a number of chapters in this volume (see chapters 9, 10, 12, and 13). Given the attention devoted to this problem in this volume and in the field at large, it is worth noting some specific issues.

One concerns the parametric form of the model governing the change process. Most models are defined by expressing the *hazard rate* of an event—or the *transition rate* (or *intensity*) when a shift to one of several states is possible—as a specific function of relevant time dimensions (e.g., age and duration), measured covariates, and perhaps an unmeasured random disturbance. Hazard (and transition) rates can be defined mathematically in several ways (see Tuma and Hannan 1984, 71–73; Blossfeld et al. 1989, 31–33), but an intuitive approach seems more useful than a formal mathematical one for this discussion. Roughly, it measures the *probability per unit of time* that an event or transition occurs in an infinitesimal interval of time among those *at risk* during the particular time interval in question. Like probabilities, rates cannot be negative; however, as measures "per unit of time," they may exceed 1. They apply to those still "at risk" of the event, i.e., to those to whom the event *could* happen.[2] Other quantities can be derived from a rate model: the probability that an event has (or has not) occurred by some time, the probability density of an event at some time, the mean length of time until an event, and so forth.[3]

Models of (hazard or transition) rates typically postulate some specific relationship between the rate and one or more dimensions of time and of some number of covariates. Substantive arguments may lead one to think that as some measure of time increases, the rate rises or falls, or perhaps first rises and then falls (or vice versa). Similarly, substantive arguments may suggest that as some covariate increases, the rate rises or falls in

　　1. For a contrary view that stresses the sensitivity of results, see Heckman and Singer (1984).

　　2. This means that the probability of an event occurring can be low even though the rate is high simply because few are still at risk. For example, the probability of dying at age 100 is low even though mortality rates are high at old ages because few people live long enough to be a risk of dying at age 100.

　　3. Models can also be postulated in terms of these other quantities, and they sometimes are. For example, accelerated failure-time models are usually based upon postulates about the mean logarithm of the length of time in some state.

value, or perhaps has an even more complex pattern of variation. Model specification involves making valid assumptions about these relationships. Researchers seek to match key features of the mathematical form of their models with what they regard as key features of real-world processes. Arguments about the realism of this match are inevitable since theory rarely gives firm guidance concerning the mathematical form. Empirical attempts to assess the match naturally follow.

One of the aspects of proper specification discussed most often concerns the way in which the rate depends on time. There is a large list of possible specifications with mathematical forms that are convenient (often an unmentioned but important property) and that can be derived in some plausible way. For rates expected to change monotonically with time, there are Weibull, Gompertz, Makeham, and Gamma models (see Tuma and Hannan 1984, 221); for those expected to change nonmonotonically, there are inverse Gaussian, log-logistic, log-Gaussian, Sickle, and Hernes models; for a completely unspecified pattern there is Cox's (1972) model or a piece-wise constant rate model (Tuma et al. 1979). These possibilities are not exhaustive. Choosing among the alternatives a priori is rarely easy. Several chapters in this volume deal with this issue (see especially chapters 9 and 10).

Another issue involves proper specification of the effects of covariates in parametric models. The most common assumption is that a covariate has "proportional" effects, i.e., that, ceteris paribus, a change in a covariate induces a multiplicative change in rates that is independent of the value of time and other covariates. This assumption, which is used in a number of studies in this volume, can be tested and modified when found to be invalid. Though not really an unresolved methodological problem, it is often a practical problem for investigators whose samples are too small to permit convincing tests of this assumption.

A related issue concerns the functional form of the dependence of rates on covariates. In a sense, this is also not an open problem because investigators can modify their models to permit a wide variety of relationships between covariates and rates. But it is again a practical problem because certain relationships become standard (the usual one being that each covariate has a log-linear effect on the rate). Deviations from such an assumption are hard to detect without large samples. Chapters 14 and 15 in this volume help by discussing ways to test such assumptions, though this does not solve the sample-size problem.

Another issue that has received a great deal of discussion in the past few years is "unobserved heterogeneity"—random variation across sample members (or over time for the same sample member) due, for example, to measurement error in covariates, to omission of key explanatory factors, or to simple random shocks to the environment. Identifying differences between the parametric form of time dependence and unobserved heterogeneity is difficult because theories of the life course have yet to provide persuasive arguments about proper functional forms for either time dependence or sources of unobserved heterogeneity. Galler and Poetter (in chapter 12 of this volume) provide an empirical example that illustrates the difficulties that result.

Some issues involving modeling change over the life course have not been touched upon in this volume. One of these is the modeling of joint change in discrete and metric outcomes—for example, jointly modeling job shifts (a change in a discrete variable) and earnings fluctuations (a change in a metric variable). Tuma and Hannan (1984) discussed the need for such models, and Petersen (1988) has indicated some ways of approaching this problem. We hope to see new efforts on this topic in the near future.

The issues discussed above mainly pertain to efforts to develop models of the occurrence of events and transitions over the life course that are theoretically grounded and that depict reality as accurately as possible. Another set of issues concerns ways of dealing with various deviations between actual and ideal data.

For example, estimators used in event history analysis almost always assume that the times of events and transitions are measured precisely, but this is never the case. Instead, information on time is always rounded or grouped. Sometimes the deviations between actual and ideal measurements are substantial: the data may tell duration in a job only to the nearest month and dates of marriage to the nearest year. Such data are said to be "grouped" as long as no events are systematically omitted. Estimators can be developed for grouped data (and have been for some models), but most investigators usually ignore this subtlety. Yet this is dangerous. Inferences can be adversely affected by this practice, as the work reported in chapter 12 of this volume suggests.

Another deviation between actual and ideal data pertains to missing data on the "dependent" variable, which with event histories means the times and nature of events and transitions. Since missing data on a dependent variable often leads to bias in linear regression analysis, it seems clear that consequences in event history analysis are likely to be at least as severe, and probably more so. We are in great need of research on the consequences of such missing data in event history analysis and on post hoc procedures for adjusting for the missing information. This type of data imperfection is essentially ignored in the present volume.

One form of missing data *is* routinely discussed in event history analysis and incorporated into the estimation procedure for a model—censoring of information on the times and states occupied *after* the end of a given observation period, i.e., right-censoring of data. Indeed, one advantage of event history analysis is that it has made treatment of this form of missing data standard. Left-censoring, a related form of missing data in which there is no information on the times and/or nature of changes *before* the beginning of the observation period, occurs somewhat less often than right-censoring but is hardly ever discussed when it does occur. Moreover, actual attempts to correct for left-censoring in empirical applications of event history analysis are exceedingly rare. The acquisition of left-censored event history data usually leads, at best, to apologies for data deficiencies that are then ignored. Although the best solution to this problem is not to collect left-censored data, in some situations it is the only type of event history data that is possible. In view of this, satisfactory methods for dealing with left-censoring in empirical analyses need to be developed.

Another rarely discussed data problem is missing data on covariates that change over time, i.e., intermittent measurement of such covariates. This problem must be considered in conjunction with a modeling issue: From the viewpoint of theory, at what point in time *should* time-varying covariates be measured? Does the transition rate at time t depend on the covariate's value at the start of some spell, at time t, or at some time $s < t$? The first is a common assumption, and it is surely reasonable in some situations. It is clearly the most typical time when covariates are measured. The second is often a plausible assumption but covariates are not always measured at the time of the event. Sometimes the third seems appropriate because there is a lag between the triggering condition and the occurrence of an event. If the rate at time t depends on the covariate's value at some other time s, then the covariate needs to be measured at s. Yet, when a time-varying metric covariate is measured intermittently, the measurements almost never occur at the theoretically relevant times but at the ones that were convenient when collecting the data. Neither the consequences of such missing information nor ways of compensating for it has yet received the treatment it deserves. Because time-varying covariates are increasingly used in event history analysis, this inattention needs to be rectified. Unfortunately, we must report that the necessary attention cannot be found in this volume.

Finally, there is a set of issues that hinge on the scheme used to sample event history data from the entire population. Much work needs to be done on these issues. First, sampling theorists need to develop sampling schemes that are designed for event history analysis. Otherwise those collecting data have little alternative except to use sampling plans developed for cross-sectional analysis, and these may be far from optimal. For ex-

ample, suppose we want to design a study of death from AIDS that will
be based on life history data (e.g., data giving times of sexual partner-
ships, drug usage, and eventually, for some, death). We strongly suspect
that certain types of sample members (e.g., intravenous drug users, ho-
mosexuals) have a much higher risk of death from AIDS than others (e.g.,
heterosexuals who do not use drugs). Is it best to sample these various
types of individuals in proportion to their occurrence in the population?
If one group is oversampled, what, if any, analytic adjustments should be
made? Hoem (1985) did some work relevant to this issue, and he and his
colleagues address yet another aspect of sample design and event history
analysis in this volume. But these efforts barely scratch the surface of the
work on sampling issues that needs to be done if empirical applications of
event history analysis to life course research are to have maximum
benefit.

The Contributions to This Volume

The chapters in this volume are arranged into three parts. The first two
parts deal primarily with some major life domain. Those in Part I deal
with job and unemployment processes, and those in Part II concern migration and family formation. Chapters in Part III raise and attempt to
resolve various methodological issues in event history analysis.

In the first chapter in Part I, Mayer and Carroll investigate the relationship between job and class mobility using data from the three birth cohorts in the German Life History Study (GLHS). They show that quite
distinct labor market processes are tapped by distinguishing between two
time dimensions: duration in a given job versus duration in a given class.
First they establish that class divisions have an important impact on the
rate of job shifts even after controlling for individual characteristics (e.g.,
education, labor force experience, occupational status of current job) and
contextual factors (industrial sector and firm size). They then show that
there are important differences between job and class mobility. While the
rate of job shifts is much higher for women than for men, women have
much greater class stability than men, which is usually to their disadvantage. Furthermore, although they find no intercohort differences in the
rate of class shifts, the rate of job shifts (within classes) increases across
the cohorts studied.

Shavit, Matras, and Featherman examine job shifts in the early careers
of Israeli men. Specifically, they compare the labor force experiences of
youths before military service and the labor force experiences of young
adults after military service. Surprisingly, they find that job stability is
greater for youths before military service than for young adults after mili-

tary service. This result may be specific to Israel, where the extended period of compulsory military service may delay serious job searching until military service is completed.

Petersen and Spilerman employ a parametric log-logistic transition rate model to study job departures from a large insurance company in the United States. Their sample, which is based on personnel records, is unusual because the data not only describe individuals' careers within the firm but also promotion opportunities in different departments. Petersen and Spilerman's findings corroborate on the firm level what Mayer and Carroll infer about the workings of internal labor markets on the basis of their results concerning firm size and industrial sector. Another significant finding in their paper, which we mentioned earlier, is that seniority in firms appears to be considerably more important than age for departure decisions.

In the study of shifts in job or class, methods of event history analysis have become important not only because the problem of right-censoring can be solved, but also because it is possible, in principle, to disentangle the multitude of time dimensions involved (age, labor force experience, seniority, job duration, class duration, and so forth). But, whereas job tenure is mainly a methodologically convenient construct in studies of job mobility, duration itself is the major time dimension of interest in studies of unemployment.

In the first of the two chapters on unemployment, Sørensen tests an analytic distinction between unemployment in what he calls "open" and "closed" economic sectors. In Sørensen's paper, the main means of distinguishing unemployment due to a lay-off from unemployment in order to search for a new job is the duration of unemployment and its predictability by individual attributes. Sørensen uses a discrete-time approximation to a continuous-time Weibull model to analyze data from the Panel Study of Income Dynamics (PSID). Notable in Sørensen's model is the incorporation of time-varying covariates and the estimation of the interaction between covariates and time. He finds that individual characteristics influence the duration of unemployment in the closed sector of the economy less than in the open sector. Unemployment duration in the open sector seems to correspond mainly to job search processes. Finally, he finds that increased compensation tends to prolong the length of unemployment, a topic that the next authors also consider.

In the second of the chapters applying event history models to the study of unemployment, Hujer and Schneider analyze West German data for the 1970s. Their major concerns are (a) to compare the transition from unemployment to employment with the move from unemployment to out of the labor force, and (b) to examine the effects of contextual labor market conditions on these two transition rates. They conclude that the processes governing the two transitions differ greatly and that moves from unemployment to out of the labor force are shaped by institutionally defined time limits for receiving compensation, i.e., the exhaustion of unemployment benefits after being unemployed for an institutionally established length of time. Somewhat surprisingly, their results suggest that the rate of moving from unemployment to out of the labor force is relatively unaffected by changes in labor market conditions. On the basis of their empirical findings, the authors also raise some doubts about the economists' usual predictions on the relationship between unemployment duration and compensation levels.

The chapters in Part II apply methods of event history analysis to topics conventionally treated within the framework of aggregate-level demographic data: migration, fertility, and marriage. These papers not only apply event history methods but in several instances also extend these methods in some way.

Wagner uses data from the German Life History Study to try to disentangle the relationship between education and rates of migration. Education may affect migration either because moves are directly related to enrolling in educational institutions at other locations or because education predisposes individuals to a more migratory life style. Among other things, Wagner finds that both long distance moves and moves to large cities involve highly qualified people to a disproportionate extent. The educational selectivity of migration does not appear to depend on the size of the place of origin, but it does depend on the size of place of the destination.

Tuma and Huinink investigate patterns in the rates of birth of the first three children of native West Germans in the period after World War II. This chapter is noteworthy in several ways. First, it demonstrates that estimates of fertility based on a small representative sample, such as the German Life History Study, compare favorably with estimates based on official census statistics. Second, their chapter shows the superiority of event history data and analysis in understanding fertility and in accounting for heterogeneity by gender, cohort, parity, and background variables. Their analyses show that the relationship between the timing of births and completed family size is multifaceted, and that information on the timing of birth yields insight into fertility processes that is not easily detected with analyses of aggregate level data. Third, their results underscore the importance and fruitfulness of basic descriptive analyses in the framework of event history analysis before proceeding to multivariate and parametric models. In particular, they find a bimodal pattern to the rate of first birth in one birth cohort, which common parametric event history models do not allow. This unexpected pattern would not have been discovered without their exploratory analyses of their event history data.

Diekmann's chapter is exemplary both for the procedures used to select parametric functional forms of time dependency and for the explication of the relations of these forms to the underlying generating mechanism. He shows that the hazard rate for both the Hernes (1972) model and the log-logistic model can be derived from a differential equation model of a social diffusion process. The models are assessed using data on age at marriage for a cross-sectional sample of West Germans and also for several U.S. birth cohorts previously analyzed by Hernes (1972). He finds that the Hernes model usually fits somewhat better than the log-logistic model, and that both of these models fit much better than the exponential model or the Sickle model proposed by Diekmann and Mitter (1983).

Like Diekmann, Wu investigates the rate of first marriage and is especially concerned with finding a model that fits well. He outlines a general way of testing whether a model of time dependency in a rate has an appropriate functional form. He also gives the details for several previously proposed models of the age dependency in the rate of first marriage: the Hernes (1972) model, the Coale-McNeil (1972) model, the log-logistic model, and the log-Gaussian model. He applies these tests to data on a large sample of U.S. white women. He finds that the last two models do not fit well at all; the first two fit much better, with the Hernes model fitting somewhat better than the Coale-McNeil model. He notes that a substantive advantage of the two better-fitting models is that they have "defective" distributions, which in this context yields the correct implication that some fraction of individuals will never marry.

Although several chapters in Parts I and II of this volume treat methodological issues as well as substantive ones, those in Part III are concerned primarily with solving some previously unresolved methodological issue in event history analysis and only secondarily with the substantive issues in their empirical applications.

The first chapter in Part III, which is by Hoem, Rennermalm, and Selmer, addresses the problem of biases that result from analyzing a sample that is restricted in a way that it is not only unrepresentative of the population but also related to the process being studied. Their particular research compares results about marriage and birth processes based on analyses of complete cohabitational histories to results based on analyses of data for only the most recent cohabitation (an artificially restricted sample generated from the complete histories actually available to them). They find that analyses of the restricted sample lead to upwardly biased estimates of the rates they studied, especially rates of marriage. Fortunately, however, they also report that the biases do not mask any general trends.

The remaining three chapters in Part III deal with some aspect of unobserved heterogeneity in rate models. Although this topic has been treated at length over the past several years by Heckman and coauthors (e.g., Heckman and Borjas 1980; Flinn and Heckman 1982; Heckman and Singer 1982, 1984, 1986), these three chapters provide new insights into this problem.

Galler and Poetter are concerned especially with the consequences of unobserved heterogeneity for analyses of the rate of leaving unemployment. They begin with short, clear reviews of both search-theoretic formulations of models of this rate and methodological approaches to unobserved heterogeneity in rate models, especially the approach developed by Heckman and Singer. They then illustrate the consequences of different specifications of duration dependence and unobserved heterogeneity in rates of leaving unemployment in analyses of two waves of data from the German Socio-Economic Panel Study begun in 1984. They compare results for two versions of three models of the rate of leaving unemployment: exponential, Weibull, and piecewise-constant (in duration) models. In one version of these three models they ignored unobserved heterogeneity; in the other they did not. They found that the sensitivity of their results to the assumption about unobserved heterogeneity was greatest for the Weibull model but also large for the exponential model. In contrast, except for the estimated intercepts, the results for the piecewise-constant model were relatively insensitive to assumptions about unobserved heterogeneity. Galler and Poetter not only provided a convincing interpretation of these results but also relate them to particular features of their data that might otherwise have been overlooked.

The next two chapters focus on testing for unobserved heterogeneity and/or misspecification in a rate model rather than on correcting for it. Blossfeld and Hamerle outline a score test based on the calculation of generalized residuals in rate models. This test, which is quite general provided that the generalized residuals can be calculated, yields a single test statistic that is asymptotically normally distributed under the null hypothesis. They illustrate this test in analyses of job-shift rates using data from the German Life History Study. They estimate Weibull and log-logistic models as a function of job duration, labor market experience and human capital; they show that the latter can be derived from the former when there is an exponential distribution on unobserved heterogeneity. Their application of the test they developed indicates the presence of unobserved heterogeneity in both models but more so in the Weibull model than in the log-logistic model.

The last chapter in this volume, which is by Arminger, also describes an asymptotic test for misspecification of a rate model—not only omission of covariates but also misspecification of the time dependence. Arminger extends earlier work by Hausman and by White, who developed similar kinds of tests for linear models. In contrast to the test discussed by Blossfeld and Hamerle, the one developed by Arminger gives not only a test statistic for misspecification of the model as a whole but also a test statistic for each parameter. The latter permits one to draw inferences about which coefficients are biased. Arminger applies this test procedure to a Weibull model of death rates of unions. He concludes not only that the model is misspecified and that the estimated regression coefficients are biased, but also that the estimated shape parameter is not significantly biased.

I

JOB HISTORIES AND OCCUPATIONAL CAREERS

2 *Karl Ulrich Mayer and Glenn R. Carroll*

Jobs and Classes: Structural Constraints on Career Mobility

Introduction

Sociological theory offers two fundamentally different views of the relationship between class and mobility. First, class structure is frequently taken to be the result of both collective and individual social mobility. According to this position, high rates of mobility contribute to the transformation or even dissolution of a given class structure. The second and opposite view holds that mobility has nothing to do with the actual constitution of class structure. Instead, mobility is seen to affect the consciousness, internal coherence, and potential for collective action of a specific class.

Much of the recent discussion about class makes use of various shades

Funding for this research was provided by the Max-Planck-Gesellschaft zur Förderung der Wissenschaften and the Deutsche Forschungsgemeinschaft (Sonderforschungsbereich 3, Mikro-Analytische Grundlagen der Gesellschaftspolitik, Projekt A 4: Lebensverläufe und Wohlfahrtsentwicklung). The data collection was carried out by Zentrum für Umfragen, Methoden und Analysen (Mannheim) and GETAS (Bremen). Carroll was a visiting scientist at the Max-Planck-Institute for Human Development and Education, Berlin, during the writing of this paper. Joachim Wackerow greatly helped with the data analysis. The idea of applying event history analysis to class mobility was first put forward by David L. Featherman. We appreciate the helpful comments on earlier drafts by William Barnett, Chuck Halaby, Michael T. Hannan, Lothar Lappe, and Reinhard Nuthmann.

of the age-old debate about the relevance or irrelevance of mobility (e.g., Wright 1979 [mobility is irrelevant]; Goldthorpe 1980 [class structure is not constituted by mobility but mobility is important for class coherence and organization]; Giddens 1973 [mobility is important for the transformation of economic categories into social collectivities]). Typically, the debate is conducted with reference to empirical research on inter-generational occupational mobility of men (Goldthorpe 1980; Mayer 1977). The class discontinuities between fathers and sons, reflecting primarily massive changes in the occupational structure over time, may indeed be consequential for class formation (e.g., if most blue collar workers are sons of self-employed farmers). However, intra-generational, work-life, or career mobility surely must have a stronger impact on class formation. Fluctuations across classes in the course of a career should undermine class loyalty as well as loosen any potential homogeneity in the material conditions or orientations of a class. Conversely, if class boundaries can be easily transcended during a work life, then the salience of assumed class distinctions might well be questioned.

In industrial societies, career class mobility takes the form of job shifts. Yet the relationship between class mobility and job mobility remains a sociological mystery. Conceptually, it is clear that every class change involves a job shift, but many job shifts do not involve a class change. Empirically, class mobility between generations, class mobility within generations, and job shifts have each been studied thoroughly but in isolation. As a result, we still do not know the answers to such basic questions as: How do classes differ with respect to job-shift patterns? Which classes protect members from the labor market and which expose them? Which classes offer passages for upward mobility? How many job shifts does it take to reach a given class?

Intra-Career Shifts and Conventional Mobility Analysis

A great number of empirical studies on social class involve the analysis of inter- or intra-generational mobility tables. With few exceptions, the data in mobility tables are cross-sectional in that they record the respective classes of fathers and sons at one specific point in time. For measures of inter-generational mobility it has become conventional to take age 14 or 15 of the respondent as reference time for recording the father's occupation or class, while the son's (respondent's) class is recorded at the time of the interview. For intra-generational mobility, the first job is used as a reference for the position of origin.

It is obvious that a finding of regular class changing may greatly undermine the empirical research based on mobility tables. Yet despite the importance of the assumption of individuals' class constancy, little is known about such phenomena. The available descriptive studies are restricted in the sense that they look at transitions only from first class to class at the time of the interview (Goldthorpe 1980), or only between a given span of years, say 1965 to 1970 (König and Müller 1986). Although breakdowns according to age groups or birth cohorts may guard against certain erroneous inferences, they do not alleviate the basic flaw. What is sorely needed is systematic evidence of the extent of class changes, something that can best be accomplished by studying the work lives of individuals.

Studying class changes among individuals has its own complications. First, as we stated above, in modern economies classes are intimately related to jobs. Yet this does not mean that a study of class changes amounts to a study of job shifts; one must change jobs to change class but one can change jobs without changing class. Second, job changes and class changes are constrained by other structural factors, most notably organizational and industrial barriers. These must be disentangled if one is to sort out the true dynamics of social class. Third, the educational system plays a crucial role in affecting and reproducing both jobs and classes. This implies that not only career histories but life histories must be collected and examined.

Although several studies have examined the relationship of job mobility and class mobility across a career (Breiger 1981; Goldthorpe 1980; Haller and Hodge 1981; König and Müller 1986; Snipp 1985), none has dealt with the full complexity of the process. Perhaps the most comprehensive treatment was our earlier paper (Carroll and Mayer 1986), in which we showed the strong complementary effects of social class, industrial sectors, and organizational size on job-shift patterns.

Yet this treatment was also deficient when viewed from a class perspective. There are still no answers to important questions: Under which conditions does class membership make a difference? How does social class affect the life chances of individuals? Have the class experiences of individuals changed across time?

In this chapter we address these questions directly, using life history data from the Federal Republic of Germany. In the next section, we elaborate the conception of class which forms the frame of reference for the empirical work and discuss theories of class mobility. Within that section we also review our previous work and discuss the theoretical questions raised therein and in others' research. We then discuss the data and models we use in the analysis. The fourth section of the paper presents our empirical findings. In the final section we discuss the broader theoretical and empirical implications of our research.

Conceptions of Class and Theories of Class Mobility

Distinguishing Classes

Any analysis of class mobility presupposes a conceptual scheme and measurement rules for mapping jobs into classes. Two ways of conceptualizing classes may be distinguished. The first we call structuralist, since it deduces class structure from theoretical reasoning. Classes are here initially defined independently of individual and collective behavior and constructs like "structural location within the social relations of production" and "latent interests" are used to this end.

The second way of conceptualizing classes may be traced back to Weber. Here the criteria of class are clearly specified: classes exist to the extent that groups share a common market condition as the decisive basis for their specific life chances (Weber, 1964, 679, 680). However, it is taken to be an empirically open question which particular classes form in a given society. As in Weber's famous definition of a social class, mobility itself might be used as a criterion to determine class boundaries. Following this direction one would attempt to establish class categories on the basis of the mobility patterns between a larger number of occupational categories (Breiger 1981, 580).

We will follow here a position where classes and their boundaries are defined independently of the mobility process on the basis of homogeneous market and working conditions. The intention is to combine into a social class "occupations whose incumbents will typically share in broadly similar market and work situations . . . , on the one hand, in terms of their sources and levels of income, their degree of economic security and chances of economic advancement; and, on the other, in their location within the systems of authority and control governing the process of production in which they are engaged, and hence in their degree of autonomy in performing their work-tasks and roles." (Goldthorpe 1980, 39). This allows us, in a next step, to ask about typical patterns of individual and collective class mobility and to relate differential mobility patterns to the criteria which served to distinguish classes: "one may think of class positions having also inherent mobility propensities which will themselves exert an influence . . . independently of that exerted by the relative sizes of classes" (Goldthorpe 1980, 39).

The class scheme which Goldthorpe has developed shows two advantages in addition to this clear theoretical rationale. It has precisely specified measurement rules to map occupations and jobs into classes which make use of the information on both occupational activity and employment status. Further, it has come to be widely used in cross-national research (Erikson and Goldthorpe 1985, König and Müller 1986, Featherman and Selbee 1989) and thus allows us to relate our findings to a growing body of literature.

Goldthorpe's classes and a brief description of their underlying occupations are as follows (all descriptions are excerpted from Goldthorpe 1980, 39–41):

> **Class I:** All high-grade professionals, self-employed or salaried; high-grade administrators and officials in central and local government and in public and private enterprises (including company directors); managers in large industrial establishments; proprietors of large businesses.

> **Class II:** Lower-grade professionals and high-grade technicians; lower-grade administrators and officials; managers in small business, industrial establishments, and in services; supervisors of non-manual employees.

> **Class III:** Routine non-manual—largely clerical—employees in administration and commerce; sales personnel; other rank-and-file employees in services.

> **Class IV:** Small proprietors including farmers and small-holders; all other "own account" workers apart from professionals: (a) with employees, (b) without employees, (c) in agriculture.

> **Class V:** Lower-grade technicians whose work is to some extent of a manual character; supervisors of manual workers.

> **Class VI:** Skilled manual wage workers in all branches of industry, including all who have served apprenticeships and those who have acquired a relatively high degree of skill through other forms of training.

> **Class VII:** (a) All manual wage workers in industry in semi- and unskilled grades; (b) agricultural workers.

Theories of Class Mobility

There is no systematic body of theory on class mobility over the life course, not the least because issues of job mobility, occupational mobility, and class mobility have tended to be confused. We shall take from the available literature and, in part, formulate ourselves a number of theses which can be tested empirically.

The Closure Thesis. This view of mobility emphasizes the closed and antagonistic nature of the class system (Parkin 1971). It associates position in the hierarchy with privilege and opportunity. Those who stand on top use their control over resources to retain their position and, when possible, to pass it on to their children. Because retention of class is usually successful, and because the hierarchy is a closed system with no additional higher locations to move into, mobility from the privileged classes will be lower than from the less privileged classes. Thus we expect an effect of closure due to advantage and exclusion as well as due to a ceiling effect.

Distance effects will operate to the extent that classes are hierarchically ordered, with the consequence of ordered mobility rates along the hierarchy. Effects of closure should be much more visible for intra- than for inter-generational mobility. It should be easier to retain privileges during one's lifetime than to pass them on to one or several children. In addition, intra-career class mobility should show lines of closure more clearly, since it is much less affected by changes in the occupational structure than mobility between generations.

It is less obvious how closure operates at the bottom of the class system. There is no way to go further down; that is, people encounter a floor effect. Furthermore, disadvantages should act cumulatively to suppress upward mobility, as a cycle of deprivation. Both conditions should decrease mobility. Also, there may be what Parkin (1974) called "solidaristic exclusion," a social exclusivity among underdogs where lack of individual power and economic resources is compensated by mutual support and collective representation, or where the pride of the working class or craft group leads to immobility even when advantageous opportunities are available outside. The question, then, is where such solidaristic exclusion, craft and trade traditions, and other kinds of collective identification will show themselves. These phenomena seem much more likely in the class of skilled workers or even production supervisors than in the class (VII) of unskilled workers.

The Structural Dominance Thesis. Recent research on social stratification has highlighted social structural explanations of attainment, as opposed to earlier individualistic explanations. Three social structures have been argued as playing the dominant role in career outcomes: organizations (Baron and Bielby 1980, 1984), industry segments (Averitt 1968, Stinchcombe 1979), and social class (Wright 1979). In an earlier paper (Carroll and Mayer 1986) we demonstrated that the effects of these three structures were complementary but not equal. At some times organizational structures would dominate the mobility process, while at other times industry segment and social class would dominate.

Internal labor markets provide a useful starting point from which to untangle this complex relationship. As is well known, firms with internal labor markets promote employees regularly and often in lockstep, on rationalized bureaucratic career ladders. Mobility within the firm can be predicted fairly well simply on the basis of time in the current salary grade (see, e.g., Petersen and Spilerman in this volume). From a Weberian view of social class, the employees of a firm with an internal labor market may be said to compose a single class to the extent that their mobility experiences are homogeneous (which, however, may not be true for entry-level and certain higher-level exempt employees). Indeed, a reasonable interpretation of the literature on internal labor markets is that it sees employees working within such a firm as having qualitatively different career chances than others—they are, so to speak, a class apart.

But the distinctiveness of an internal labor market does not arise from a simple enhancement of working conditions, job security, and promotion opportunities. Along with these factors comes a conflation of the usual social class differences. If it is to be taken as legitimate, the career ladder of an internal labor market must be rationalized in such a way that it is perceived as fair, just, and egalitarian. Consequently, rules are constructed to prevent people from moving too many levels too quickly. Likewise, personnel procedures for different occupations become standardized, often by providing manual workers with better than usual conditions of work.

Where, then, will social class be the dominant structure shaping career mobility? The key to the answer lies in the conceptualization of class itself. Marx's original formulation rested squarely on the analysis of the social relations of production as it concerned the exploitation of labor. Nowhere was this more visible than in the thriving industry of his time, which he and Engels studied at length: textile manufacturing. The class framework we use here emphasizes both authority relations and market circumstances. Neither should be a particularly strong factor in internal labor markets (which often include considerable union power) or in industrial sectors where authority relations are blurred by professionalism and other status characteristics. Instead, we argue that social class structures mobility in markets and in industrial sectors where labor relations are exploitative and where property rights are weak.

The Life Course Thesis. Class mobility in a career may be not only frequent but also structured systematically in correspondence with age or labor force experience. There is clear evidence that men change classes across their careers. In a recent study, König and Müller (1986) compare the career mobility of men in West Germany and France between 1965 and 1970. In Germany, 13% moved between classes (defined according to the Goldthorpe class scheme), in France 21%. The authors find a clear age dependency. Looking at the fifteen-year brackets from ages 20–34, 35–49, and 50–64, the proportion of men mobile between classes declined in Germany from 12 to 9 to 5%, and in France from 30 to 14 to 8%. In comparing the first and current occupations of a large sample of American men, Snipp (1985), finds that over 23% of those with a manual first job shifted later into a non-manual job. Shifts in the other direction were almost as prevalent. Similarly, Goldthorpe's data (1980, 51–52) shows striking differences between first class, based on first full-time job, and class held in 1972 for men aged 35 and over. Over 65% of these men started out in one of the two lower classes; by 1972 fewer than 43% remained in these classes. In the other direction, classes I and II showed remarkable increases. Only 9% had a first job in either of these two classes, but by age 35 over 27% did.

Is there any age-related pattern to this jumping from class to class? Two bodies of theory suggest there is. The first has been around in mobility literature for some time and is occasionally referred to as the "counter-mobility thesis" (see Girod 1971, Bertaux 1974, Bernard and Renaud 1976). It argues that career mobility eventually moves one back to the class of his or her parents, but only after some initial shifting around, usually of a downward character. Offspring of upper-class parents, in particular, are seen as likely to move downward early in their careers and then to advance, generally back to the upper classes, by middle age.

A second body of relevant thought comes from the job search literature (see March and March 1981). Many of the models found here also suggest a lot of early shifting between classes but not necessarily in the direction suggested by the counter-mobility theorists. Instead, this literature stresses the stability arising from good person-job matches, which often require time and experience to obtain. The intervening period is characterized by the instability created by poor person-job matches. Both the counter-mobility thesis and the job search model stress the roles of individual action and career achievement.

Higher rates of early class mobility could also occur because class boundaries are less capable of discriminating between young persons than between older ones. Cultural, linguistic, educational, and property attributes—the material from which social barriers are made—are more equally distributed among youth. They are also more easily disguised and imitated at the younger ages. All this serves to make social classes much more permeable for the young than for the middle-aged or elderly.

In contrast, we also have to consider the possibility that age groups as such constitute specific labor market segments where both very young and very old workers are statistically discriminated against and tend to be confined to marginal employment. We also know from the economic literature (Oppenheimer 1974) that young persons can afford to enter employment where substantive interests are more important than the calculation of income returns. The "life cycle squeeze," with its constraints of providing economically for a growing family without a fully employed wife, may force people to change jobs with the consequence of a change in class position. Thus, according to the life course thesis, one would hypothesize that social class mobility is much more likely in the early working life.[1]

The Rationalization Thesis. Work and labor relations have changed profoundly across history. Many social theorists believe these deep transformations are continuing today in an especially intensified manner. Two general arguments have been advanced about the nature of post-industrial changes in the labor force and, hence, the class structure of modern societies of the Western democratic-capitalist type. The first of these is optimistic and has been argued most forcefully by Bell (1973). Post-industrial society is based on information, he argues, and it is characterized by the automation of work, increasing demand for service-oriented jobs, and a rise in the number and status of administrative, managerial, and, in particular, science-based professional positions. The overall macroscopic trend involves the upgrading, so to speak, of the average status and of the total distribution of jobs in the entire labor force. Similar predictions can be derived from the long-standing debate on sectoral transformation and, specifically, tertiarization (Müller 1983).

The second and counterargument is pessimistic. As put forward by Braverman (1974), it sees modern work as becoming more rationalized in the technical sense of specialization and control. Productivity may increase, especially in the short term, but the cost is an increasingly alienated labor force which becomes further detached from any control over its work and therefore the lives of its members. While possibly being temporarily offset by the growth of the service sector, the overall long-term trend is a degradation of work, especially as it concerns specific occupations and industries.

Goldthorpe and Payne (1986) contend that the two arguments have implications that should be discernible in secular mobility trends. If the workforce is being upgraded, they contend, then the expansion of administrative and managerial positions should be accompanied by enhanced mobility opportunities for individuals not starting from these classes. Conversely, if the overall trend is one of degradation, then they claim that upward mobility should be constricting and that mobility into the manual classes should be on the rise. They find that their English and Welsh data do not fully support the implications of either argument, but that the data are in closer agreement with the upgrading trend; the degradation argu-

1. Since the sample comprises respondents only up to age 53 we have not taken up here the complexities of life course changes in career patterns in the pre-retirement phase. We would expect here considerable amounts of downgrading and downward mobility for older manual workers.

ment is "flatly contradicted" (p. 19). West German data on inter-generational occupational mobility clearly supports the upgrading thesis up to 1970, under the assumption that degradation does not overwhelmingly take place in a set of tasks without a change in job titles (Mayer 1979a, 1979b).

The consideration of specific task-content leads to a more sophisticated version of the degradation argument. It holds that degradation does not necessarily imply a shift in the overall distribution of classes, but rather a transformation in the nature and content of jobs within a given class. Thus the "expansion of administrative and managerial positions is more apparent than real. This is so because many of these positions have either been themselves degraded into essentially subordinate ones, involving only routine tasks, or have been created by an upgrading of such subordinate positions of no more than a nominal or cosmetic kind" (Goldthorpe and Payne 1986, 20). In the German discussion the latter position has been put forward by Kosta, Krings, and Lutz (1970), whereas for many years the major dogma was the middle-of-the-road position of polarization of work, allowing simultaneously for both upgrading and degrading processes (Kern and Schumann, 1970).

Once one allows for changes in job content that are not observable via mobility between jobs, there is no way to arrive at clear empirical conclusions at the level of the total class structure. However, one major implication of the rationalization thesis is that classes have become internally differentiated in a job-related sense. To quote Goldthorpe (1980, 54), "the channels of mobility have changed without affecting its extent." Thus we hypothesize that job mobility within classes has increased steadily in the transition to the post-industrial era.

A closely related idea brings the educational system into play. Noting that the large mass enrollments of modern educational systems have increased the "credentialed" population enormously, Goldthorpe distills from Parkin (1971, 62–67) the implication that, rather than tightening the bond between educational qualification and social class, the surfeit has actually loosened (or "counterbalanced") it. Thus, in addition to a diminution of the effects of parent's class over the lifetime, one may also expect a lessening and a loosening of the effects of education in a rationalized society.

The Reproduction Thesis. Although class structures change—incrementally or in sudden upheavals—they should be fairly stable from the perspective of most persons' lifetimes. Such a postulated inertial tendency requires special explanation (Hernes 1976). There are at least two insightful directions in which to search for an answer. First, class structures, like any other social institutions, must be reproduced on a daily basis. Certain jobs, organizations, "industries" (e.g., child care) and, not least, the state, are devoted to reproductive functions. More significantly, class structures reproduce themselves on a daily basis because the social relations of production are necessary conditions for the existence of wage earners and employers. The conditions for physical, material, and cultural reproduction are determined by the market wage (Marx 1970 [1867], 181f.).

The second important aspect of reproduction theory concerns inter-generational class continuity. The current debate here is over the intervening mechanisms of transmission, while widespread class inheritance is often taken for granted. Class may be reproduced inter-generationally in a direct way through differential access to family capital, privilege, and social contacts. Others have been persuaded by Bourdieu and Passeron (1971) that inter-generational reproduction is more indirect, operating primarily through the educational system. Despite the apparently egalitarian and meritocratic nature of modern education, Bourdieu holds that upper-class families get more from it for their children by virtue of higher investments in cultural capital, which allows fuller exploitation of curricula, facilities, and teachers. In addition, upwardly mobile families use their newly acquired financial capital to invest in the educational and cultural capital of their children.

We are interested in the timing of class reproduction in the life course, an issue that might clarify the debate over direct and indirect inter-generational class transmission. By the life course thesis above, we argued that early class positions are less stable than those entered later in life. The observation of counter-mobility, whereby the children of upper-class parents drop in class stature initially and then return to their parents' class, suggests a specific avenue and timing of reproduction. By looking at the different effects of education and family background at different points in a career, it seems reasonable to expect that education forms class membership most strongly early in the career, while family background has stronger and delayed effects late in a career.

Data and Models

We use retrospective data from the German Life History Study directed by Karl Ulrich Mayer. Three cohorts of men and women born in the years 1929–1931, 1939–1941 and 1949–1951 were sampled and interviewed by GETAS, a professional survey research firm. The sample of 2172 persons is representative for the Federal Republic and West Berlin. Details of the sampling plan, field procedures and data coding can be found in Mayer and Brückner (1989).

Our analysis involves primarily the job history component of the Life History Study. For each respondent, data were collected on the dates of the beginning and ending of each job held. Respondents were also asked to identify the occupation, wage rate, industry, and size of firm for each job. Changes in jobs were flagged when they occurred within the same firm.

These basic data were used to code the structural variables of interest on social class and industrial sector. For the class schema we adapted Goldthorpe (1980) using rules developed by Walter Müller and his associates at the University of Mannheim for the German occupational structure. For industrial sectors, we used the sevenfold schema of Stinchcombe (1979). Our previous paper describes the rationale and coding behind this schema in great detail, so we refrain from discussing it here except to note that the sectors where labor relations are believed to be most exploitative are labeled "capitalist" and "small competitive." Internal labor markets are most prevalent in the "bureaucratic" and "large-scale engineering" sectors. Both of these groupings are pertinent to the structural dominance thesis. (Details on the mapping of industrial branches into the classification by Stinchcombe can be found in Carroll and Mayer [1986].)

Most of the analyses reported below use rate functions to model the effects of variables of interest on job shifts and class shifts. Rate functions specify as the dependent variable the construct

$$r(t) = \lim_{dt \to 0} \frac{\text{Pr (change between } t, \ t + dt | \text{state at } t)}{dt} \qquad (2.1)$$

where the probability is of a job or class change between times t and $t + dt$, given that a job or class is held at time t (see Tuma and Hannan [1984] or Blossfeld, et al. [1986, 1989]). To model the effects of independent variables, we use the proportional hazards model of Cox (1972). This model specifies that

$$r(t) = h(t) \exp(b_1 X_1 + \ldots + b_k X_k) \qquad (2.2)$$

where the b coefficients measure the size of the effects of the X exogenous variables; $h(t)$ is an unspecified nuisance function which is assumed to affect each sample unit identically. For estimation, we use partial likelihood techniques (Cox 1975), which yield unbiased and efficient estimates under reasonable assumptions (Efron 1977).

Other analyses which we report below use the conventional techniques of ordinary least squares and logistic regression. The following is a complete list of the variables we use, along with their assigned names.

Cohort 1939–1941: An indicator variable that takes the value 1 for respondents born in the second cohort of the sample (between 1939 and 1941 inclusive); otherwise the value is zero.

Cohort 1949–1951: An indicator variable that takes the value 1 for respondents born in the third cohort of the sample (between 1949 and 1951 inclusive); otherwise the value is zero.

Sex: An indicator variable that takes the value 1 for female respondents and the value 0 for men.

Experience: Measured as the number of months elapsed since entry into the first job.

First job: An indicator variable that takes the value 1 for the first job held by a respondent; the value is 0 for all subsequent jobs.

Job status: Scale of social prestige of occupation. Based on the extensive work of Wegener (1985) using German survey data.

Education: Scale of highest level of general education completed. Takes the value 1 if Volks-/Hauptschulniveau (elementary school); 2 if Mittlere Reife (middle school degree); 3 if Abitur or Fachabitur (high school degree).

Training: Scale of highest level of occupational education completed. Takes the value 1 if no vocational training; 2 if apprenticeship; 3 if Meister-/Techniker-degree (technical training); 4 if Fachhochschulniveau (technical college degree); 5 if Universitätsabschluß (university degree).

Log size of employing organization: Natural log of number of employees in organization.

Empirical Analysis

Table 2.1 provides descriptive information on the distribution of social classes in the life history data. The work histories of these three cohorts of 2172 West Germans comprise 6732 jobs or employment episodes. Of these, a majority are in skilled and unskilled manual classes. Fewer than 5% are in the higher professional, administrative, and managerial class. Social classes are not equally distributed across industrial sectors. For illustration, we have chosen three very different sectors and present in Table 2.1 the distribution of jobs in each. The large-scale engineering sector contains an abundance of skilled and unskilled manual jobs. Proportionally, the classical capitalist sector contains even more: over two-thirds of the jobs fall into these classes. By stark contrast, the professional sector has far fewer jobs of these kinds; the bulk of its jobs are in the higher and lower professional positions.

Table 2.1. Distribution of Social Class in West Germany Across the Life Course

Social Class	All Jobs by Sector				First Jobs by Cohort					Mean Jobs per Class Episode
	All Jobs	Large-Scale Engineering	Classical Capitalist	Professional	First Jobs	Cohort 1929–1931	Cohort 1939–1941	Cohort 1949–1951	All Class Episodes	
I. Higher professional, administrative, managerial	273	68	16	116	53	11	15	27	180	1.52
II. Lower professional, administrative, managerial	900	131	55	324	229	46	67	116	528	1.70
III. Routine non-manual	943	143	103	201	377	100	127	150	627	1.50
IV. Small employers, proprietors, self-employed	345	16	30	9	113	60	37	16	285	1.21
V. Lower technical, manual supervisors	422	152	74	29	65	9	25	31	286	1.48
VI. Skilled manual	1514	574	299	35	591	162	227	202	795	1.90
VIIa. Semi- and unskilled manual, nonagricultural	1605	460	409	164	378	169	130	79	1185	1.35
VIIb. Semi- and unskilled manual, agricultural	197	0	4	0	115	86	24	5	146	1.35
Total	6199	1544	990	878	1921	643	652	626	4032	1.54

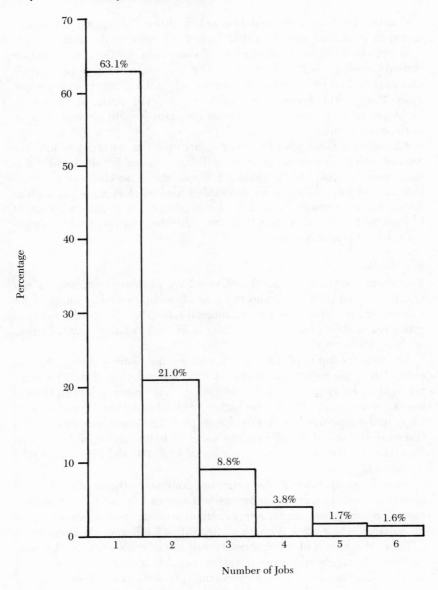

Figure 2.1. Distribution of Jobs per Class Episode

One way to examine these data is to look at the distribution of first jobs across the different cohorts. From Table 2.1 it appears that from the period 1945 to 1970 (the time of entry of these cohorts) the class structure shifted "upward" in its distribution. The professional and upper service classes (I and II) increased in abundance while the manual classes, especially the unskilled and semi-skilled class (VII), declined. The self-employment and small business class (IV) also steadily dwindled as an initial entry point.

Aggregating these job episodes to class episodes (changes in jobs are ignored unless they occur across two distinct classes) results in 4032 distinct spells for analysis. As Table 2.1 shows, the mean class episode consists of 1.54 jobs, although for the skilled manual class it goes as high as 1.90. Figure 2.1 shows the distribution of jobs per class episode. As might be expected, it is highly skewed to the right: the greatest number of class episodes contain only a single job.

Job Mobility

Elsewhere (Mayer and Carroll 1987) we have presented estimates of the effects of social class on various types of job mobility when controlled for cohort, sex, education, and organizational size. The class coefficients are estimates relative to the omitted class, semi- and unskilled manual workers in agriculture (VIIb).

A number of things about the estimates are noteworthy. First, with the exception of the self-employment class IV, the ordering of the classes in terms of mobility propensities conforms to that expected by the closure thesis. In most equations, the higher professional class (I) is the least likely of the employed classes to change jobs. The lower service class (II) is next in the ordering, followed by lower technical and manual supervisory jobs (V), then by routine non-manual jobs (III) and the manual jobs (VI and VII).

Second, consistent with the structural dominance thesis, the effects of social class are significant for across-firm moves but not for within-firm moves. By these estimates, internal labor markets seem to smooth over the usual effects of class, perhaps by instituting a different class regime.

Third, the effects of occupational status are overwhelmed by the class variables. In no equation does the status variable achieve statistical significance.[2] This runs counter to a strong interpretation of the closure thesis, such as that advanced by Blau and Duncan (1967). Obviously the class

2. This result contrasts with the estimates of models—not reported here—where class conditions are left out as predictors of the rate of job change or of class change. In such models occupational status shows significant effects.

scheme is able to catch quite homogeneous socioeconomic groupings, where the internal status differentiation is too small to affect mobility propensities. In contrast, general educational resources remain effective. This implies that school qualifications not only determine access to a given class, but also act as a mobilizing force in job shifts up to a point where skills match the job requirements.

It is noteworthy that occupational training is consequential in addition to class membership for three types of job shifts. It is negatively related to downward mobility, mobility across firms, and upward mobility across firms. That vocational resources prevent slipping confirms our theoretical expectations. However, that such resources apparently tend to tie workers to their firm seems surprising in the light of theories which postulate an occupational labor market transcending firms (Sengenberger, 1975). It seems rational that firms want to keep the most qualified workers, and obviously they are able to do so by offering sufficient incentives within the firm. Another contradiction to the labor market theory is provided by the finding that skilled workers, not unskilled workers, are most prone to lateral moves across firms.

Fourth, contrary to the life-course thesis, first jobs usually show a lower rate of movement than subsequent jobs. This somewhat unusual finding is perhaps the result of applying controls for experience and job status. An alternative hypothesis is that many of the first jobs are held after three-year apprenticeships and often in the same firms. Therefore they are less likely to show the characteristics of a job-search period.

Industrial Sector

In Mayer and Carroll (1987) we have also investigated social class and industrial sector simultaneously. According to the findings reported there, class distinctions are important for job mobility in the capitalist sector (food, wood, leather, textiles, printing) and in the small competitive sector (sales, retail, hotels, restaurants, personal and domestic services). Social class is without statistically significant effects in the professional, bureaucratic, and large-scale engineering sectors. As argued in the structural dominance thesis, the more knowledge-based and bureaucratic sectors most likely superimpose their own mobility regimes within internal labor markets.

Job, Sector, and Class

How do changes in job or sector interrelate with changes in social class? Table 2.2 presents conditional probabilities of changing social class, by origin and destination class, given a change in job or industrial sector. Notice first the strong bonding power of social class. Most job changes,

Table 2.2. Conditional Probabilities of a Change in Social Class Given a Change in Job or Sector

Origin Class	Destination Class (conditional job change/sector change)							
	I	II	III	IV	V	VI	VIIa	VIIb
I	82.1/77.3	4.5/4.5	2.7/4.5	8.1/9.0	0/0	1.8/4.5	0.9/0	0/0
II	11.2/6.9	73.2/62.1	9.3/17.8	2.2/4.0	1.0/1.1	0.4/1.1	2.8/6.9	0/0
III	1.3/1.4	18.3/17.9	57.8/50.3	4.7/5.2	1.6/2.1	2.9/3.4	13.2/19.3	0.2/0.3
IV	2.8/2.2	6.1/14.3	6.7/12.1	36.1/5.5	3.9/2.2	7.2/13.2	28.3/50.5	5.6/0
V	5.6/6.8	13.2/17.8	6.0/11.0	9.3/6.8	58.1/46.6	5.6/6.8	2.1/4.1	0/0
VI	1.5/0.9	3.6/5.5	2.6/6.4	3.1/3.6	13.1/8.8	62.1/41.9	13.9/32.5	0.1/0.3
VIIa	0.6/0.6	2.8/3.1	7.1/9.4	2.9/4.1	3.1/1.1	10.5/10.9	71.3/68.3	1.7/2.4
VIIb	0/0	1.2/1.9	2.9/4.9	8.8/1.0	1.8/1.9	7.0/11.7	48.5/76.7	28.8/1.9

Note: Probabilities add from left to right and may not equal 100 because of rounding.

40

even when associated with sectoral changes, do not involve changes in social class. This is especially the case for the professional classes (I and II) and the semi- and unskilled manual class (VIIa). Only in the self-employed and manual agricultural classes does a job change typically involve a class change, and both of these types of events are almost true by class definition.

For those who do change class at the time of a job change, moves of a short "distance" are the norm. Noteworthy exceptions to this rule are the high proportions of moves from the self-employed class (IV), and from the routine non-manual class (III), into the semi- and unskilled manual class (VIIa). Overall, however, the findings are consistent with the closure thesis.

Class Mobility

Table 2.3 presents partial likelihood estimates of the rate of leaving any social class as a function of the various independent variables. The leftmost column reports the base model without any class independent variables. The next column to the right reports a model including the origin classes as dummy variables (again, the farm workers are the omitted contrast). The remaining estimates report the basic model calculated separately for each origin class.

We note several important features of these estimates. First, the strong cohort effects disappear when moving from rates of job shifts to class shifts. Substantively, this finding is consistent with the rationalization thesis: class barriers have not become easier to transcend, although mobility between jobs within classes seems to have increased.

Second, the effects of the sex variable change in sign across two types of analysis. Whereas in the job shifts, women moved more frequently, in the class shifts they move less frequently. This finding is not an artifact of the class compositions of women's jobs, as the models which control for class origin clearly show.

Third, human capital theory, as exemplified by the labor force experience variable, seems to have few implications for class mobility. Whereas this variable has strong negative effects on job-shift patterns, its predictive power diminishes to almost nil in the class-shift models once origin class is taken into account.

Fourth, the effects of first class agree with those of first job. Entry class does not appear to be a fluctuating, transitory state. Rather, it exerts considerable holding power and the rate of class shift actually rises once first class has been left. This suggests that the life-course thesis does not lead to an adequate image of class mobility during working life.

Fifth, size of firm or organization continues to have strong negative effects on the rates of mobility between jobs and classes. This effect persists

Table 2.3. Partial Likelihood Estimates of Models of the Rate of Class Change (standard errors shown in parentheses)

Independent Variables	All Origins (w/o class-independent variables)	All Origins (classes as dummy variables)	Origin Class							
			I	II	III	IV	V	VI	VIIa	VIIb
Cohort 1939–41	.069	.081	−.012	−.315	−.105	.498	−.210	.058	.160	−.213
	(.067)	(.067)	(.619)	(.215)	(.196)	(.265)	(.266)	(.116)	(.152)	(.247)
Cohort 1949–51	.063	.074	.146	−.684*	.030	.777*	−.458	.036	.165	.514
	(.079)	(.081)	(.737)	(.249)	(.208)	(.354)	(.331)	(.137)	(.188)	(.632)
Sex	−.288*	−.205*	−1.58	.108	−.369*	−.566*	.594	.027	−.065	−.436*
	(.065)	(.071)	(1.20)	(.190)	(.181)	(.272)	(.361)	(.155)	(.154)	(.229)
Education	.296*	.393*	.644	.316*	.232	.279	.681*	.636*	1.01*	.759
	(.066)	(.069)	(.485)	(.144)	(.147)	(.260)	(.206)	(.151)	(.180)	(.732)
Training	−.079	−.038	−.746*	−.357*	.109	−.319	.537*	.060	.423*	−.069
	(.048)	(.051)	(.311)	(.104)	(.147)	(.210)	(.193)	(.162)	(.151)	(.370)
Experience	−.005*	−.005*	−.006	−.006*	−.005*	−.009*	−.004*	−.003	−.003	.003
	(.001)	(.001)	(.005)	(.002)	(.002)	(.003)	(.002)	(.002)	(.002)	(.004)
First class	−.227*	−.414*	−.460	−.645*	−.347	−.420	.125	−.212	−.328	−.836*
	(.083)	(.086)	(.861)	(.251)	(.220)	(.417)	(.316)	(.199)	(.174)	(.340)

Job status	−.013*	−.002	−.018	.021*	−.024*	.022*	.019	.003	.003	−.021
	(.002)	(.003)	(.012)	(.007)	(.007)	(.008)	(.010)	(.009)	(.007)	(.013)
Log organiza-tion size	−.086*	−.065*	−.311*	−.052	−.065	−.071	−.028	−.069*	−.032	.029
	(.014)	(.015)	(.143)	(.044)	(.044)	(.153)	(.051)	(.026)	(.029)	(.156)
Origin class										
I		−2.68*								
		(.333)								
II		−1.53*								
		(.173)								
III		−.854*								
		(.137)								
IV		−1.19*								
		(.164)								
V		−1.16*								
		(.161)								
VI		−.695*								
		(.118)								
VIIa		−1.02*								
		(.122)								
Chi square	168.8	324.4	17.5	34.3	35.7	35.4	53.0	34.9	66.7	28.8
Degrees of freedom	9	16	9	9	9	9	9	9	9	9
No. of events	1239	1239	16	124	179	75	89	91	239	114

*p ≤ .05.

43

in the face of controls for origin class, which supports our earlier conclusion that organizational structures shape careers independently of class and industrial sector (Carroll and Mayer 1986).

Sixth, class differences in mobility are strong and ordered in a fashion somewhat like that suggested by the closure thesis. The higher service and professional class (I) exerts the greatest constraining force, manifested in a rate of movement about 90% lower than the rate for farm workers (VIIb). The other classes are even more consistently ordered than in the job-shift rates.

We also searched for interaction effects between cohort and education on the rates of exits from given classes, following the hypothesis that the influence of education on class mobility lessens over historical time. Except for one instance we found no such historical trend or change. The exception is a higher positive rate of exits from class II in the middle cohorts. This suggests superior upward mobility chances during the career brought about by favorable returns to education for the particular path leading from the middle to the higher levels of the class hierarchy.[3]

Entry into Initial Class

The strong effects of the first class episode suggest that entry into the first class may be a much different process. It is also the process where evidence of reproduction theory should be most clearly visible. For these reasons, we estimated models of initial class entry separately. Here, however, waiting time is relatively unimportant. It will measure primarily the level of education. It is also not clear when the "clock" for such a waiting time should begin. Thus, we report estimates of logistic response models for initial class entry. They are found in Table 2.4.

As might be expected in Germany (Blossfeld 1985; König and Müller 1986), the educational and vocational degrees have a strong impact on the initial class entered. Such certified qualifications act as gateways or elevators to class position. Once educational and occupational training are taken into account, the socioeconomic resources of the family of origin— measured here by the occupational prestige of father's job when the respondent was 15 years of age—do not additionally influence the class entry of children. The major exception to this pattern is entry into class IV, where superior resources of the family of origin ease entry into self-employment and low status of the father keeps children in the working class.[4]

3. The beta coefficient of the interaction between education and the birth cohorts of 1939–1941 is .5424 (standard error .273).

4. If one estimates these models without the education and training variables, all origin effects except for entry into classes III, IV, and VI become highly significant. Also the changes in educational composition show up in differences between cohorts.

Table 2.4. Logistic Response Models of Initial Class Entry

Independent Variables	Entry Class							
	I	II	III	IV	V	VI	VIIa	VIIb
Constant	-3.75*	-1.36*	-2.11*	-7.80	-5.29	-3.93	-5.47	-7.05
	(.509)	(2.87)	(.378)	(n.e.)	(3.51)	(n.e.)	(3.51)	(3.79)
Cohort 1939–41	.049	.138	.064	-.019	.319	.102	.089	-.598*
	(.263)	(.123)	(.088)	(.119)	(.219)	(.092)	(.086)	(.137)
Cohort 1949–51	.086	.180	.148	-.299	.488*	.013	.078	-1.15*
	(.239)	(.116)	(.088)	(.162)	(.209)	(.094)	(.100)	(.263)
Sex	-.385*	.445*	1.16*	-.036	-.342*	-1.12*	-.104	-.412*
	(.196)	(.093)	(.088)	(.112)	(.159)	(.081)	(.080)	(.118)
Father's job prestige	.007	.001	.000	.215*	.010	-.012*	-.005	-.011
	(.005)	(.003)	(.003)	(.006)	(.006)	(.004)	(.004)	(.008)
General education								
Middle school degree	-.366	.108	.238	-.415	-.321	-.353	-.170	1.76
	(.551)	(.144)	(.142)	(.491)	(.288)	(.246)	(.225)	(3.76)
High school degree	1.49*	1.57*	.189	-1.37	.426	-1.15*	-.652*	-4.40
	(.523)	(.199)	(.218)	(.740)	(.396)	(.419)	(.316)	(7.49)
Occupational training								
Apprenticeship	-1.27*	.196	.912*	.793	1.91	3.02*	1.79	-.114
	(.484)	(.245)	(.341)	(.712)	(3.49)	(.329)	(3.50)	(.158)
Technical training	1.90*	1.62*	1.57*	-3.91*	3.82	.967	-2.37	-4.65
	(.994)	(.690)	(.766)	(1.97)	(3.53)	(.904)	(n.e.)	(n.e.)
Technical school degree	.200	-.377	.369	-2.46	.699	-5.10*	-1.46	1.20
	(.603)	(.433)	(.713)	(n.e.)	(3.58)	(1.69)	(n.e.)	(n.e.)
University degree	1.14*	-.137	-3.00*	2.44	-6.23	1.04	-2.77	1.49
	(.482)	(.303)	(.864)	(1.35)	(13.9)	(1.12)	(6.99)	(n.e.)
Log likelihood	-113.8	-441.3	-674.6	-321.7	-213.5	-607.5	-568.1	-283.9
Chi square	178.5	575.2	631.9	325.1	226.6	490.8	482.2	185.2
Degrees of freedom	679	679	679	681	679	680	681	682
No. of events	46	190	314	105	55	484	295	99

*$p \le .05$.

45

The gender variable shows strong signs of class segregation occurring at time of entry into the labor force. Women are channeled into classes II and III in high proportions, while they are much less likely than men to move into all the other classes. Coupled with the strong negative effects of sex on class mobility after entry (Table 2.3), this strongly suggests that most sex segregation is career-long (see also Blossfeld 1988).

Later Class Entry

Given an initial class, what are the conditions under which mobile individuals enter specific classes? We now turn to this question by examining partial likelihood estimates of models with class-specific destination states. That is, we model the destination class as a competing risk model. The estimates are presented in Table 2.5.

Entry into the class of higher administrative, professional and managerial positions strongly depends on higher formal schooling and is severely restricted for women. Although the number of such positions has clearly

Table 2.5. Partial Likelihood Estimates of Models of the Rate of Class Entry (standard errors shown in parentheses)

Independent Variables	Destination Class						
	I	II	III	IV	V	VI	VIIa
Cohort 1939–1941	.025	.456*	.230	−.131	.265	.138	−.025
	(.245)	(.185)	(.200)	(.198)	(.171)	(.209)	(.127)
Cohort 1949–1951	−.229	.575*	.443*	.093	.224	−.087	.050
	(.296)	(.204)	(.226)	(.239)	(.211)	(.271)	(.155)
Sex	−1.42*	−.016	1.33*	−.099	−1.61*	−1.04*	−.447*
	(.319)	(.158)	(.194)	(.190)	(.257)	(.244)	(.125)
Education	1.36*	.894*	.249	.151	−.355	−.562	−1.01*
	(.184)	(.133)	(.180)	(.204)	(.220)	(.356)	(.258)
Training	.026	−.182	−.349*	.099	.450*	−.518*	−.268*
	(.118)	(.100)	(.138)	(.140)	(.144)	(.192)	(.119)
Experience	−.005	−.000	−.003*	−.006*	−.003	−.009*	−.005*
	(.003)	(.002)	(.002)	(.002)	(.002)	(.002)	(.002)
First class	.052	.263	−.635*	−.879*	.538*	−1.34*	−.001
	(.321)	(.220)	(.218)	(.229)	(.250)	(.238)	(.171)
Job status	−.006	−.011*	−.003	−.011	−.025*	−.026*	−.018*
	(.005)	(.005)	(.006)	(.006)	(.007)	(.008)	(.005)
Log organization size	−.005	.020	−.025	−.233*	−.033	.061	−.281*
	(.045)	(.033)	(.039)	(.045)	(.034)	(.040)	(.032)
Chi square	183.6	72.3	100.3	47.3	117.9	91.4	198.9
Degrees of freedom	9	9	9	9	9	9	9
No. of events	91	191	152	141	189	121	334

*$p \leq .05$.

Note: Class VIIb had too few observed entries to allow for estimation.

increased over time, we detect no cohort effect. One must, therefore, assume that the cohort differences are compositional and hidden in the effect of schooling. The class of qualified, semi-professional white collar positions (II) is, in contrast, increasingly accessible to the younger cohorts and is equally open for women and men. General schooling is important and there is a negative effect of occupational status; that is, moves into class II tend to equilibrate status and start from lower jobs. If persons have a good education and start their careers in lower prestige jobs, they have a good chance to move into class II.

Class III, lower white-collar work, is a destination port for members of the youngest cohort and for women, people with little or no vocational training. It is not a condition typically entered after the first class episode. Becoming self-employed (class IV) tends to occur later in the career and is more likely the smaller the size of the prior employing firm. Thus, self-employment appears to be one way of overcoming the limited opportunities within small firms.

Class V (technicians, foremen, production supervisors) is a domain of men and a career step for skilled manual workers early in the working life. How does one get into skilled work during the career? This is somewhat of an enigma, since this type of move should usually occur immediately after an apprenticeship. According to these results this move is most prevalent for men with little training and with destination jobs of lower occupational prestige. Finally, semi- and unskilled jobs are more likely to be entered later in their career by men who come from small firms, with little education and little vocational training.

We also estimated these models for moves into second and subsequent classes, including father's occupational prestige as a proxy measure for the socioeconomic resources of the family of origin. Delayed effects of origin not mediated by education shows to be significant only for later moves into class II.[5] Therefore we find that the thesis of class reproduction by means of the educational system is supported in an even stronger manner than suggested above. This mechanism not only operates, as we expected, at the time of entry into the class structure but also during the working life.

Jobs within Classes

We now take up a final but intriguing research question: How can the number of jobs within a class episode be explained? Recall that one argument, the rationalization thesis, held that job differentiation within

5. The beta coefficient for the effect of father's prestige on the rate of entry into class II is .0074 (standard error .003).

classes has increased steadily throughout the twentieth century while class mobility has not. Our inability to find evidence of cohort effects in the rates of class mobility suggests that part of this thesis may be correct. We now examine the other, more interesting, part directly.

Our research strategy was to estimate ordinary least squares regression models with the number of jobs within the class episode, and its natural logarithm, as dependent variables. Such an approach makes it necessary, of course, to control for duration in the class episode and whether or not the episode was censored. The resulting estimates can be found in Table 2.6.

Across the hierarchical models estimated we find very consistent results. First, in all equations there are strong cohort effects signaling a trend of an increasing number of jobs per class episode over time. Second, the number of jobs is generally higher in the first class spell. This is not an effect of the longer average duration of the first class episode since this is partialed out. There is therefore a genuine situation of higher job mobility early in the career. Third, the experience variable bears out the long-established finding of decreasing job mobility during the career.

More interesting are the findings for the various classes. By definition, self-employment reduces job mobility. The classes with the highest partial effect on number of jobs are the two manual classes of skilled and unskilled workers (VI and VII) and the lower service class (II). They are different in the sense that job mobility among blue collar workers is most likely horizontal mobility for small wage gains, whereas in class II career-like job sequences will be the rule. We do find here a curious difference between blue collar and white collar positions without qualification (III, VII). In the unqualified blue collar class, job moves are frequent. They do not appear to be particularly pronounced in the (mostly female) lower white collar sector. We do not have a ready-made explanation for this difference in labor market structure.

Conclusion

Initially we raised a number of issues of a theoretical and empirical kind which will now be discussed in the light of our findings.

Does the distinction between job and class mobility matter? Yes, indeed it does. Although the average number of jobs per class episode is, at 1.54, not particularly striking, most job *changes*—even when connected to sectoral shifts—do not involve changes in social class. This pattern becomes even more pronounced when we exclude self-employment, where job changes almost always imply a move to another (wage earning) class. Also, the gross number of jobs per class episode (Table 2.1) or the net explanatory power of particular classes (Table 2.6) show large differences between classes in exposing their members to job shifts. These results confirm our expectations about the higher job mobility of unskilled, semi-skilled, and, to a lesser degree, of skilled workers. We did not expect to find, however, that the qualified clerical and semi-professional employees experience more job shifts than the routine non-manual employees.

Further, this distinction brings out quite clearly the different labor market experiences of men and women. Most employed women enter into the lower- and middle-level service classes III and II, where they experience greater job mobility than men but less class mobility; they become locked into the more disadvantaged positions. The distinction between jobs and classes has also proven to be useful in the assessment of inter-cohort changes. In contrast to increases in job mobility from the older to the younger cohorts, we find stability in class mobility. This lends credibility to our assumption that the cohort differences in job shifts are not an artifact of the retrospective method. Substantively, we take this to be evidence for an increase in the degree of job differentiation, in support of the rationalization hypothesis.

Is the class structure a central, macro-social condition for shaping job trajectories? Particularly in the German case a societal class structure is not only a derivative of the economic order, but on a national level is also patterned and modified by legal provisions of labor law, social security law, agreements of collective bargaining, and the institutions of general education and vocational training. We find abundant evidence that the determining force of class membership does not vanish once we take industrial sector, size of firm, and individual resources into account.

However, class effects on either the rate of job change or the rate of class change do not spread evenly. They are definitely modified according to industrial sector, whether the moves are within or across firms, and according to the size of the employing organization. The less the firm or sector conforms to the market model, the weaker the influence of class structure on working lives. Conversely, job trajectories in "systems of open positions" (Sørensen 1983) are not governed exclusively by attributes of the person and the job. The class structure intervenes, as posited by the structural dominance thesis.

The impact of class structure on career mobility can probably be captured best by an image of inertia. Classes hold people and predetermine their evolving life to a considerable extent. Against the life course thesis we do not find that first class episodes are of shorter duration. The opposite appears to be the case, extremely so where the entry class is the lower service class (II) or the unskilled worker class (VIIa). Forty percent of our respondents stayed in their initial class during the periods observed for each cohort.

This mobility quota seems to contradict the image of inertia and self-

Table 2.6. Models of Within-Class Differentiation by Job Shifts within Class (standard error shown in parentheses)

	Dependent Variable							
Independent Variables	Number of Jobs	Log. Number of Jobs	Number of Jobs	Log. Number of Jobs	Number of Jobs	Log. Number of Jobs	Number of Jobs	Log. Number of Jobs
Constant	.930	.001	1.06	.056	1.08	.016	.709	−.154
Duration	.005*	.002*	.004*	.002*	.004*	.002*	.004*	.002*
	(.000)	(.000)	(.000)	(.000)	(.000)	(.000)	(.000)	(.000)
Censored	.056	.024	−.069	−.037	−.091	−.041	−.073	−.034
	(.055)	(.023)	(.060)	(.025)	(.061)	(.025)	(.060)	(.025)
Cohort 1939–41	.274*	.129*	.229*	.108*	.238*	.109*	.244*	.109*
	(.060)	(.025)	(.060)	(.025)	(.061)	(.025)	(.060)	(.025)
Cohort 1949–51	.368*	.192*	.235*	.129*	.248*	.130*	.238*	.121*
	(.064)	(.027)	(.068)	(.028)	(.068)	(.028)	(.068)	(.028)
First class			.183*	.097*	.230*	.126*	.234*	.118*
			(.065)	(.027)	(.080)	(.033)	(.080)	(.033)
Experience			−.002*	−.001*	−.002*	.001*	−.001*	−.001*
			(.000)	(.000)	(.000)	(.000)	(.000)	(.000)
Sex			.015	.014	−.020	.007	.011	.026
			(.051)	(.022)	(.054)	(.022)	(.057)	(.024)
Class spell no.					.050	.027	.046	.025
					(.042)	(.018)	(.042)	(.017)

50

Education					.028 (.044)	.008 (.018)	.069 (.047)	.029 (.019)
Training					−.068* (.032)	−.012 (.014)	−.037 (.034)	−.0001 (.014)
Class								
I							−.011 (.154)	−.017 (.064)
II							.230* (.115)	.126* (.048)
III							.139 (.107)	.075 (.044)
IV							−.278* (.120)	−.125* (.049)
V							.070 (.127)	.030 (.053)
VI							.366* (.104)	.199* (.043)
VIIa							.573* (.105)	.249* (.043)
R^2	.134	.164	.157	.197	.160	.198	.196	.241

*$p \leq .05$.

Note: Class VIIb had too few observed entries to allow for estimation.

51

reproduction. We therefore have to add a number of qualifications. Class VIIb, farm workers, is a highly transitory state where only 17% of our respondents stay their whole working life and from which almost 60% move to unskilled jobs. Likewise class V, manual supervisors and lower technicians, has many properties of a "career stage" which most persons enter from skilled manual jobs and almost 50% leave again for routine or initial level white collar positions or self-employment. Also the majority of men in class III experience upward mobility to class II or self-employment. Of the men ever having been in class II, one-third make their way up to class I. Class closure is highest in the most privileged classes (I and II) and lowest among the skilled workers (VI). Thus, we have to stress not only the long mean duration in a given class (about 16–17 years) but also the fact that origin class strongly patterns the direction and destination of a class change.

3 *Yossi Shavit, Judah Matras, and David L. Featherman*

Job Shifts in the Career Beginnings of Israeli Men

Introduction

Events in the early stages of careers are important determinants of socio-economic attainments in subsequent phases of the life course. Models of socioeconomic attainment (e.g., Blau and Duncan 1967; Featherman and Hauser 1978) demonstrate considerable stability in occupational prestige between jobs held early and late in the life course. Indeed, much of the importance of education in the attainment process is mediated by its effects on occupational allocation early in life. Hogan (1982) demonstrates that the temporal ordering of entry into the labor force, school leaving, and other such milestones in the transition to adulthood also affects ultimate attainment. Coleman (1984) argues that some of the occupational advantages of whites over blacks in the United States is due to the fact that whites are more likely to accumulate work experience while still in school and to return to school after initial phases of employment (see also Freeman and Wise 1982). Osterman (1980) shows that job instability in late adolescence is detrimental to orderly career formation in early adult-

This study was supported by a grant from the National Institute on Aging (PO1 AG04877). Seymour Spilerman provided helpful comments on an earlier draft. Nao Tsunematsu provided computational assistance.

hood. In short, the process of entry into the labor force seems to be an important nexus in the socioeconomic life course and worthy of the attention it has been receiving (Ornstein 1976; Osterman 1980; Spenner, et al. 1982).

In many countries a substantial majority of persons under 20 years of age are not in the labor force at any moment in time. Some have not yet entered the labor force for the first time while others have withdrawn temporarily (Hauser 1979). For those adolescents who are out of school, labor force participation may be erratic and unrewarding (e.g., Osterman 1980; Mare, et al. 1984; Coleman 1984; Matras, et al. 1984). When compared to adults, youths are more likely to be unemployed (e.g., Mare, et al. 1984), to hold jobs for shorter periods of time (e.g., Osterman 1980), and to work in low-paid, dead-end type jobs, which are abundant in the secondary labor markets (e.g., Brown 1982). In short, youths are said to be a marginal group in the labor force and to suffer from handicaps similar to those suffered by ethnic and racial minorities and by women (Osterman 1980).

One cause for the marginal status of adolescents in the labor market is their higher rate of job turnover. Job changes often involve spells of frictional unemployment. Furthermore, as persons leave jobs, they often fail to realize investments of time and on-the-job training.

In this paper we consider several theoretical explanations for the job instability of adolescents. We then employ Israeli job-history data to describe and model differences in job stability between adolescents and young adult men. We measure and compare the bearing of labor market and of life-course factors on age variation in job stability among Israeli young men.

Instability of Youth Employment

Spilerman's (1977) work on careers provides useful conceptual tools with which to analyze the dynamic aspects of labor force participation (Spenner, et al. 1982). Careers are defined as structured sequences of work roles that persons occupy over time. Careers vary in the level of occupational rewards their constituent jobs bestow upon workers at any point in time. They also vary in the extent of continuity they provide. Some persons embark upon careers that involve numerous job changes, while others remain in one job for a long time. Some careers link progressively more rewarding jobs, while others manifest an erratic pattern of change in reward level.

Spilerman distinguishes between *orderly* and *chaotic* careers. The former refers to job sequences with a consistent improvement in reward level; the latter refers to sequences that lack a unilineal process. Frequent shifts among jobs can be either beneficial or detrimental to socioeconomic attainment (Spilerman 1977; Berg 1970; Coleman 1984). Their potential benefit lies in the fact that movement is necessary if upward mobility is to take place. However, rapid shifts may also reflect inability to accumulate on-the-job training and experience, or to enjoy promotion opportunities within the firm.

Increasing job stability over time or over successive ages in the life course implies an orderly career, given, also, consistent improvement in reward level. Job instability over time or successive ages implies maladaptation to the labor force and is detrimental to socioeconomic achievement. But early work-life job instability associated with upward moves may imply an ordered career, provided it is succeeded ultimately by increasing job stability.

Characteristics of Adolescents

Several explanations have been proposed for the growth in job stability as persons move from adolescence to adulthood. Adolescence is said to be a moratorium during which people try out various social roles and refrain from long-term social obligations (Erikson 1968). Most adolescents are not yet married, nor are they, at this stage, expected to support their parents. Consequently, they do not value a steady income as much as older workers do. In the labor force this is reflected in the high turnover of youths among jobs and in repeated entries into and exits from the labor force.

The transition into adulthood (both aging and the transition into adult roles) involves a gradual change into a more stable pattern of employment. Frequent shifts may be beneficial in adolescence when young workers are still searching for ever better jobs. An orderly career, namely one that leads the incumbent to social success, exhibits a gradual decline in the rate of job changes: as workers grow older, marry, and bear children, they become less likely to risk fresh starts. With age, instability of employment comes to signify a maladaptation to the demands of the labor market and is progressively detrimental to socioeconomic attainment.

Needs of Firms

The difference in preferences of younger and older workers has been asserted to be compatible with the different needs of firms in the economy (Osterman 1980). Some firms require unstable employees. These firms are typically characterized as belonging to the secondary labor market. They are often small firms with a labor-intensive production process which requires little training of workers. Adolescents are said to be suitable workers for such firms: on the one hand, they do not value promotion opportunities or job security; and on the other, they can easily get access to jobs in the secondary economy where prior experience is not required. By contrast, primary labor market firms are typically large, capital-intensive, and require workers who are willing to undergo training. Since training of workers is costly, primary-sector firms prefer to employ older workers who are likely to stay with the firm for long periods of time (Thurow 1975). Similarly, within the various industrial sectors in the economy, some occupations and jobs require stable workers, whereas others are more suitable to casual labor.

Osterman argues that the compatibility between the needs of firms and the sociopsychological nature of age groups account for the differential concentration of age groups in occupations and industries. However, the sectoral concentration may have a reciprocal causal relationship with youth employment patterns. Brown (1982), for example, suggests that youth unemployment is due in part to the fact that adolescents are over-represented in occupations which are more strongly associated with spells of unemployment. Similarly, the instability of adolescent workers may be due to their concentration in industries which do not provide continuity of employment within firms and jobs. Clearly, the two explanations are not mutually exclusive: adolescents' patterns of employment may result from both the nature of adolescence and the nature of the jobs they hold. One objective of the present analysis is to contrast the magnitudes of the two effects in explaining age variations in job instability.

Labor Force Experience
The third factor that singles out youth from adult workers is their lack of opportunity to make substantial investments in their own human capital. Wages, earnings, job stability, and employment are positively related to educational attainment and to experience in the labor force (e.g., Mincer 1974; Featherman and Hauser 1978; Hachen 1983). Educated workers are perceived by employers as being more productive. Consequently, such workers manage to secure entry into the more rewarding jobs which, in turn, they are less likely to leave (Carroll and Mayer 1986). Furthermore, employers are said to invest more heavily in the training of educated workers for the requirements of the job. Once the investment has been made, trained workers are less likely to be dismissed (Thurow 1975). Many adolescents have not yet had the opportunity to complete their course of studies and many enter the labor force while still in school or between spells of schooling (e.g., Coleman 1984). Thus, adolescents may simply exhibit labor force behavior which is characteristic of less educated workers in general. Similarly, adolescent workers have not had the opportunity to accumulate experience in the labor force. In the eyes of employ-

ers, experience, like formal schooling, is an indicator of potential productivity on the job (e.g., Mincer 1974; Bills, in progress). Furthermore, experienced workers are more likely to have completed their search for a career, to "settle down" in jobs, and to leave them less readily (Carroll and Mayer 1986).

Education and Youth Unemployment

Working youths are a negatively selected group within each cohort. As noted earlier, in industrialized societies schooling is normatively extended later into adolescence and early adulthood. Mare and his associates (1984) suggest that as education is historically prolonged, only the least able of each successive cohort ever experience full-time work before the age of 18. They argue that youth unemployment is due, in part, to the fact that the pool of working youths consists primarily of persons who are least able; otherwise they would have still been in school.

The adult labor force, on the other hand, consists of a more representative subset of the ability distribution. Thus, with age, as more able persons leave school and enter the labor force, the modal pattern of careers becomes more orderly, stable, and rewarding. This intriguing hypothesis is consistent with findings reported by Mare and his associates on rates of employment in the transition from youth to adulthood. However, the data which they employ do not include measures of ability. Consequently, they test the hypothesis indirectly within the framework of a statistical model of selection bias. Our data enable us to test for selectivity effects on job instability in adolescence.

In summary, the labor market experience of youths is said to display higher rates of job turnover. Four factors are said to account for this phenomenon: the sociopsychological nature of adolescence, the industrial and occupational concentration of youthful workers, the human capital profiles of young workers, and their negative selection from among the total cognitive-ability distribution. In the present study we contrast the relative importance of labor market, human capital, life course, and selection effects on job stability in Israel.

Data

The data which we employ consist of 2,144 retrospective life histories obtained in interviews with a national probability sample of Jewish Israeli men born in 1954 (Matras, et. al. 1984). The interviews were conducted during 1980–1981 when the respondents were about 27 years old. The interviews consisted of two sections: (1) retrospective life histories on various areas of activity, and (2) details of current employment, family characteristics, social participation, attitudes, and income. The life history section of the interview schedule reconstructs residential, educational, employment, family formation, and military service histories. Within each of these domains of activity, the respondent was asked to list each event, to describe it in some detail, and to date it. For example, in the domain of employment, the following information is available on each job held since age fourteen: date of entry and exit, occupation and industry codes, number of hours worked per week, number of subordinates, whether or not respondent changed a job title or section within the firm, and dates of changes. In addition, information is also available on whether or not the job change involved a change of employer. Retrospective data on income were not collected because, due to Israel's high inflation rates, respondents were often unable to recall either nominal or real income figures. The interview data were merged with military records, which provide information on psychometric intelligence measured at about age 17.

Most Israeli men spend about three of their late-adolescent years in military service. Because of its near-universality, military service has acquired the status of a major rite of passage. It is perceived as a major demarcator between youth and adulthood. This is illustrated in Figure 3.1, where we plot the percentage employed (whether full- or part-time) at the beginning of each half-year age interval for ages 14 to 26. The pat-

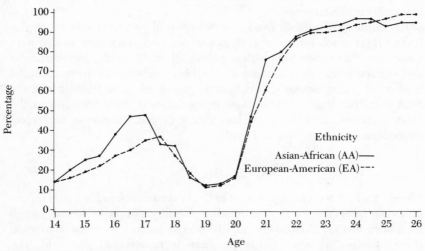

Figure 3.1 Percentage of the Cohort Who Were Employed, by Ethnicity and Age

terns are plotted separately for persons of Asian-African origins (there-after AA) and for those of European-American birth or ancestry (EA).[1]

About 14% of the cohort reported employment at age 14. This percentage increased sharply among the AA youths to a peak of 49 percent at age 17.0, and increased more gently for the EA youths to a peak of 35 percent at age 17.0. The percentage employed dropped sharply at ages 18 through 20, when most of the young men were performing compulsory military service. After the military service ages, the percentage employed recovered dramatically, reaching about 85 percent by age 22. Subsequently there was a less dramatic but steady increase in the percentage employed, exceeding 90 percent at ages 24 and 25.

The major difference between the ethnic groups is seen in the much larger proportion of AA's who worked prior to military service. This probably reflects their lower rates of secondary-school attendance (e.g., Shavit-Streifler 1983). Yet, despite documented ethnic differences in the attendance of higher (post-military) education, there was only a negligible difference between the groups in employment in the ages 20 through 26. This may reflect the fact that Israeli students in post-secondary education typically work, at least in part-time jobs. An earlier report on the 1954 cohort took note of the intensity of employment commitments in early adolescence. Specifically, it reported that a large proportion of jobs taken prior to military service were in fact full-time jobs and were held for at least five months (Matras, et al. 1984).

We define a job as a spell during which a person is employed by a given employer. As of the time of interview, the 2,144 members of the sample had had some 8,222 distinct and identifiable jobs. In about 7% of these jobs the respondent was self-employed. Such jobs are also deleted from the analysis because the processes that determine the likelihood to "shift" from self-employment are probably very different from those that determine shifting from jobs in which the worker is an employee. One hundred and thirty jobs were entered before age 14. These are deleted because in the interview schedule, respondents were asked to list jobs that were undertaken after that age. Also deleted are all jobs held prior to the respondent's immigration to Israel (155 jobs). Of the remaining 7,500 jobs, two-thirds were entered at the post-military-service ages (21–27). About one-fourth (22.7 percent) were entered by age 18—that is, at the post-

1. Geo-cultural origin and, in particular, the distinction between Asian-Africans and European-Americans is a major basis of social differentiation in Israel (cf. Smooha, 1978). It is highly correlated with all indicators of socioeconomic attainment. We present the patterns separately for the two groups because it would be unacceptable to assume ethnic homogeneity of the patterns.

primary—school ages. Finally, 10.7 percent were jobs entered at the military service ages (18–20).

The analysis employs partial likelihood proportional hazard (Cox 1972) models which are estimated in SAS's PHGLM procedure (Harrell 1982). With 7,500 spells, the estimation proved very time-consuming. In order to save computer time, a 33% random representative sample of respondents was drawn from the original sample of 2,144 persons. The subsample consists of 738 respondents who were employed in 2,448 jobs, which constitute 32.4% of all the jobs selected.

The units of analysis are job spells, that is, records which pertain to each of the jobs held by individuals. For each spell we define eight sets of variables. The first is the duration of employment of the respondent in the job measured in months. This variable provides the basis for calculating the rate of leaving the job. Longer durations reflect smaller hazard rates because, by definition, persons with high hazards of leaving jobs are unlikely to remain in them for long durations. Mean duration varies with age, from 12.03 to 13.85 (see Table 3.1). Second, we recognize two censoring events, the interview and military conscription. All job spells that ended within two months of induction are defined as censored. Conceptually, this corresponds to the notion that time of induction is determined by processes that are external to labor market processes. Some (if not most) adolescent jobs would have continued longer if the worker had not been obliged to enlist at a specific age. By defining conscription as a censoring event, we will focus on those modes of job-termination initiated by either the employee or the employer (but not by military service). The proportions of job censored by either event are presented in Table 3.1.

The third set of variables are dummy variables representing the age category of job entry. Fourth is a set of variables that characterize the job to which the spell pertains. Four job characteristics are included in the analysis. The prestige score of the job title (Kraus 1976) ranges from a possible 3 to 98. It is entered into the model as a proxy for the overall "desirability" of the occupation. We hypothesize that workers are less likely to leave "good" jobs. Thus, we expect the effect of prestige on the hazard rate to be negative. Public is a dummy variable coded 1 if the job was held in one of several industries that are monopolized (or almost monopolized) by the state, local authorities, or other public agencies (e.g., education, health, welfare, religious services, etc.). About 30% of the Israeli labor force is employed in the public sector. One important characteristic of public employment is that it assures many workers of job security and provides promotion opportunities within the various agencies and public firms. Thus, we expect that the hazard rate of leaving public sector jobs is lower than the hazard rate of leaving other jobs. NSubs is

Table 3.1. Means and Standard Deviations of Job Spell Variables by Age at Which Job Was Entered

	Age Group					
	14–17		18–20		21–27	
Variable	Mean	S.D.	Mean	S.D.	Mean	S.D.
Job characteristics						
PUBLIC (public sector)	0.02	0.13	0.13	0.34	0.09	0.29
PRESTIGE (prestige of occupation)	19.98	13.27	24.30	16.68	31.81	22.08
NSUBS (number of subordinates)	0.41	1.66	1.50	5.47	2.13	8.07
HOURS (number of hours worked per week)	42.75	10.89	46.34	13.03	46.13	13.86
Worker's human capital						
SECONDARY (some secondary education)	0.72	0.45	0.64	0.48	0.58	0.49
MATRICULATION (high school diploma)	0.04	0.19	0.15	0.36	0.10	0.30
UNIVERSITY (some higher education)	0.00	0.06	0.04	0.20	0.11	0.31
DEGREE (a university degree)	0.00	0.04	0.02	0.13	0.13	0.34
EXPERIENCE (months of labor force experience)	5.16	9.72	17.77	20.17	32.63	28.72
Life course variables						
STUDY (enrolled in school at end of job spell)	0.35	0.48	0.10	0.30	0.14	0.35
MARRIED (married at end of job spell)	0.02	0.13	0.24	0.43	0.46	0.50
CHILD (parent at end of job spell)	0.01	0.11	0.17	0.38	0.29	0.45
IQ (verbal and analytic intelligence)	51.65	18.20	54.97	18.86	57.63	17.72
Social background						
POPSEI (father's occupational prestige)	33.37	13.43	37.27	18.88	35.49	16.51
ETHNIC (Sephardi origins)	0.82	0.38	0.75	0.43	0.75	0.43
DURATION (Months in the job)	12.03	11.94	13.00	12.80	13.85	12.30
Censored by interview	0.01	0.11	0.09	0.28	0.35	0.48
Censored by military conscription	0.34	0.47	0.17	0.38	0.01	0.08
Number of jobs	602		247		1599	

61

the number of workers who were subordinate to our respondent on that job. We expect that workers who are in positions of authority had accumulated on-the-job training in the firm and are more likely to be retained by their employers. Hours is the number of weekly working hours. Full-time workers are less likely to leave jobs than are part-time workers. Thus, NSubs and Hours are expected to have negative effects on the hazard. These job characteristics are expected to account for some of the age differences in job stability because younger workers are less likely to be employed in the public sector, but are more likely to hold low-prestige occupations, to have little job authority, and to work part-time.

A fifth set of variables measures human capital at the time the worker entered the job. Older workers have had time to accumulate more education and work experience than young workers. We hypothesized that job stability is positively affected by the educational credentials workers bring to the job. Educational credentials are entered into the model as four dummy variables that correspond to some extent of secondary education; secondary education plus a matriculation diploma; some university education; and a university degree (a B.A. or higher). The omitted category is "no secondary education." Experience measures the number of months of labor force experience that the worker has brought to the current job. We expect that, with time in the labor force, workers become more committed to their jobs and exhibit more job stability.

The next variable, IQ, is measured by the military screening examinations which most Israeli men are required to take at age 17. The test consists of a Raven (Raven 1958) matrices test of analytic intelligence and a test of verbal intelligence (see Shavit and Featherman [1988] for some details on the tests.) As suggested (Mare, et al. 1984), adolescent workers are typically less intelligent as measured by these tests than are adult workers. From Table 3.1 we learn that the mean intelligence score of those holding jobs entered in adolescence (14–17 years) is 51.65, whereas the mean IQ scores of those with jobs entered in the 21–27 age category is 57.63. The six-point difference is about one-third of a standard deviation.

The seventh set of variables includes three dummy variables—study, married, and child—that indicate whether or not the respondent was in school, married, or a parent at the end of the job spell in question. We expect the effect of school enrollment on the hazard to be positive because students are more likely to work in temporary (summer) jobs. The effects of marital status and being a parent are expected to be negative because workers who must support families are less likely to shift among jobs. Controlling for these variables is expected to attenuate age-group differences in job stability.

The eighth set of variables that characterize each job spell are two in-dicators of worker's socioeconomic and ethnic origins. Popsei is the pres-tige of father's occupation when the respondent was a teenager, and ethnic is a dummy representing Asian-African ethnic origins. Adolescent work-ers are disproportionately of AA origins (because the school drop-out rates of this group are higher [Shavit-Streifler 1983]) and of low socioeconomic background. To the extent that these two variables affect job stability, they must be controlled in our models.

Age Differences in Job Stability

In Table 3.2 we present estimates of several models of job leaving. The model in the first column is estimated with censoring defined by the time of interview. The parameter estimates of the model indicate that respon-dents in the oldest of the three age intervals were least likely to leave their job at any small point in time. The effect of the 18–20 age stage is also negative but small, and is not significantly different from the effect of the omitted age category (14–17). These results indicate that job stability increases across the three stages of the early life course.

Table 3.2. Proportional Hazards Models of Job Shifts: All Non-Self-Employed Jobs Entered since Age 14

Independent Variables	Model							
	1†	2	3	4	5	6	7	8
AGES 18–20	−0.089	0.117	0.073	0.120	0.017	0.131	0.307*	0.479*
AGES 21–27	−0.511*	−0.093	−0.104	−0.044	−0.161*	0.149*	0.220*	0.586*
POPSEI			0.004*	0.005*	0.002	0.003	−0.000	0.001
ETHNIC			0.135*	0.142*	0.186*	0.101	0.182*	0.190*
PRESTIGE				−0.004*				−0.004*
PUBLIC				−0.511*				−0.533*
NSUBS				−0.024*				−0.023*
HOURS				0.002				0.008*
SECONDARY ED.						−0.093		−0.344*
MATRICULATION						0.108		−0.505*
UNIVERSITY						−0.421*		−0.947*
DEGREE						−0.418*		−1.246*
EXPERIENCE						−0.007*		−0.005*
IQ					0.007*			0.009*
STUDY							0.691*	1.025*
MARRIED							−0.311*	−0.309*
CHILD							−0.590*	−0.517*
CHI-SQUARE	103.12	7.29	12.53	47.53	28.57	69.20	252.15	387.80

*Parameter at least twice its standard error.

†Censored by interview only. All other models censored by interview and conscription.

In the second model (and all the remaining models in the table), both the interview and military conscription are defined as censoring events. This dramatically reduces the parameter estimate of the older age category. Although still negative, the effect of having entered a job in the early twenties is much reduced when compared to Model 1. Model 3 adjusts the age effects for socioeconomic background, with little change in the effects of the age variables. We conclude provisionally that conscription is a major cause of job leaving among adolescents, and that when this factor is controlled, job stability is only slightly greater in early adulthood than in adolescence.

Models 4 through 7 correspond to the explanations for age differences in job stability which were discussed earlier. Model 4 tests the hypothesis that adolescent instability is due to the kind of job in which adolescents are employed. As expected, the rate of leaving a job was inversely related to occupational prestige and to job authority. Similarly, public sector employment attenuates the propensity to leave a job. The effect of hours-worked-per-week is positive but not significant. The inclusion of the four job characteristics in the model reduces the contrast between the youngest and oldest age categories by over 50%.

In Model 5 we control for psychometric intelligence. Contrary to our expectation, the effect of this variable on the hazard is positive and its inclusion in the model accentuates the difference between adolescence and early adulthood. Model 6 indicates that post-secondary education and labor force experience are conducive to stable employment. The inclusion of these variables in the model reverses the sign of the age effect. Net of human capital differences between the ages, adolescents appear more stable workers than young adults.

In Model 7 we control for the three life course variables. As expected, students are relatively unstable workers, while married men and parents are more stable than single workers. Furthermore, the net effects of age in Models 7 are significant and positive. Model 8 indicates that when controlling simultaneously for all the independent variables, adolescents are significantly and substantially more stable in their jobs than young adults.

In summary, the major reason for the greater tendency of Israeli adolescents (compared to young adults) to leave their jobs is military conscription. In addition, the types of jobs they hold, their lower levels of human capital, and their student and family roles also contribute to adolescent job instability. We find it interesting that when all of these factors are controlled, adolescence appears to be a period of greater stability in employment than the other age ranges. We will discuss this point in the final section of the paper.

The Destinations of Job Shifts

We noted at the outset that a job shift can be both an instrument for social mobility (when workers shift to better jobs) or an indication of "disorderliness" of a career segment. We also suggested that, as workers grow out of adolescence, their labor market behavior becomes more career-oriented in the sense that they seek to improve their positions by upward shifts. In terms of our model, this translates into the expectation that the rate of moving into a better job is greater for young adults than for adolescents and that the rates associated with unemployment or less desirable destinations are greater in adolescence.

Following Sørensen and Tuma (1981) and Carroll and Mayer (1986) we distinguish between upward, downward, and lateral job shifts. Upward shifts are defined as moves into jobs in which the occupational prestige score is higher by five points or more than that of the job of origin. Downward shifts involve a loss of occupational prestige of five points or more. Shifts into jobs with similar prestige scores are defined as lateral moves. In addition we also take cognizance of moves into "non-employment."[2]

Among jobs begun in adolescence, only 24.8% were followed directly by other jobs. In the first column of Table 3.3, the most prevalent destination is military service: 33.7% of job spells were terminated within two months of induction into military service, 25.1 percent were followed by spells of school enrollment, and 15.3 percent of were followed by three months or more of being non-employed.

Of jobs entered in the 18–20 age category, 27.1% were followed by

Table 3.3. Job Spells by Age at Which They Were Entered: Percent Distribution by Destination of Subsequent Shifts

Destination	Age 14–17	Age 18–20	Age 21–27
Upward move	5.7	8.9	12.3
Downward move	3.3	13.0	9.4
Lateral move	15.8	19.4	22.5
Military service	33.7	17.4	0.6
Non-employment	15.3	27.1	14.0
School	25.1	5.7	6.0
Censored by interview	1.1	8.5	35.2

2. Unemployment is conventionally defined as a state of seeking employment while being out of a job. Our data base does not contain information on job search behavior. Consequently we employ the term *non*-employment in reference to periods during which respondent was not employed, was out of school, and was not in military service.

spells of non-employment, 17.4% were followed by induction into military service, and 41.3% were followed by direct entry into other jobs. In the oldest category, 35.2% of jobs were censored by the interview, 14% were followed by non-employment, and 44.2% were followed by other jobs.

In Table 3.4 we present models of job leaving which are conditional on the destination of the move. In Model 1 we focus only on departures which led directly to other jobs. All departures which were not followed (within two months) by another job are defined as censored. The greater stability at adolescence is even more pronounced than in the last column of Table 3.2 (compare 0.840 and 1.169 to 0.479 and 0.586). It would seem that much of adolescent instability was associated with moves into destinations other than immediate, subsequent jobs; namely, back to school.

Interestingly, respondents were more likely as older workers than as adolescents to move in all three directions (columns 2, 3, and 4), including into less prestigious jobs. If careers become more orderly with age, we would have expected the propensity of workers to make downward moves to diminish with age. The results contradict this expectation. Rather, the

Table 3.4. Proportional Hazards Models of Job Shifts by Destination

Independent Variables	Shift to Another Job				Shift to Non-Employment
	Any Job 1	Upward 2	Downward 3	Lateral 4	5
AGES 18–20	0.840*	0.776*	1.872*	0.545*	0.572*
AGES 21–27	1.169*	1.477*	1.488*	0.961*	0.341*
POPSEI	0.002	0.007	0.001	−0.003	−0.000
ETHNIC	0.160	0.056	−0.036	0.323*	0.108
PRESTIGE	−0.005*	−0.044*	0.038	−0.010*	−0.001
PUBLIC	−0.451*	−0.587	−0.097	−0.454*	−0.691
NSUBS	−0.021*	−0.023	−0.052	−0.012	−0.061*
HOURS	0.001	0.007	−0.002	0.000	0.010*
SECONDARY ED.	−0.070	0.144	−0.172	−0.130	−0.401*
MATRICULATION	−0.183	1.032*	−1.155*	−0.702*	0.314
UNIVERSITY	−0.319	0.271	−1.527*	−0.200	−0.730*
DEGREE	−0.734*	0.615	−1.727*	−1.241*	−0.796*
EXPERIENCE	−0.004*	−0.009*	−0.003	−0.002	−0.005*
IQ	0.000	0.002	−0.007	0.001	0.005
STUDY	0.181	0.179	0.093	0.247	—†
MARRIED	−0.214*	−0.229	−0.531*	−0.101	−0.793*
CHILD	−0.574*	−0.278	−0.638*	−0.720*	−0.473
CHI-SQUARE	163.88	128.52	126.21	111.34	196.79

*Parameter at least twice its standard error.
†No variance in the independent variable for the uncensored cases.

findings suggest that younger workers were least likely to move, irrespective of destination.

Even among jobs that led into spells of non-employment the effects of the older age categories are positive and significant, though smaller than the comparable effects in the other columns of Table 4. Thus, respondents as young adults were more likely to shift into non-employment, but they were less likely to do so than they were to make other types of moves.

Several additional findings appear in Table 3.4. First, the effect of prestige is negative with respect to upward shifts, and is positive with respect to downward shifts. This probably reflects ceiling and floor effects: the higher the prestige of the current occupation, the more difficult it would be to find an even better job. Conversely, the higher the prestige of the current job, the greater the number of less prestigious jobs available.

Employment in the public sector inhibits movement in any direction. Tenure in the public sector shields workers from shifting to non-employment, but its effect is also negative with respect to upward mobility. Finally, the effect of education is positive with respect to upward job mobility and is negative in the other columns.

Summary and Discussion

Adolescent workers are said to occupy marginal positions in the labor force. Their income and occupational prestige are low, they are more frequently unemployed, and they are less likely to benefit from promotion opportunities within and across firms than older workers. The marginal position of youths has been attributed in part to their erratic pattern of labor force participation and job instability. In the present study we have analyzed work history data for a sample of young Israeli men in an attempt to describe and explain differences in job stability between adolescence and early adulthood. We conclude that respondents were indeed somewhat less stable workers as adolescents than as young adults. The single most prevalent reason for leaving a job among adolescents was military conscription. Controlling for the interference of conscription explains a major part of the relative instability of adolescent workers. In addition, adolescents were more likely to be students, single, and childless. These characteristics are, as one would expect, conducive to job instability. Age-group differences in job characteristics and human capital affect stability in ways very similar to those revealed by previous studies (Sørensen and Tuma 1981; Carroll and Mayer 1986) and explain some of the age differences in job stability.

When all of these factors are controlled, our respondents appear to have been more stable workers as adolescents than as young adults. They were less likely to shift from one job to the next at any point in time, irrespective of whether the move involved upward, downward, or lateral mobility along the occupational prestige hierarchy. They were also less likely to shift from employment to non-employment. Thus these findings are clearly at odds with a model that assumes that with age (at least in early adulthood), workers' careers become more orderly. We find no indication that in Israel the transition into adulthood involves either stabilization in jobs or that job shifts are more likely to be in an upward direction.

How do we account for the inherent stability of teenage workers in Israel? At this point we can only offer some speculation. Most adolescent jobs begin between ages 16 and 18, within two years or less of conscription. These jobs are probably viewed by their incumbents as temporary because the date of induction is pre-set to age 18 or so. On the one hand, such jobs may be discarded more readily. On the other hand, several factors may operate to counter job instability at this stage of the life course. First, adolescent workers may find it difficult to obtain jobs because employers are reluctant to hire workers who are about to leave for an extended military service. Therefore, adolescents attempt to hold on to their current jobs. Second, employers are normatively—and under certain conditions also legally—obliged to rehire their adolescent employees after the latter are discharged from military service. Therefore, preconscription workers may hold onto jobs in order to guarantee their future employment. Finally, adolescents may simply "wait out time" in their jobs. Why bother leaving a job and risk unemployment when conscription is near?

The near-universality of military service has several implications for the process of the transition to adulthood. As an important rite of passage it delays the ages at which cohorts of men begin to marry, and it also delays the ages of post-secondary education. Our findings suggest that it also reverses the tempo of career formation. Whereas adolescence is a time of relative stability and stagnation, the search for career lines and experimentation with different types of jobs begins in the post-military ages, as is reflected in the higher rates of movement in the 21–27 age category.

4 *Trond Petersen and Seymour Spilerman*

Job Quits from an Internal Labor Market

Introduction

Bureaucratic career incentives form the major reward structure under which most white collar workers in the United States are employed. Rewards are attached primarily to positions rather than to performance within jobs. Individual advancement comes about through movement between positions, and individuals are promoted from lower to higher positions on the basis of past performance and future potential. Good performance in the present frequently is rewarded with a promotion in the future (see, e.g., Stinchcombe 1974, chap. 5; 1983, 181–83; Rosenbaum 1984, 244).

We gratefully acknowledge the financial support of the National Institute of Aging (grant no. AG04367), and from the National Science Foundation (grant no. SES-82-18534). The first author also wishes to acknowledge partial support for computational expenses from the Milton Fund of Harvard University (grant no. 31-995-2003-2). We are grateful to James Duke for research assistance. The first author benefited from seminar discussions of the paper at the Max-Planck-Institute für Bildungsforschung in West Berlin and at Harvard University. In particular we thank Glenn Carroll, Tom Colbjørnsen, Gudmund Hernes, Karl Ulrich Mayer, Aage Sørensen, Annemette Sørensen, and Nancy Tuma for comments. We are also grateful to Tormod Lunde, who wrote the computer routine for generating the numbers for Figure 4.1 and Table 4.8. Mary Visher commented extensively on the entire paper.

Incentive structures of this type have two major effects.[1] First, they provide employees with the motivation to perform well in order to increase the likelihood of a future promotion (see, e.g., Stinchcombe 1974, 125; Williamson 1975, 78). Bureaucratic career incentives share this effect with other types of incentives, such as piece rates and production bonuses, which are used widely among blue collar employees. The second effect of bureaucratic career incentives is to reduce turnover by making it more costly for the employee to leave an organization (see, e.g., Doeringer and Piore 1971, 29–30, 57–58; Osterman 1984; Granovetter 1986, 25).[2] Good performance in the past can be observed and assessed by the current employer, but not easily by prospective employers. Earning a future promotion, therefore, to a large extent is contingent on remaining in the same organization.[3]

This paper addresses the second effect of bureaucratic career incentives: their impact on turnover. Much of the internal labor market literature has focused on turnover, yet there has been relatively little empirical research on the relation between internal labor markets and turnover. Apart from instances of dismissals or layoffs, departure from a firm reflects an employee's decision. The options faced by the worker are either to remain with the firm, earn the current salary, and accept the prospects for future promotion; or to leave for employment elsewhere or, possibly, for non-employment. In contrast, the decision to promote and, more generally, the structuring of career ladders and advancement rules are made by the firm; at least in the short run they cannot be manipulated by employees and their organizations. However, the ways career ladders and pro-

1. In addition to these obvious effects bureaucratic career incentives may also operate as a divide-and-conquer device, which alleviates conflict between management and workers (hierarchical conflict) and promotes competition between workers (lateral conflict) (see Burawoy 1979, chap. 8; Edwards 1979, chap. 8). Whether management intentionally created bureaucratic career incentives as a divide-and-conquer device or whether it is just a by-product beneficial to management is subject to debate (see Jacoby 1985).

2. Steady salary increases within a given job may accomplish the same end. From the employer's perspective a hierarchy has some additional advantages. First, it serves to filter and select employees for jobs involving greater responsibility and authority, promoting only those of superior performance (see Rosenbaum 1984, chap. 2). Second, large salary differences at the same job may be difficult to legitimize even if they reflect differences in performance, since employees seem to care about local differences and make comparisons with others at the same level (see, e.g., Dessler 1984, 323; Frank 1985, chaps. 2–3).

3. There are additional and sometimes alternative means for reducing turnover, such as tying rights and fringe benefits to length of service. Abraham and Medoff (1985) provide evidence that among white collar employees merit appears to be the most important determinant of promotions and hence earnings, while among blue collar employees seniority is more important.

motion prospects are formulated affect individual departure decisions. The decision to leave is related to the promotion and career policies of the organization.

In order to address the relationship between departure decisions and organizational reward structures we ask the following questions. How do employees respond, in terms of quit behavior, to the structure of opportunity within an organization? Are they more disposed to remain when they occupy positions with strong prospects for future advancement? Conversely, are they more likely to leave when prospects for advancement are poor? When employees have reached high status levels within an organization are they less apt to depart—net of seniority—than workers in low positions? Finally, how do the reasons for departure vary with organizational characteristics and individual background variables?

The literature on turnover and career moves within and between organizations is extensive. For a detailed review, see Bluedorn (1982) and Granovetter (1986). In brief, both pecuniary (wages and fringe-benefits) and nonpecuniary (satisfaction and authority relationships) job features have been examined for their impact on departures (For a comparison of the importance of pecuniary versus nonpecuniary factors, see Bartel [1982]). Most studies report that departure rates depend strongly on the level of current rewards, seniority in the organization, and the employee's age; that is, for a given level of individual resources departure rates decline for all three variables (see, e.g., Blau and Kahn 1981; Felmlee 1982; Freeman and Medoff 1984, chap. 6; Tuma 1976, 1985; Carroll and Mayer 1986; Flinn 1986; Meitzen 1986; Waite and Berryman 1986; Kandel and Yamaguchi 1987). The *intention* to quit, as opposed to the actual quitting, depends in the same way on these variables (see Sørensen and Fuerst 1978; Halaby 1986). Several studies address how promotion rates within organizations depend on individual resources and organizational characteristics (White 1970; Wise 1975; Medoff and Abraham 1980; Sandefur 1981; Sørensen and Tuma 1981; Halaby 1982; Bielby and Baron 1983; Rosenbaum 1984, chap. 3; Skvoretz 1984; White and Althauser 1984; Abraham and Medoff 1985; Tuma 1985; Carroll and Mayer 1986; DiPrete and Soule 1986; Hartmann 1987). The studies show that the rate of promotion declines with seniority and with the level of current rewards.

No study, to our knowledge, addresses how departure decisions or quit behavior depends on the structure of opportunity in an organization; for example, how departure decisions vary with promotion rates.[4] The pre-

---

4. Three partial exceptions to this statement are Konda and Stewman (1980), Halaby (1986) and Meitzen (1986). Meitzen's study of quit behavior controlled for whether a job slot

sent study takes some steps towards assessing this dependence. Also, no study distinguishes between different types of voluntary departures; for example, those taken for reasons related to career advancement and those taken for personal reasons, such as tending to the needs of the family.[5] Most studies of departures assume that workers leave jobs voluntarily for reasons tied to career advancement. The current study, in contrast, directly investigates the reasons for voluntary job separations, distinguishing those that occurred to meet personal needs from those that took place for career reasons.

This paper therefore extends the existing literature in two ways. First, we assess the relationship between departures and organizational opportunity structures. Second, we examine the reasons voluntary departures occurred. To this end, in the empirical investigation, we use unique longitudinal data on a single hierarchically organized bureaucracy. We utilize information about the timing of each move within and out of the organization as well as the type of the move, employing a multi-state hazard rate model.

The remainder of the paper is organized as follows. In the next section we develop the research questions for the empirical investigation. Then we describe the data, the personnel records of a large U.S. insurance company. The following section discusses our statistical method, a multi-state hazard rate model. The concluding sections present the results.

Departures and Careers: Research Questions

Employees leave organizations for a variety of reasons. We consider two reasons that are the outcomes of choices made by employees: leaving for career reasons and leaving for personal reasons. Career reasons are defined as pursuit of better opportunities, higher earnings, better working conditions, and more interesting or suitable work in jobs outside the organization. Personal reasons include tending to family needs, such as children or illness, or departure due to relocation of the employee's spouse (see Table 4.1). In both cases the employee or his or her family makes the

---

allowed for salary increases. Halaby's study of the intentions or declared likelihoods of looking for other jobs controlled for whether the employee thought it likely that he or she would be promoted in the current job. Konda and Stewman report estimates of promotion and departure probabilities for several grade and seniority levels in a police organization, but do not discuss the relationship between the two, although they postulate a relationship in the theoretical discussion.

5. A partial exception is Bartel and Borjas (1977), who, using panel data, distinguished between departures for job-related and for personal reasons. However, they had no data on promotions.

Table 4.1. Definition of Variables Used in the Analysis

Definition of Destination States

State 1: Left for career reasons
   a. Higher earnings
   b. Better working conditions
   c. Greater opportunity
   d. More interesting or suitable work
State 2: Left for personal reasons
   a. Nearer home or better transportation
   b. Change of residence
   c. Household duties
   d. Illness in family
State 3: Promotion within company
   Any move leading to a salary grade level higher than the grade currently occupied

Educational Levels

0 Less than four years of high school
1 High school graduate (4 years)
2 High school graduate (4 years) plus secretarial or business school
3 College courses or certificates, less than 60 credits
4 College courses, 60 or more credits but degree not received
5 Junior or community college degree
6 Bachelor's degree
7 Graduate school courses, advanced degree not received
8 Master's degree
9 Doctorate

Organizational Variables

Division:	Job Focus:	Location:
1 Agency	1 Machine operator	1 Home office
2 Corporate	2 Secretary/steno	0 Other city
3 Group	3 Typist	
4 Individual	4 Figure clerk	
5 Investment	5 Other clerk	
	6 Accounting claims/contract analysis	
	7 Math/programming	
	8 Sales staff	
	9 Underwriting/investment	
	10 Not applicable	
	11 Other codes	

decision to move, in contrast to cases where the employee is fired or laid off.

When an employee decides between remaining with or leaving the organization, he or she typically applies some cost-benefit calculus, weighing the expected value of remaining against the expected returns from leaving. If the expected value of leaving is higher than that of remaining, the employee will quit.

How are these expected values determined? Consider first the expected value of leaving an organization for career reasons. That value depends, in large measure, on the alternatives available elsewhere as compared to prospects within the organization. If the employee's rewards within the organization are already high, opportunities outside the company are likely to be less attractive. We can state this as a research question, which refers to the employee's positions within the organization:

Research question 1: Are employees with higher current rewards less likely to quit, either for personal or career reasons, keeping other things such as seniority and age constant?

That the rate of departure declines with the level of already obtained rewards is not novel (see Sørensen and Tuma 1981; Tuma 1985; Carroll and Mayer 1986; Kandel and Yamaguchi 1987). What is novel is the exploration of the issue within a single hierarchically organized company, allowing a more detailed examination of the effects of the reward structure.

Consider next the expected value of remaining in the organization. For a given level of current rewards, this clearly will depend on the probabilities of getting promoted in the future. In positions with poor promotion opportunities, the expected value of remaining in the organization is low. Thus, our second research question is:

Research question 2: Are departure rates low in structural positions where promotion rates are high and vice versa, keeping other things constant?

This question relates directly to the concerns of the literature on internal labor markets: To what extent is turnover influenced by the structuring of career opportunities in a sector of an organization (see, e.g., Doeringer and Piore 1971, chap. 2; Williamson 1975; Osterman 1984; see also Becker 1975, chap. 2)?

The next issue relates to the contention that career ladders are needed in order to reduce turnover for employees with high amounts of firm-specific human capital, often referred to as idiosyncratic skills (see Doeringer and Piore 1971, 15–16; Williamson 1975, 62). Although we have no measure of firm-specific skills, we do have measures of seniority in the company, which can serve as a proxy for the former. Under the firm-specific skills interpretation of the employer's interest in reducing turnover, one would expect turnover to decline with the buildup of seniority. An alternative explanation for the decline in turnover with the amount of time spent in the company is that departures are primarily related to the life cycle (see also Rosenbaum 1984). The longer employees have been with an employer, the older they are, and therefore the fewer years they have left in the labor force to discount the costs of a job quit. We assess the impact of both age and seniority on the rate of departure. In particular, we analyze the relative weight of age and firm-specific seniority in turnover decisions. If the age effect is stronger than the seniority effect, one would surmise that turnover is primarily a phenomenon related to life cycle choices, due either to the number of years left in the labor force over which the costs of a departure can be amortized, or to age-related psychological costs of quitting. If, in contrast, the seniority effect is the stronger, turnover is primarily related to the buildup of firm-specific capital; that is, it is a structural phenomenon, relatively independent of life cycle choices. We hope to make some progress towards distinguishing between a life cycle and a firm-specific capital interpretation of quit decisions. Hence, our third research question is:

Research question 3: Which temporal variable is more relevant in explaining the two types of turnover: age, in which case turnover should be seen as principally a life cycle phenomenon; or seniority, in which case turnover is related primarily to the buildup of firm-specific human capital?

Consider finally the expected value of leaving for personal reasons. We hypothesize that this will depend on the employee's sex. Managing a household and nurturing children are still activities for which women bear the principal responsibility. When family needs require one or the other spouse to withdraw from work and career, we expect that women will be more likely to do so. This translates into a research question about the effects of demographic characteristics:

Research question 4: Are women more likely than men to leave the organization for personal reasons, keeping other factors constant?

It is well-known that women have higher turnover rates than men (see, e.g., Viscusi 1980; Blau and Kahn 1981; Hachen 1988; Ehrenberg and Smith 1988, 368–70; for contrary albeit very partial evidence, see Weiss 1984). That women withdraw more often from work for family reasons is also well known (see, e.g., Ehrenberg and Smith 1988, 328–30). However, to our knowledge no study distinguishes the quit rate for family and personal reasons from the quit rate for career reasons (a partial exception is Bartel and Borjas 1977), and hence no estimate is available on how men and women differ in these respects.

Data and Variables

The data used in this study are taken from the personnel records of a large U.S. insurance company. During the 1970s the company employed approximately 16,000 individuals at any given point in time. We use the personnel records pertaining to the career experiences of every employee who was either in the company as of 1970 or entered between 1970 and December 1978. Detailed information is available about the timing (year, month, and day) of promotions, demotions, and departures. Employees who voluntarily left the company were asked to state the main reason for doing so. Altogether nineteen reasons are recorded.

The company is hierarchically organized into salary grade levels, from grade 1 (the lowest) through grade 20 (the highest). The vice-presidents are not included in this grade scheme. The hierarchy is explicit in written documents and is clearly perceived by the employees. Internal labor markets are well developed. Vacant positions are posted within the company and employees are encouraged to apply for the jobs. Positions are made accessible to job-seekers outside the company only when no suitable internal replacement can be found. Further details on the company are given in Spilerman (1986). See also Noyelle (1987, chap. 5) for a discussion of internal labor markets in the insurance industry.

We analyze the rate of leaving a grade level for each of the three reasons discussed in the preceding section. We do this by means of survival analysis (see Tuma and Hannan 1984, pt. 2). The dependent duration variable in the analysis is the number of months an employee spends in a salary grade level before promotion, demotion, departure from the organization or censoring (end of study, December 1978) occurs. A salary grade level can be left for several reasons. In our general formulation we consider fifteen mutually exclusive and exhaustive reasons. In the present paper we report only the analysis for the three reasons discussed earlier: the grade level was left because the employee (1) terminated employment for reasons tied to his or her career; (2) terminated employment for personal, usually family, reasons; (3) was promoted to a higher grade level. We deal with dismissals and demotions (quite rare) in a separate paper, which includes an extended analysis of the structure of promotion (Spilerman and Petersen 1988). Definitions of the three reasons as well as of the other variables in the analysis are reported in the Table 4.1.

The rates of leaving a grade level for any of the three reasons—career, personal, or promotion—are predicted using three sets of covariates: demographic, human capital, and organizational. The demographic variables are race and sex. The human capital variables are educational level (from 0 through 9; see Table 4.1); seniority in the company, measured as the number of months the employee has spent in the company as of the starting date of the current salary grade level; and the employee's age at the time he or she entered the current grade level. Duration is measured as the number of months spent in the current salary grade. The rate of leaving a grade level at duration t in the grade depends on t, thus allowing for duration dependence, positive or negative. The organizational variables are the division in which the employee works, his or her job focus (a company-specific occupational code), and location (see Table 4.1). The job focus variable applies to all jobs in salary grades 1–12. The company rarely assigns job foci to the managerial and administrative positions in grades 13 and above.

In the present analysis job focus, division, and location are included mainly as control variables, although we will comment on the effects of division and location because they speak to research question 2. The job focus variable carries substantive interest in its own right, and is dealt with in separate papers (see Spilerman and Petersen 1988). In the statistical analysis we fix the seniority and age variables at their values at the date a grade level was entered, but allow them to change when a change in grade level occurs. That is, we let them depend on time between, but not within, grade levels. The covariates division, job focus, and location are treated as time-dependent, within as well as between grade levels. Thus if an employee changed his or her job focus while remaining in the same grade level this is taken into account in the analysis (for details see Petersen 1986a, 1986b).

By introducing both seniority in the company and duration in the grade level we allow for the possibility that duration in a grade may have a different effect than seniority in the company, on, say, the rate of getting promoted. The behavior of the employee may be governed by two clocks—duration in grade and seniority in company—with possibly opposite effects.

The focus of the present analysis concerns the demographic, human capital, location, division, and duration effects on rates of promotion and the two types of departures we have outlined.

Methods

We specify a continuous time transition rate model. Let the rate of leaving salary grade level s for reason j after duration t in the grade be

$$\lambda_{sj}[t|x(t)] \;=\; \lim_{\Delta t \downarrow 0} P_s[t \le T < t + \Delta t, J = j \mid T \ge t, x(t)]/\Delta t, \quad (4.1)$$

where T is a random variable denoting duration in grade s, and J another random variable denoting the reason for which the grade was left. $x(t)$ is the set of covariates that influences the rate, evaluated at duration t and possibly summarizing the employee's history in the company up to duration t in grade s. The index s runs from 1 through 20, one for each of the salary grade levels, while j runs from 1 through 15, one for each of the fifteen reasons for leaving the grade. $P_s[\cdot]$ denotes a probability.

Equation 4.1 is an instantaneous transition rate. Roughly, it gives the probability of leaving salary grade level s for reason j after duration t in that grade but before duration $t + \Delta t$, given the covariates in $x(t)$ and given that the employee was in grade s at duration t (where t denotes the number of months the employee already has spent in the grade and Δt equals one month).

The overall hazard rate of leaving grade s is given as

$$\lambda_s[t \mid x(t)] \;=\; \sum_{j=1}^{J'} \lambda_{sj}[t \mid x(t)], \quad (4.2)$$

where J' is equal to 15. Here we report only estimates of $\lambda_{.1}$, $\lambda_{.2}$, and $\lambda_{.3}$ (transitions made for other reasons are here treated as censored observations). Also, estimates are reported only for grades 2, 4, 7, and 12–15 (the latter four grouped together). The points to be made come through by considering this subset of grades, and the savings in the number of tables is enormous.

From 4.1 and 4.2 it follows that the probability that grade s was left for reason j, given that it was left after duration t, is

$$P_s[J = j \mid T = t, x(t)] \;=\; \lambda_{sj}[t \mid x(t)]/\lambda_s[t \mid x(t)]. \quad (4.3)$$

Thus the parameters pertaining to the rates not only tell us how long an employee waits before experiencing a transition, but also the probability of a specific type of transition, given that one occurred. Equation 4.3 has the form of a multinominal logit model, and its interpretation is well known.

We stress that the specifications in 4.1 and 4.2 make no assumption about independence of the different reasons (for discussions of this point see Prentice, et al. 1978, 545–47). An objective of this analysis is to investigate how the departure rates are related to the promotion opportunities in the company, and any assumption of independence would be inappropriate. Specifically, we assess how the departure rates in various structural positions in the company vary with the promotion rates in the same positions. If departure rates are high in positions where promotions rates are low, and low when promotion opportunities are high, then the relationship between departures and promotions is negative. The higher the promotion rate, the lower the departure rate.

Each of the transition rates is given a log-logistic specification (see Kalbfleisch and Prentice 1980, 27–28), as follows:

$$\lambda_{sj}[t \mid x(t)] = (\gamma_{sj} + 1)t^{\gamma_{sj}} \cdot \exp[\beta_{sj}x(t)]/\{1 + t^{(\gamma_{sj} + 1)}\exp[\beta_{sj}x(t)]\}, \quad (4.4)$$

where $\gamma_{sj} > -1$ and the parameters β_{sj} and γ_{sj} are to be estimated.[6] Without going into the details, this specification is particularly suitable in the present context. We assume that in the initial months in a grade duration has a positive effect with respect to promotion (you are not likely to be promoted immediately upon entering a grade). The promotion rate reaches a peak and then declines, as it becomes apparent that the employee is being passed over. Thus we expect the promotion rate to be bell-shaped (see also McGinnis 1968). With respect to departures—either for personal or career reasons—our priors are more complex. Because duration adds to seniority, there may be a negative association with the rate. However, net of seniority (which is included in the model), the effect may be positive, in that, having been passed over for promotion, an employee may be more willing to leave. Because the log-logistic specification can also portray increasing and declining rates, it is utilized for departures as well as promotions.

The interpretation of the parameters pertaining to the explanatory variables is the usual: a variable with a positive parameter increases the rate and one with a negative parameter decreases it. In other words, a positive parameter translates into a shorter waiting time for an event of the specific type, while a negative sign translates into a longer waiting time.

The parameter estimates are obtained by the method of maximum likelihood, as described in Petersen (1986a, 1986b).[7]

Descriptive Statistics

Table 4.2 gives descriptive statistics for the variables used in the analysis, other than division and job focus, which are not central to the present

6. The parameters of the transition rate in equation 4.4 were estimated by the method of maximum likelihood, using the algorithm described in Petersen (1986a).

7. Blossfeld, Hamerle, and Mayer (1986) explain (chap. 6, esp. 181–246) and list (Appendix 2, 262–72) the computer program used in the present article. The algorithm was developed in Petersen (1986a).

Table 4.2. Descriptive Statistics for Variables Used in the Analysis by Salary Grade Level (excluding division and job focus)

Variables	Salary Grade Level			
	2	4	7	12–15
	Mean (standard deviation)			
Duration (months)[a]	14 (14)	19 (17)	22 (18)	22 (18)
Seniority (months)[b]	6 (11)	27 (39)	83 (91)	150 (120)
Age (years)[b]	24 (8)	28 (10)	31 (10)	37 (9)
Educational level[c]	1.7 (1.3)	2.6 (1.9)	3.2 (2.3)	5.2 (2.3)
	Proportions			
Race				
White	.67	.73	.80	.94
Black	.23	.18	.13	.04
Asian	.02	.02	.02	.01
Hispanic	.08	.06	.05	.01
Sex				
Female	.90	.90	.66	.20
Male	.10	.10	.34	.80
Educational level				
0 or 1	.61	.46	.38	.14
2	.13	.12	.08	.02
3	.16	.14	.15	.11
4 or 5	.07	.11	.10	.08
6, 7, 8, or 9	.03	.16	.29	.66
Location[d]				
Home	.33	.33	.64	.64
Other	.67	.67	.34	.34
Destination states				
Remained in grade[e]	.04	.16	.26	.29
Left the company	.46	.35	.15	.09
Career reasons	.13	.12	.05	.03
Personal reasons	.11	.09	.03	.005
Other reasons	.22	.14	.07	.05
Promoted from grade	.49	.48	.58	.60
N (employees)	8894	8122	3235	4838

[a]The mean number of months spent in a grade level, including censored observations.
[b]Measured as of starting date of entry into grade level.
[c]The mean of the educational scale running from a low 0 to a high 9, see Table A1.
[d]Measured as of the date the grade either was left or censoring occurred.
[e]Censored observation.

study. When appropriate, means and standard deviations are reported, otherwise the proportions of employees having a certain value on a variable are given.

Table 4.2 shows that the four variables—duration in grade level, seniority, age, and education—all increase from one grade level to the next. Employees higher up in the hierarchy have been longer in the company, are older, and are better educated.

The proportions of white and of male employees increase as we move up the hierarchy. The home office has a higher concentration of employees in the upper grade levels than do offices elsewhere.

In Table 4.2 five destination states are considered: the employee was still in the grade level at the time the study ended (a censored observation); he or she left the company due to career, personal, or other reasons; or he or she got promoted from the grade. In the analysis of rates we focus only on promotions, career, and personal reasons for leaving the company.

We see that the proportions who left the company, for any of the three reasons considered, decline sharply with grade level. This may in part reflect the fact that employees in the higher grade levels are older and therefore less likely to leave. It may in part be that the higher grade levels offer their employees more opportunities. The alternatives available elsewhere may be less attractive to those higher up in the hierarchy.

Further, we see that the proportions being promoted from a grade increase with the grade level. This may reflect, in part, higher promotion rates in the higher grade levels, but also the fact that the departure rates are lower in higher ranks, so that more employees remain in the company until a promotion occurs.

Analysis of Rates

We report the results on rates in two parts. First, we discuss the effects of the independent variables on the three rates, for each grade level considered. Then we discuss how the rates depend on the grade level.

Effects of Independent Variables

The estimates of the three first rates of the multi-state hazard in equation 4.4 are given in Tables 4.3, 4.4, 4.5, and 4.6, one table for each set of grades. In each table two different specifications of the rates are considered. In Panels A only the demographic variables enter (race and sex), and, of course, duration. In Panels B we add the human capital and organizational variables.

The models in Panels B improve the fit significantly compared to the models in Panels A, using a likelihood ratio test statistics, indicating that

Table 4.3. Estimates of the Parameters of the Multi-state Hazard Rate Model for Destination States 1, 2, and 3 from Salary Grade Level 2 (estimated standard errors in parentheses)

	Panel A: Demographic Effects Only		
	Destination State		
Independent Variables	Departure for Career Reasons	Departure for Personal Reasons	Promotion within Company
Constant	−3.834 (.136)	−5.778 (.233)	−6.036 (.108)
Duration (in grade)	−.074 (.030)	−.018 (.033)	1.227 (.027)
Race[a]			
Black	−.591 (.084)	−.573 (.091)	−.472 (.057)
Asian	.153 (.273)	.084 (.309)	.568 (.206)
Hispanic	−.500 (.124)	−.259 (.129)	−.265 (.084)
Female (=1)	−.330 (.108)	1.356 (.216)	−.294 (.081)
−Loglikelihood[b]	6415.1	5680.7	18014.1

	Panel B: Demographic, Human Capital, and Organizational Effects		
	Destination State		
Independent Variables	Departure for Career Reasons	Departure for Personal Reasons	Promotion within Company
Constant	−2.101 (.220)	−4.976 (.297)	−6.521 (.159)
Duration (in grade)	−.001 (.031)	.044 (.034)	1.300 (.028)
Race[a]			
Black	−.290 (.090)	−.368 (.097)	−.559 (.061)
Asian	.106 (.286)	−.115 (.323)	.527 (.207)
Hispanic	−.232 (.130)	−.069 (.133)	−.338 (.087)
Female (=1)	−.875 (.123)	1.169 (.223)	−.113 (.081)
Age (years)	−.035 (.004)	−.010 (.004)	−.021 (.002)
Seniority (months)	−.034 (.004)	−.036 (.004)	−.016 (.002)
Educational level[c]			
2	.049 (.100)	−.073 (.110)	−.266 (.074)
3	.069 (.093)	.086 (.103)	.157 (.067)
4 or 5	−.289 (.137)	.215 (.134)	.052 (.095)
6, 7, 8, or 9	.312 (.184)	.485 (.188)	−.041 (.158)
Job Focus[d]			
1	.328 (.123)	.168 (.125)	.290 (.088)
2	.135 (.122)	−.195 (.124)	.165 (.088)
3	.504 (.100)	.059 (.107)	.219 (.070)
4	.033 (.133)	−.054 (.141)	.459 (.094)

Continued

Table 4.3. Estimates of the Parameters of the Multi-state Hazard Rate Model for Destination States 1, 2, and 3 from Salary Grade Level 2 (estimated standard errors in parentheses) (*continued*)

Division[e]			
2	−.751 (.196)	−.361 (.199)	.497 (.122)
3	−.560 (.122)	−.373 (.128)	.647 (.095)
4	−.532 (.119)	−.278 (.131)	.547 (.094)
5	−.320 (.196)	.169 (.199)	.565 (.149)
Location			
(1 = Home)	−.959 (.103)	−.582 (.105)	.274 (.060)
−Loglikelihood[b]	6207.3	5588.7	17849.4

Note: The parameters of the multi-state hazard in equation (4.4) were estimated by the Method of Maximum likelihood, using the algorithm described in Petersen (1986a). Number of employees in grade level 2 is 8894.

[a] Excluded groups: whites and Native Americans.

[b] The loglikelihood is partioned into three parts, one for each of the three rates. The loglikelihood pieces for the full 15 state hazard are not reported in the table. They are of no use in performing tests of interest for current purposes.

[c] Excluded group: High School Graduate or less education.

[d] Excluded group: Job foci with codes 6 and higher.

[e] Excluded group: Agency.

human capital and organizational variables add to the explanatory power of the model.[8]

Tables 4.3–4.6 contain a great deal of information (a full summary of the results is given in Table 4.7). Here we report only the most salient points, of which there are seven. First, in all grades women have lower rates than men of leaving the company for career reasons, but much higher rates of leaving for personal reasons, which speaks to research question 4. This no doubt reflects the different roles of men and women in the labor force. Women often leave jobs to take care of their families or because their husbands took a job somewhere else, whereas men rarely leave for those reasons. Hence, women appear to have lower job attachment, not because they tend to move from one to another employer more frequently than men, but because they more often have to withdraw from work in order to deal with family obligations. If women could arrange for alternative ways of dealing with family obligations, or if the obligations were more equitably distributed between the sexes, women would in fact constitute a more stable labor force than men, assuming the quit rate for

8. The value of the chi-square statistics is computed as follows. Let L_1 be the loglikelihood for a hazard with the added variables and L_0 for the hazard with those variables excluded. Minus twice the difference between L_0 and L_1 yields the value of the chi-square statistics. The degrees of freedom are equal to the number of parameters added between the model with L_1 and the model with L_0.

Table 4.4. Estimates of the Parameters of the Multi-state Hazard Rate Model for Destination States 1, 2, and 3 from Salary Grade Level 4 (estimated standard errors in parentheses)

	Panel A: Demographic Effects Only		
	Destination State		
	Departure for Career Reasons	Departure for Personal Reasons	Promotion within Company
Constant	−4.114 (.153)	−5.953 (.246)	−5.843 (.110)
Duration (in grade)	−.131 (.033)	−.083 (.037)	.983 (.026)
Race[a]			
Black	−.366 (.099)	−.465 (.120)	.053 (.062)
Asian	.247 (.223)	.410 (.257)	.250 (.193)
Hispanic	−.847 (.188)	−.077 (.162)	−.170 (.099)
Female (= 1)	−.342 (.114)	1.111 (.219)	−.549 (.080)
−Loglikelihood[b]	5614.0	4475.8	17437.4

	Panel B: Demographic, Human Capital, and Organizational Effects		
	Destination State		
	Departure for Career Reasons	Departure for Personal Reasons	Promotion within Company
Constant	−2.724 (.286)	−4.457 (.367)	−6.173 (.187)
Duration (in grade)	.039 (.034)	.033 (.038)	1.103 (.027)
Race[a]			
Black	.011 (.107)	−.292 (.125)	−.142 (.065)
Asian	−.040 (.233)	.227 (.278)	.024 (.195)
Hispanic	−.366 (.202)	.164 (.175)	−.374 (.100)
Female (= 1)	−.522 (.129)	1.057 (.228)	−.258 (.087)
Age (years)	−.031 (.005)	−.031 (.005)	−.024 (.002)
Seniority (months)	−.038 (.002)	−.017 (.001)	−.005 (.001)
Educational level[c]			
2	.077 (.128)	.139 (.131)	−.060 (.080)
3	.334 (.117)	.026 (.131)	.253 (.076)
4 or 5	.211 (.125)	−.137 (.151)	.229 (.085)
6	.433 (.115)	.284 (.132)	.187 (.087)
7, 8, or 9	.215 (.233)	−.331 (.316)	.332 (.184)
Job Focus[d]			
1	.005 (.266)	−.238 (.269)	−.316 (.141)
2	.396 (.171)	−.133 (.182)	−.093 (.115)
3	.302 (.217)	−.014 (.221)	−.251 (.130)
4	.146 (.211)	−.295 (.248)	−.237 (.139)
5	−.037 (.129)	−.198 (.146)	−.341 (.097)

Table 4.4. Estimates of the Parameters of the Multi-state Hazard Rate Model for Destination States 1, 2, and 3 from Salary Grade Level 4 (estimated standard errors in parentheses) (*continued*)

Division[e]			
2	−.449 (.220)	−.727 (.246)	.848 (.116)
3	−.459 (.134)	−.384 (.143)	.732 (.090)
4	−.749 (.162)	−.290 (.152)	.648 (.094)
5	−.523 (.192)	−.899 (.250)	.650 (.094)
Location			
(1 = Home)	−.737 (.119)	−.395 (.122)	.422 (.060)
−Loglikelihood[b]	5162.9	4310.3	17186.7

Note: The parameters of the multi-state hazard in equation (4.4) were estimated by the Method of Maximum likelihood, using the algorithm described in Petersen (1986a). Number of employees in grade level 4 is 8122.

[a]Excluded groups: whites and Native Americans.

[b]The likelihood is partioned into three parts, one for each of the three rates. The loglikelihood pieces for the full 15 state hazard are not reported in the Table. They are of no use in performing tests of interest for current purposes.

[c]Excluded group: High School Graduate or less education.

[d]Excluded group: Job foci with codes 6 and higher.

[e]Excluded group: Agency.

career reasons would remain unchanged. With respect to promotion, in the lower grades, 2, 4, and 7, women have lower rates of promotion than men, while in the higher grades, 12–15, they are at an advantage relative to men.

Second, in all grades blacks have the lowest rates of departure and promotion, particularly in grades 2, 4, and 7. This means that they remain longer in each grade level. In part they do so because they wait longer before getting promoted, and in part because they wait longer before quitting the company. Their lower rates of promotion probably reflect the disadvantage of being black in general, not of being black in this particular company, otherwise one would have expected higher quit rates for blacks. They would have sought jobs in other companies with more favorable treatment of minorities, had such companies existed. This point can only be appreciated by considering the multi-state hazard estimated in this paper, and not from the hazard for promotion alone.

Third, age and seniority in the company have negative effects on all three rates in all grade levels. The older a person is and the longer he or she has been in the company the less likely he or she is to get promoted or to leave. An increase in seniority of one year has about ten times the negative effect on departure rates as has a similar increase in age, while on the rates of promotion, seniority and age have about equal effects. This speaks to research question 3. Seniority also tends to have a greater neg-

Table 4.5. Estimates of the Parameters of the Multi-state Hazard Rate Model for Destination States 1, 2, and 3 from Salary Grade Level 7 (estimated standard errors in parentheses)

	Panel A: Demographic Effects Only		
	Destination State		
	Departure for Career Reasons	Departure for Personal Reasons	Promotion Within Company
Constant	−5.026 (.285)	−8.320 (.491)	−5.756 (.127)
Duration (in grade)	−.172 (.076)	.175 (.112)	.967 (.037)
Race[a]			
Black	.428 (.228)	−.151 (.358)	−.133 (.107)
Asian	.171 (.733)	1.307 (.554)	.279 (.322)
Hispanic	−.015 (.399)	−.836 (.744)	.114 (.160)
Female (= 1)	−1.008 (.174)	1.505 (.361)	−.777 (.075)
−Loglikelihood[b]	1011.7	727.7	8319.0

	Panel B: Demographic, Human Capital, and Organizational Effects		
	Destination State		
	Departure for Career Reasons	Departure for Personal Reasons	Promotion Within Company
Constant	−4.428 (.790)	−7.301 (1.07)	−6.637 (.268)
Duration (in grade)	−.001 (.088)	.430 (.138)	1.246 (.040)
Race[a]			
Black	.319 (.246)	−.519 (.409)	−.375 (.109)
Asian	−.048 (.811)	.821 (.629)	−.240 (.346)
Hispanic	.230 (.437)	−1.205 (.809)	.137 (.161)
Female (= 1)	−.412 (.224)	2.145 (.491)	−.105 (.087)
Age (years)	−.015 (.017)	−.033 (.016)	−.034 (.005)
Seniority (months)	−.018 (.002)	−.008 (.002)	−.003 (.001)
Educational level[c]			
2	.747 (.408)	−.479 (.586)	.183 (.154)
3	.137 (.349)	−.406 (.464)	.325 (.114)
4 or 5	−.015 (.418)	.148 (.401)	.472 (.127)
6	.732 (.308)	.600 (.366)	.757 (.117)
7, 8, or 9	.429 (.392)	.047 (.586)	.940 (.156)
Job Focus[d]			
1	.471 (.527)	.613 (.881)	−.072 (.203)
2	.310 (.459)	−.660 (.483)	−.831 (.167)
6	.256 (.324)	−.527 (.483)	.084 (.124)
7	−.132 (.392)	.398 (.411)	.050 (.147)
8	.438 (.356)	−.348 (.423)	.278 (.137)
9	.111 (.357)	−.013 (.497)	.259 (.137)
10	−.169 (.373)	.000 (.399)	.062 (.123)

Table 4.5. Estimates of the Parameters of the Multi-state Hazard Rate Model for Destination States 1, 2, and 3 from Salary Grade Level 7 (estimated standard errors in parentheses) (*continued*)

Division[e]			
2	−.477 (.525)	−.921 (.495)	.679 (.180)
3	−.131 (.401)	−1.134 (.403)	.796 (.155)
4	−.372 (.472)	−.642 (.404)	.810 (.160)
5	−.248 (.556)	−.875 (.605)	.528 (.211)
Location			
(1 = Home)	−.443 (.231)	.318 (.290)	−.142 (.089)
− Loglikelihood[b]	937.3	682.8	8051.0

Note: The parameters of the multi-state hazard in equation (4.4) were estimated by the Method of Maximum likelihood, using the algorithm described in Petersen (1986a). Number of employees in grade level 7 is 3235.

[a] Excluded groups: whites and Native Americans.

[b] The likelihood is partioned into three parts, one for each of the three rates. The loglikelihood pieces for the full 15 state hazard are not reported in the table. They are of no use in performing tests of interest for current purposes.

[c] Excluded group: High School Graduate or less education.

[d] Excluded group: Typist, Figure Clerk, Other Clerk, and Other Codes.

[e] Excluded group: Agency.

ative impact on career departures than on terminations for personal reasons. Because seniority correlates with a buildup of firm-specific skills (e.g., knowledge of procedures, development of collegial ties) and the accumulation of rights in the firm (e.g., a pension), departure for career reasons declines rapidly with seniority. Personal and family considerations, however, are less tied to seniority.

Fourth, the effects of duration are interesting. In all grades the parameters for duration on the rate of promotion are positive. This means that the probability of experiencing a promotion in, say, the next month increases with duration in the grade, up to some point, after which it decreases. The hazard has a bell-shaped function. On the two other rates the effect of duration is ambiguous, and varies with the grade. In grade 2, for example, duration has a negative effect on the rate of leaving for career reasons, while it has a bell-shaped effect on the rate of leaving for personal reasons. Both effects, however, are quite small. Figure 4.1 illustrates the shapes of the three hazards as functions of duration for grade 2.

Fifth, we see that location has a positive effect on the rate of promotion in grades 2 and 4, but negligible effects in grades 7 and 12–15. In grades 2 and 4 the effects of location on the two departure rates are negative. The interpretation of this finding seems simple. In the home office in the lower grade levels opportunities for promotions are high, and departure rates are consequently low. The results indicate that departure rates are

Table 4.6. Estimates of the Parameters of the Multi-state Hazard Rate Model for Destination States 1, 2, and 3 from Salary Grade Levels 12–15 (estimated standard errors in parentheses)

	Panel A: Demographic Effects Only		
	Destination State		
	Departure for Career Reasons	Departure for Personal Reasons	Promotion within Company
Constant	−6.486 (.278)	−8.777 (1.05)	−7.066 (.110)
Duration	.021 (.080)	−.064 (.325)	1.191 (.034)
Race[a]			
Black	.814 (.351)	.126 (1.04)	.061 (.160)
Asian	.666 (.792)	[b]	.266 (.350)
Hispanic	.613 (.606)	1.332 (1.08)	−.045 (.295)
Female (=1)	−.362 (.243)	1.595 (.454)	.289 (.075)
−Loglikelihood[c]	1217.3	200.6	12804.1

	Panel B: Demographic, Human Capital, and Organizational Effects		
	Destination State		
	Departure for Career Reasons	Departure for Personal Reasons[d]	Promotion within Company
Constant	−5.438 (.792)		−5.884 (.241)
Duration (in grade)	.286 (.087)		1.380 (.036)
Race[a]			
Black	−.189 (.379)		−.401 (.160)
Asian	−.241 (.863)		−.122 (.369)
Hispanic	−.093 (.633)		−.438 (.315)
Female (=1)	−.686 (.268)		.277 (.077)
Age (years)	−.034 (.014)		−.050 (.004)
Seniority (months)	−.014 (.001)		−.001 (.000)
Educational level[e]			
2 or 3	.980 (.553)		.180 (.114)
4 or 5	1.036 (.551)		.199 (.136)
6	.611 (.498)		.026 (.098)
7	.901 (.518)		.181 (.123)
8 or 9	.721 (.514)		.427 (.123)
Division[f]			
2	.342 (.368)		.106 (.126)
3	.362 (.370)		.332 (.122)
4	−1.155 (.519)		.141 (.125)
5	.411 (.367)		.663 (.129)
Location			
(1 = Home)	−.092 (.224)		−.059 (.070)
−Loglikelihood[c]	1082.6		12526.0

not independent of the promotion rates, and that consideration of the multi-state hazard yields valuable insights.

Sixth, it is striking how the rates of departure in grades 2, 4, and 7, for both career and personal reasons, are higher in division 1 (agency) than in divisions 2–5, while the rates of promotion are much lower in division 1 than the other divisions. As with location, this speaks to research question 2: the rates of departures are higher in those structural positions where promotion rates are lower. Also, as with location in the company, employees in salary grades 12–15 do not respond to promotion patterns in the same way as employees in grades 2, 4, and 7.

Finally, the effects of education are mixed. Education has a clear positive effect on promotion in all grades but grade 2. No similar inference can be drawn regarding the departure rates of grade 2 and the other grades.

Differences in Rates between Grade Levels

In the preceding section the effects of covariates were assessed, keeping the grade level constant. Now we turn to an analysis of the effect of the grade level itself, keeping covariates constant, thereby addressing research question 1.

This analysis can be accomplished in a variety of ways, depending on which values of the covariates one chooses to keep constant. We focus on how the three rates vary with grade level for two groups of employees:

Table 4.6. Notes to Table 4.6

Note: The parameters of the multi-state hazard in equation (4.4) were estimated by the Method of Maximum likelihood, using the algorithm described in Petersen (1986a). Number of employees in grade levels 12–15 is 4838.

[a]Excluded groups: whites and Native Americans.

[b]No Asian left the company from grade levels 12–15 for personal reasons. Hence their estimated rate of departure for personal reasons is 0, and the effect parameter is β(Asian) = $-\infty$ (estimate of minus 28 million). Deleting the term for Asians from the hazard yielded identical results in terms of the other parameter estimates and in terms of the loglikelihood.

[c]The likelihood is partioned into three parts, one for each of the three rates. The loglikelihood pieces for the full 15 state hazard model are not reported in the table as they are of no relevance for the tests performed in this paper.

[d]Too few transitions were made for this reason to allow estimation of the cause-specific hazard with any reasonable level of stability in the parameter estimates. The estimates varied drastically with small changes in the specification of variables.

[e]Excluded group: High School Graduate or less education.

[f]Excluded group: Agency.

Table 4.7. Summary of Effects of Independent Variables on the Three Rates by Grade Level

Variables	Grade 2			Grade 4			Grade7			Grade 12–15		
	λ_{21}	λ_{22}	λ_{23}	λ_{41}	λ_{42}	λ_{43}	λ_{71}	λ_{72}	λ_{73}	λ_{k1}	λ_{k2}	λ_{k3}
Duration	0−	0+	+ +	0+	0+	+ +	0−	+	+ +	+	0−	+ +
Race[b]												
Black	−	−	−	0	−	−	0+	0−	−	0−	0+	+ +
Asian	0+	0−	+	0−	0+	0+	0−	0+	0−	0−	− −	0−
Hispanic	0−	0−	−	0−	0+	−	0+	0−	0−	0−	0+	0−
Female[c]	−	+ +	0−	−	+ +	−	0−	+ +	0−	−	+ +	+
Age	−	−	−	−	−	−	−	−	−	−		−
Seniority	−	−	−	−	−	−	−	−	−	−		−
Education[d]	?	+	?	?	?	+	?	?	+ +	?		+
Location	−	−	+	−	−	+	0−	0+	0−	0−		0−

Note: Computed from Panels B of Tables 4.3–4.6. The entries mean that the variable:
+ +   increases the rate strongly;
+   increases the rate;
0+   has a small or insignificant positive effect on the rate;
0−   has a small or insignificant negative effect on the rate;
−   decreases the rate;
− −   decreases the rate strongly;
?   has an ambiguous effect on the rate.
The effects on λ_{k2}, where k denotes grades 12–15, are computed from Panel A of Table 4.6, since too few transitions were made for personal reasons in grades 12–15 to estimate the other effects reliably. See note d in Table 4.6 and the proportions and the N's in Table 4.2.
[a]The rates $\lambda_{.1}$, $\lambda_{.2}$, and $\lambda_{.3}$ are for leaving the company for career reasons, leaving it for personal reasons, and getting promoted within the company. The subscript k in λ_{kj} denotes grades 12–15. See table 4.1 and pp. 72–77 for more precise descriptions of the three reasons.
[b]The race effects are measured relative to being white.
[c]The effect of being female is measured relative to being male.
[d]The entries summarize the effects of educational dummy variables.

white males and white females. For the two groups, we further fix the age and seniority variables—evaluated at the time a salary grade level is entered—at 30 years and 12 months, respectively. We set education equal to more than high school but less than a complete college education. In grades 2, 4, and 7, job focus is set equal to secretary/stenographer (i.e., job focus 2). In grades 12–15 job focus is not relevant. Division of the company is set equal to agency (division 1) and location in company is set equal to home office. Since the rates exhibit duration dependence we also need to choose values for the duration in the grades for which we want to assess the rates. We estimate the rates after 12 and 24 months' duration in

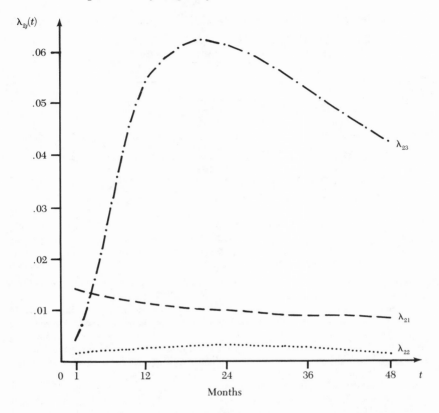

Figure 4.1. The Three Destination-Specific Rates in Grade 2 as Functions of Duration in the Grade
Note: The curves are drawn on the basis of the parameter estimates in Panel B of Table 4.3. The three rates λ_{21}, λ_{22}, and λ_{23} are for leaving the organization from grade 2 for career reasons, for personal reasons, and for getting promoted from grade 2, respectively. The rates have been calculated while fixing the explanatory variables at the following values: sex equal to male; race equal to white; age (measured as of the date salary grade level 2 was entered) equal to 30 years; seniority (measured as of the date salary grade level 2 was entered) equal to 12 months; education equal to more than high school but less than a complete college education; job focus equal to secretary or stenographer; division equal to agency; location equal to home office.

the grade levels. The estimates of the rates are computed from Panels B of Tables 4.3–4.6.

Table 4.8 gives the estimated rates for each grade and sex. Two things are striking in the table. First, we see that the rate of getting promoted is more or less the same across the grades (signified by $\lambda_{.3}$), with the excep-

Table 4.8. Estimated Rates after 12 and 24 Months' Duration in Grade Level for Selected Values on Independent Variables by Grade Level

	After 12 Months					
Grade Level	Rates for White Men			Rates for White Women		
	$\lambda_{.1}$	$\lambda_{.2}$	$\lambda_{.3}$	$\lambda_{.1}$	$\lambda_{.2}$	$\lambda_{.3}$
2	.011492	.001894	.050360	.005210	.005817	.045580
4	.018236	.001503	.050037	.011833	.004188	.041343
7	.005715	.000447	.011142	.003875	.003714	.010091
12–15	.007816	.000122	.040477	.004048	.000602	.050131

	After 24 Months					
Grade Level	Rates for White Men			Rates for White Women		
	$\lambda_{.1}$	$\lambda_{.2}$	$\lambda_{.3}$	$\lambda_{.1}$	$\lambda_{.2}$	$\lambda_{.3}$
2	.010093	.001909	.061049	.004900	.005600	.058051
4	.015330	.001510	.055371	.010626	.004077	.049959
7	.005344	.000598	.021610	.003700	.004753	.019915
12–15	.008625	.000117	.056693	.004720	.000572	.063247

Note: The rates are computed from Panels B of Tables 4.3–4.6, except in the case of the rates of leaving for personal reasons (i.e., $\lambda_{.2}$) from grade levels 12–15. The latter rates are computed from Panel A of Table 4.6. Other than sex, race, and duration (the values for which are given above), the values of the covariates for which the rates are assessed are: Age (measured as of the date a salary grade level was entered) equal to 30 years; seniority (measured as of the date a salary grade level was entered) equal to 12 months; education equal to more than high school but less than a complete college education; job focus equal to secretary/stenographer (i.e., job focus 2), which is of relevance only in salary grades 2, 4, and 7; division equal to Agency (i.e., division 1); location equal to home office. See also pp. 000–000.

The rates $\lambda_{.1}$, $\lambda_{.2}$, and $\lambda_{.3}$ are, respectively, for leaving the company (from the relevant grade level) for career reasons, leaving it for personal reasons, and for getting promoted within the company. See Table 4.1 and pp. 72–77 for more precise descriptions of the three reasons.

tion of the rates of promotion in grade level 7, which are substantially lower than the promotion rates in the other grades. This suggests that pyramidal organizational structures need not constrain careers in the higher echelons of the hierarchy more than careers in the lower ranks. Employees in the upper echelons of the hierarchy are as likely to be promoted as those lower down (see also Stewman and Konda 1983). The important point in this company is that the process of promotion is not driven by vacancy (see White 1970), but by merit. In vacancy-driven systems the crucial factor is the ratio between number of jobs at grade k and number of jobs at grade $k + 1$, a ratio which need not decline with k. In the merit-driven system, the employee's performance is the crucial factor determining whether a promotion occurs, since promotions involve changes in grade level but not necessarily in occupational duties.

Second, we see that the rates of leaving the company, for both of the two reasons considered, decline dramatically with grade level. In particular, the rate of leaving for personal reasons becomes very close to zero in the highest grade levels. The ratio of the rate of leaving for personal to the rate of leaving for career reasons is about the same in grades 2, 4, and 7, but then drops dramatically in grades 12–15, for both women and men. As shown in Table 4.2, only half a percent of those in grades 12–15 left for personal reasons, while as many as 11 percent in grade 2 did. This speaks to research question 1, that for a given promotion rate, the departure rate will decline with the level of achievement already obtained in the corporation.

One may speculate on the reasons for the second finding. One plausible explanation is that for employees in the higher grades the relative value of staying in the company is higher than for those in lower grade levels, in the sense that the alternatives available outside are not as attractive as those available in the company.

Summary of Findings and Implications

We have studied the determinants of voluntary departures for career and personal reasons from a large internal labor market. We assessed how quit rates were related to promotion rates in the organization, to the employee's position in the organization and to demographic and human capital characteristics. The company studied is hierarchically organized in salary grade levels. Using a multi-state hazard rate model we predicted the rates of getting promoted from a grade level and the rates of leaving it for either career or personal reasons.

Several findings were reported. Here we summarize the most important. First, it was shown that women have lower rates than men of leaving for career reasons, but much higher rates of leaving for personal reasons. This probably reflects the basic social difference between men and women in dealing with family obligations.

We considered simultaneously the effects of age, seniority, and duration in grade level on the three rates. Age and seniority, measured at the date a grade level was entered, had negative effects on all three rates in all grade levels. Duration in grade level, in contrast, had a bell-shaped effect on the rate of getting promoted. Given the log-logistic formulation of the hazard rate, this means that the probability of experiencing a promotion increases with time during the initial months in a grade level; it then peaks and declines. The effects of duration in grade level on the two rates for departure were ambiguous, either weak or insignificant.

Second, it was shown that the rates of departure are lower in the higher echelons of the organization, even controlling for seniority, whereas the rates of promotion remain more or less constant as one moves up the career ladder. Thus, employees who have reached positions of high achievement are less likely to leave than those lower in the hierarchy.

Third, it was found that in structural positions where rates of promotions are high—that is, in the organization's home office in grades 2 and 4 and in divisions 2–5 in grades 2, 4, and 7—the rates of departure are low. This suggests that the process governing leaving should not be studied independently of the process governing internal promotions. To understand the first process we need also to study the second.

We conclude by discussing some implications of the findings. First, we shall comment on the implications for our understanding of organizational departures and promotions. Specifically, we address the implications of the striking age, seniority, and duration effects. Tables 4.3–4.6 (Panels B) revealed that the effects of duration in grade level on the probability of a promotion are strong, significant, and consistently bell-shaped, in all four grade levels. The duration effects on departures, in contrast, were small, followed no pattern, and in five of seven rates were insignificant.

As a general rule, one ought to exercise restraint in interpreting duration effects. In the present case, however, the patterns revealed were so striking as to justify some speculation. The findings suggest that the process of promotion follows a renewal process, where the relevant clock is time since the last promotion, as indicated by the strong, significant, and consistently bell-shaped effects of duration in grade. Departure, in contrast, is not a renewal process (with time since last promotion as the relevant time marker), as illustrated by the weak and generally insignificant effects of time since last promotion on the rates of departure. Instead, the process seems to depend on total time in the company, as picked up by the significant and strong negative effects of seniority.

It might be objected that our estimated effects of duration on the rates of promotion are artifacts of unmeasured variables not included in the models (see Heckman and Singer 1982). We think this is not the case. Our reason becomes apparent by comparing Panels A and B of Tables.4.3–4.6. For departures, the effects of duration, in most of the rates, decline when the variables in Panels B are added to those in Panels A; the effects approach zero or become insignificant. For promotion, in contrast, controlling for the additional variables amplifies the effects of duration in all grade levels, indicating that the effects probably correctly reflect individual level dynamics as opposed to unmeasured heterogeneity.

Overall, seniority has about ten times the negative effect on the rates of departure than age has; an increase in seniority of one year lowers the rate about ten times more than the same increase in age. This holds for both departure rates in all four groups of grade levels studied. Seniority may be interpreted as a proxy for relationship-specific investments. The more seniority, the higher the firm-specific investment, and the more will be lost by a departure. Hence the effect of seniority on the rate of departure should be negative. Age effects relate to behavior over the life-cycle. The older the employee, the fewer remaining years in the labor force to recoup the costs of a departure, which translates into a negative effect on the rate of departure.

On the basis of the present results it seems that the effects on departures of relationship-specific investments are much stronger than the life-cycle effects, which speaks to research question 3.

Our final comment concerns the implications for our understanding of gender-based stratification. The findings that females withdraw from the company for personal reasons more often than men, for career reasons less often, and—in the low grades—experience lower rates of promotion than men, warrant some speculation. In stratification research one typically correlates current achievement with human capital, organizational, and labor market characteristics. In general, it is found that women with resources comparable to men fare worse than their male counterparts. This is taken as evidence of discrimination.

One might adopt the view that the process of stratification should be studied in a life cycle perspective. Thus, employees move from positions of lower to higher status partly on the basis of their performance and credentials, but partly by virtue of being situated in career and promotion systems where the likelihood of getting ahead is high, provided one stays within the system. If one accepts this point of view, the current findings have important ramifications. In concordance with other studies we found lower rates of promotion for women, at least in the lower echelons of the company, which can be taken as evidence that women are at a disadvantage relative to men. We also found that women, more often than men, withdraw for personal reasons, primarily in order to deal with family obligations; at the same time they are less likely to depart for career reasons. The issue therefore becomes: To what extent can the differential achievements of men and women be attributed to differential treatment by employers, and to what extent to the different constraints men and women face from family obligations? If a substantial part of the difference is attributable to the choices women make in order to accommodate family constraints, the implication is clear. In order to advance equality of achievement between men and women, the creation of equality of opportunity in the workplace is insufficient. Employers and local governments must supplement this with child care arrangements and flexible time provisions to reduce the burden of household demands. Given such provisions, a more equitable distribution of household duties between men and women must develop.

5 *Aage B. Sørensen*

Employment Sector and Unemployment Processes

Introduction

Unemployment is an important and carefully monitored social indicator. The level of unemployment in a society is generally considered a measure of its social and economic welfare and is, therefore, of considerable political significance. By this indicator, most Western societies have not been doing well in recent years. Unemployment rates have remained stubbornly high, not only in the United States, where unemployment traditionally is high, but also in many European countries where unemployment was low to very low in the sixties and early seventies.

Traditionally, unemployment is considered a variable in macroeconomic theory to be manipulated through measures that affect aggregate demand. The main measure of unemployment, the so-called unemployment rate, is a statistic that measures how many people are affected by unemployment. It may well be the relevant variable for macroeconomic theory, but it is not a measure that tells us much about individual unem-

This chapter was first presented as a paper at the Eleventh World Congress of Sociology in New Delhi, India, August 18–22, 1986. The research reported here was supported by a grant from the National Institute of Aging (grant no. 1P01AG02877-01). I am indebted to Nancy Williamson and Jessica Sewell for valuable research assistance.

ployment processes. The rate is a proportion formed by counting in the numerator the number of people looking for work at a point in time (the survey week) and in the denominator the total number of people in the labor force.[1] The measure is not a rate in the technical sense of the term unless it can be assumed that all unemployment durations are of equal length.

The number of people looking for work in a particular week is a count of the number of unemployment spells in existence in that week. The spells are created by people leaving or being forced out of their jobs. Spells are terminated by people reentering employment or leaving the labor force. The count of spells or people unemployed at a point in time will be determined by the rate at which spells are created and by the rate at which they are ended. If the creation and termination of unemployment spells are completely determined by the demand for labor and if the labor market is homogeneous, then aggregate demand should indeed govern the number of spells to be observed at a point in time and the usual method of measuring unemployment is adequate. If, on the other hand, the creation and duration of spells are governed by forces other than the business cycle, then the unemployment rate as conventionally measured is not informative about the mechanisms that govern unemployment; nor are aggregate demand policies likely to be effective in reducing employment. If unemployment processes are determined by individual characteristics, or if the labor market is not homogeneous, aggregate demand policies risk creating excessive demand for some groups or in some sectors and result in wage inflation, while failing to reduce the unemployment for other groups or in other sectors of the labor market.

The experiences of the last decade suggest that the conception of unemployment processes as homogeneous may not be adequate, because the macroeconomic policies that go with this conception seem to have failed to reduce unemployment. In fact, the concern for inflation seems by now to have led to an almost complete abandonment of any attempt to directly reduce unemployment in the aggregate in many countries. The wage inflation is what one would expect to result from aggregate demand increases in a heterogeneous labor market with a great deal of variation in individual unemployment processes. In fact, the labor market surveys used to measure unemployment, such as the CPS, show a great deal of individual and labor market variation in the proportion unemployed.

Theory that would explain individual variation in unemployment comes

1. This is the U.S. definition and the one recommended by the International Labor Organization. Many European countries also use measures based on counts of the insured instead of, or in addition to, the survey measure.

mainly from microeconomics. Particularly prominent is a view that unemployment is generated by an individual's search for better jobs in a highly dynamic employment system. In search models, persons choose to be unemployed in order to engage in a productive search for better jobs. Unemployment is a part of the natural turnover in the labor market (e.g. Hall 1970). Unemployment compensation and welfare benefits make it economically possible for individuals to quit their jobs rather than having to search for better jobs in their spare time. The view implies that unemployment is a transient and voluntary phenomenon not effectively dealt with by increasing aggregate demand. It is especially likely to be engaged in by young people experimenting with their employment and by those groups where the economic losses of engaging in a job search are relatively small: those who may have alternative sources of support, such as married women, and low-paid workers who are not much worse off on welfare or unemployment compensation.

The conception of unemployment as search is consistent with some of the main features of the distribution of the unemployed according to demographic characteristics and also consistent with an increase in overall levels of unemployment as income support programs become more generous. The conception is not consistent with the fact that a high proportion of those who report themselves as unemployed also report that they did not voluntarily quit their jobs, but were laid off. Some of those may be argued to not be unemployed at all: the temporarily laid off who have jobs they will return to (Feldstein 1975). The rest of the laid off can still be said to be voluntarily unemployed, arguing from contract theory that they choose to sign employment contracts that ensure them high and fixed wages in partial compensation for uncertain employment (Azariadis 1975). Both search theory and contract theory imply that unemployment spells should be of short duration. There is considerable evidence for a preponderance of short unemployment spells from research using longitudinal data. In fact, spell lengths will be overestimated from cross-sectional surveys of the unemployed reporting on their completed lengths of spells such as the Current Population Survey (CPS) (Salant 1977). Still, the theory and the spell distribution that is consistent with the theory may understate the welfare consequences of unemployment as argued by Clark and Summers (1979), who show that most of the experience of unemployment is felt by a few who have very long spells of unemployment. This result dampens the benign view of unemployment as a short-term experience that is widely shared and in fact is not completely unavoidable in a dynamic economy.

A more comprehensive view of the unemployment process than offered by search and contract theories should be able to account not only for short spells, but for the overall distribution of spell lengths. This means a focus on the dynamics of the unemployment experience. It seems difficult to provide such a comprehensive view without taking into account that people may change during their unemployment spells in a manner that increases or decreases their chances of reemployment. This suggests investigations of the manner in which spell lengths depend on variables that change over the spell, as reflected in the form of duration dependence of the unemployment process. Such an investigation is the purpose of this paper.

Microeconomic theory sees unemployment as a voluntary individualistic affair in sharp contrast to the undifferentiated and involuntary view of unemployment assumed in macroeconomic theory. Microeconomic theory pays very little attention to the specification of the labor market context for unemployment processes that would condition individual-level processes. It may be surmised that processes generated by search and processes resulting from anticipated layoffs are unlikely to occur in the same labor markets. Still, the emphasis in the economic theory is exclusively on individual choice rather than on the social structures that condition those choices. Similarly, if indeed the overall length distribution of spells reflects individual change, the sources of such change cannot be identified by microeconomic theory. These sources presumably have something to do with the labor market context for unemployment processes, especially the opportunities offered by different labor market structures.

Sociologists of the labor market have in recent years done a great deal of research on labor market structures using a variety of conceptions: dual economy sectors, internal versus external labor markets, primary versus secondary labor markets. This research has rarely focused on unemployment, with the exception of Schervish (1983).[2] Instead the research has continued the traditional emphasis on socioeconomic attainment processes. However, a proper specification of labor market structures for the study of career and attainment processes should also have implications for the study of unemployment processes. Such a conceptualization and a specification of its relevance for the study of unemployment, in particular the dynamics of the process of ending unemployment, will be presented in the next section.

Unemployment Durations and Labor Market Structures

Much sociological research on the labor market is concerned with identifying labor market forces that cause variation in socioeconomic attain-

---

2. Quantitative sociological research on unemployment events is in general very rare. For one of the few recent exceptions, see DiPrete (1981).

ment. These efforts produce a great deal of description about the relative importance of individual versus "structural" characteristics for observed levels of attainments, where these "structural" characteristics are a variety of industry, firm, and organizational variables. While this research is useful for the identification of the places where people are likely to receive higher pay, the research has been less useful in increasing our understanding of how labor market structures interact with individual attributes in producing attainments (Sørensen, 1983). This understanding is more likely to be obtained from the study of the mechanisms that create labor market processes in different labor market structures. It will be a study of mechanisms that link people and their characteristics to jobs or positions providing different levels of earnings and other rewards.

Distinguishing between closed and open employment relations appears to be especially useful for the identification of different mechanisms of labor market processes. Originally proposed by Weber (1968), the distinction is elaborated upon and applied to employment relations in Sørensen (1977a, 1983). Open employment relations are here defined as employment relations that are freely available to anyone with the needed qualifications. In particular, the access to open employment jobs is not constrained by the employment decisions of those in jobs at a particular moment of time, for open employment relations will be of short duration for specific tasks. These are the employment relations assumed in the neoclassical theory that sees labor markets as competitive and basically similar to markets for other goods. In such markets, competition establishes prices that are wage rates and that are tied to the productivity of individuals in the manner described by marginal productivity theory. For given demand schedules, equally productive persons will obtain equal wage rates. Only if there are barriers to mobility creating unequal demand schedules or lack of perfect information will unequal wage rates for identical people be observed.

Closed employment relations are available to new employees only if the present incumbents of jobs have decided to leave their positions, either for a better job or for retirement. Employment relations tend to be of longer and indefinite durations because they can only be reestablished when vacancies occur in jobs. Closed position systems emerge for reasons of technology and/or contractual problems, in the manner suggested by internal labor market theory (Doeringer and Piore 1971; Williamson 1975). In internal labor markets wage rates and other rewards are characteristics of jobs, not of individuals, as administrative arrangements rather than market competition establish the match between individual characteristics and job rewards. Changes in wage rates reflect changes in jobs and are not necessarily tied to changes in individual productivity, as is the case in competitive systems. Historically and organizationally, the specific mobility regimes of promotion systems establish the correspondence between individual characteristics and jobs, so that identical individuals usually will not receive identical wage rates even if there is no uncertainty.

The vacancy competition mechanism created in closed employment relations and the wage competition mechanism created in open systems produce very different labor market processes. Still, it is possible to show that both mechanisms can be used to account for the main features of observed attainment processes (Sørensen, 1979, 1984). Thus both mechanisms would generate the typical shape of the experience earnings profile observed. However, in wage competition, growth in the early years reflects increases in productivity brought about by on-the-job training and experience, while in vacancy competition, growth reflects the utilization of mobility opportunities established by promotion schemes without necessarily reflecting growth in productivity.

Closed and open employment systems also generate very different unemployment processes. Ideal type versions of both systems should not generate any unemployment at all. In completely open systems with perfect information and no state intervention, everyone should be able to find immediate employment at some wage rate. In completely closed systems no employees should be forced to leave their jobs. When unemployment occurs in open systems, it is a result of either imperfect information or the existence of minimum wage laws that prevent some from being employed at the wage rate that corresponds to their productivity. The former situation is the one assumed in microeconomic search theory. Because it takes time and effort to obtain information, people choose to leave their jobs in order to devote their time to search for better jobs. People set an aspiration level and continue to search until they receive a wage offer that matches their aspiration level or reservation wage. The search period corresponds to a period of unemployment. The decision to engage in search should be heavily dependent on the individual's reservation wage as determined by skills, experience, and ability in relation to his or her current wage. The length of search should be determined by the rate at which wage offers at different levels appear in relation to the individual's reservation wage or aspiration and the cost of searching. The creation and termination of unemployment spells in open position systems should be strongly dependent on individual characteristics.

In closed systems, unemployment processes again will be set in motion by demand chocks in product markets. However, the internal labor market firms that are characteristic of closed position systems do not adjust to product demand changes by changing wage rates, as in open position systems. Rather they adjust by changing the quantity produced and laying off workers in response to lower product demand. Since the very forces that create closed employment relations make it costly to lose workers in which firms have made specific on-the-job training investments, layoffs tend to be initially short-term and to have promise of recall. Typically a whole production unit is laid off. Hence, except for possible seniority rules imposed by collective agreements, layoffs should be unrelated to individual characteristics if the "risk set" is properly specified.

Quite different hypotheses about the relation between individuals, firms, and unemployment processes in the two systems follow from these considerations. For the case of unemployment durations or the rate of reemployment, these hypotheses are elaborated in the next section with a special emphasis on the different mechanisms determining unemployment duration.

Unemployment Durations in Closed and Open Employment

The typical unemployment spell in open employment systems is produced by a voluntary quit for search. In closed employment systems, the spell should result from a temporary layoff. In open systems, the spell is ended by the acceptance of a wage offer that matches the reservation wage chosen by the individual. In closed systems the spell is ended by the recall. This simple scenario, of course, assumes several things: first, that quits from open employment and layoffs from closed employment are the only modes of job separation; second, that people during unemployment spells do not move from one sector to another.

There is a third mode of job separation in both systems: dismissal. Theoretically, such separations should be frequent in open employment. They should be the exception, by definition, in closed employment. Empirically they are rare. The standard CPS question about dismissals suggests that only a very small proportion of those unemployed have been dismissed. This may, of course, reflect response bias resulting from reluctance to admit having been fired. It also may result from the unemployment spell being very short after dismissal. They presumably are caused by a discrepancy between a person's performance and the current wage rate. Reemployment opportunities are more ample the lower the wage rate. If the spells are very short they are underrepresented in cross-sectional counts of spells, because of length bias (Salant 1977) caused by the selectivity of spells sampled by the cross-sectional survey (Sørensen 1977b). In longitudinal data, such as those employed here, spells caused by dismissals may be more adequately represented. However, whether they originate in open or closed employment, they should result in search.

It is useful to conceive of the search process as similar to the job-shift process (Sørensen 1987). The period of search is a job spell, the task being the search. The rate of shift out of a job can in general be argued to be determined by the current rewards obtained in the job in relation to the potential rewards, where the latter are determined by the individual's resources as measured by education, ability, and skills. If only money matters, the main variables should be the current wage in relation to the reservation wage. An example of empirical support for a negative partial effect of rewards and a positive effect of resources on the rate of shift is presented in Sørensen and Tuma (1981). For unemployment spells, the rewards of the "job" are unemployment compensation, welfare, support from other family members, and leisure. The potential rewards are those hoped for from the search and again should reflect the person's skills, experience, and other resources. As in job shift we should expect that the larger the discrepancy between these two sets of variables, the more likely it is that better employment can be found and the higher the rate of reemployment.

If job offers appear at a constant rate, we should expect time-constant rates of reemployment if the individual's aspiration for better employment or his reservation wage remains constant. Time-constant rates mean that the rate at which spells end should be the same regardless of how long the person has already been searching. Departures from the assumption of a constant rate of job offers would be caused by cyclical changes. They are difficult to model with the data used here. Given the quite short periods under consideration, it seems reasonable to ignore such changes in the employment offer distributions. Presumably, however, there are differences by locale in the distribution of job offers. Such variation is a source of unmeasured heterogeneity.

It may not be reasonable to assume that a person's aspiration level or reservation wage remains unchanged indefinitely during a search. The longer the search continues without success, the more discouraged the individual becomes. This should lead to a lowering of the aspiration level and an increased probability of reemployment. One should therefore expect positive duration dependence in spells of unemployment due to search; that is, the rate of reemployment should increase as the spell progresses (Lippman and McCall 1976a).

The rate of reemployment after an unemployment spell due to search should then be a question of the individual characteristics that determine the aspiration level or reservation wage, the amount of income available during the spell, and the duration of the spell already completed. These hypotheses will be tested below, with emphasis on establishing the predicted positive duration dependence.

The length of temporary layoffs from closed employment should, as noted, not depend on individual characteristics, but should be completely determined by the rate of recall. This rate in turn should vary between firms, reflecting their particular production schedules. This heterogeneity in the rates of recall, when left unmeasured, should produce observed negative time dependency in the rates of reemployment. This phenomenon of spurious time dependency due to unmeasured heterogeneity is well known and results from the changing composition of those remaining in a particular state (here, of being unemployed), since those with high rates of reemployment leave first.

Temporary layoff is an ambiguous state. What starts as a temporary layoff may become an indefinite layoff. Such a shift would result in genuine negative time dependency in the rate of reemployment if the unemployed remains in the closed employment sector. The job structures of closed employment are such that new hires tend to take place only at the bottom of the job ladder because of the need to maintain promotion schedules and training arrangements. The unemployed from the closed sector tend to have firm-specific skills and experiences that are less employable in other firms. Thus as the chance for recall diminishes, the rate of reemployment should also decrease.

The negative time dependence in closed employment sectors may be argued to change eventually by a shift into the open employment sector and search in a competitive labor market. The prediction then should be that the positive time dependency eventually becomes positive as the rate of reemployment also becomes dependent on individual characteristics.

I hypothesize that sources of both positive and negative true time dependency should be identifiable by labor market structures. However, unmeasured heterogeneity will also show up as negative time dependency regardless of the labor market structure to which the individual is exposed. The predicted differences therefore may only show up as more or less negative time dependency.

These hypotheses are tested below, using data on employment spells from the Panel Study of Income Dynamics (PSID).[3] In the present analysis no direct measures of labor market structures are introduced. Such measures, relying on occupational and industry variables, are being constructed in current research. Here, I shall rely instead on the individual characteristics of race and labor force experience as indicators of labor market experience, assuming that blacks and inexperienced individuals

3. For a description of the study see, for example, Morgan and Duncan (1983).

are more likely to be located in the open employment sector. Similar information on whether or not the individual returned to the same employer after the unemployment spell will be used to indicate closed employment.

Data and Methods

The present analysis uses the 1982 PSID information about spells of unemployment. Respondents in the 1982 wave were asked about their current employment status. If they answered "unemployed" or "temporarily laid off" they were asked a series of questions about the amount of welfare, unemployment compensation, and other support they were receiving. If employed they were asked if they had been unemployed in 1981, and about the timing of the spells. The present analysis used information about the most recent spell including spells in progress at the time of interview (treated as censored) for male heads of households. This produced 579 spells from the 3,384 male heads of households who responded to the survey in 1982.

PSID contains a variety of information about the unemployment experiences of male heads. From this information a number of variables were constructed. They are described in Table 5.1. A few comments about some of these variables are in order. The variable CHNP is a measure of unemployment compensation received in 1981, derived by dividing the total amount of compensation received by the number of hours reported to be unemployed. This is an average figure that does not reflect unemployment compensation received before 1981. Less than half of the respondents received any unemployment compensation. The dummy vari-

Table 5.1. Variables and Their Means and Definitions

Name	Mean	Definition
CHUN	.45	1 if received unemployment compensation, 0 otherwise
CHNP	$2.81 (CHUN = 1)	Hourly unemployment compensation in 1981
HAHE	$7.39	Average hourly wage in 1981
NBF	.05	1 if benefits lost, 0 otherwise
SAEP	.52	Return to same employer
MFTW	.54	1 if full-time labor force experience less than 6 years, 0 otherwise
MWHI	.55	1 if respondent is white, 0 otherwise
CEN	.55	1 if spell not censored, 0 otherwise
TIME	14.44 (CEN = 1) 22.42 (CEN = 1)	Number of weeks unemployed
LOGT		Logarithm of TIME

able CHUN measures this. The variable HAHE is the respondent's average wage rate in 1981. Here it is used to measure the respondent's resources in the manner suggested by the conception of the search process as a job-shift process. This wage rate will be partly endogenous to the unemployment process, and a better measure would be the respondent's predicted wage rate (Atkinson, Gomulka, and Micklewright 1984). An attempt was made to obtain predicted wage rates using variables (education and experience) available in the present analysis to estimate a wage equation for the whole sample of male heads. The resulting predicted wage rates for the unemployed did not have a significant effect on the reemployment rates and the apparent unreliability may produce bias in other coefficients. Hence, despite the possible endogeniety, the actual wage rates were used.

In some spells, thirty-two to be exact, the unemployed lost unemployment compensation during the spell. This was taken into account in computing the hourly unemployment compensation. In addition, the unemployment compensation variable is treated as a time-varying covariate in the analysis. Finally, the time-dependent covariate NBF was constructed to indicate that unemployment compensation was lost.

The measure of the duration of the unemployment spell was obtained using information about the duration in weeks of the most recent spell in 1981 or the number of weeks of unemployment completed for those unemployed at the time of interview. As shown in Table 5.1, there is a considerable amount of censoring present. Given the censoring, the most informative description of these data is provided by the Kaplan-Meier estimate of the survivor function, providing an estimate in the presence of censoring of $F(t)$, that is, the proportion remaining unemployed by time t. Selected values of the survivor function are presented in Table 5.2. While there indeed are a number of short spells of unemployment, the median is more than twelve weeks. There are a fairly substantial number of long spells—20% are estimated to last more than a year.

Table 5.2 Selected Values of the Kaplan-Meier Estimate of the Survivor Function, $F(t)$

Week (t)	$F(t)$	$N(t)$
0	1.00	579
1	.94	532
2	.87	488
4	.77	412
8	.67	347
12	.57	276
26	.34	109
39	.24	59
52	.21	24

From this information event history models for the rate of reemployment can be estimated with variables listed in Table 5.1 as co-variates. A
fully parameterized model such as the Weibull or the Gompertz would
seem desirable. These models would allow the estimation of a time-
dependency parameter from which the direction of the duration dependence could be inferred. However, available software did not permit the
estimation of the interaction between covariates and the time dependency.[4] Because the statistical significance of such interactions is of interest here, the discrete time approximation to the continuous time models
proposed by Allison (1982) was chosen. This approach also easily allows
for the incorporation of time-varying co-variates.

Allison shows that a discrete time approximation allows for a very flexible formulation of most event history models. Using a slight generaliza-
tion of the framework proposed by Allison, general models of the sort

$$p_i(t) = f[A(t) + \mathbf{B}\mathbf{X}_i] \tag{5.1}$$

can be estimated with the proper specification of f. Here $p_i(t)$ is the probability that an event takes place in period t for individual i, $A(t)$ is a vector
of constants denoting the time dependency, and $\mathbf{B}\mathbf{X}_i$ is a set of covariates
characterizing individual i. A particularly attractive specification of the
function for $p_i(t)$ is

$$p_i(t) = 1 - \exp\{-\exp[A(t) + \mathbf{B}\mathbf{X}_i]\} \tag{5.2}$$

because it will provide estimates that approximate those that would have
been obtained had the proportional hazards or the Cox model been estimated for the underlying continuous time model. In particular, these estimates will not be dependent on the length of the time interval. This
specification can be estimated using the complementary log-log "link"
specification in GLIM.

If $A(t)$ is further specified as

$$A(t) = a_0 + a \log t_i \tag{5.3}$$

we obtain an approximation to the Weibull model. Interactions may here
be tested using interaction terms involving $\log t$ and the covariates.

The discrete time approximation demands that the data, whose unit of
analysis is spells, be converted to observations on each time unit for each
individual. This produces an enormous amount of information—here,
about 10,000 observations. Since the event is quite rare and it was neces-

4. Such interactions can be estimated for the Gompertz model in RATE (Tuma 1979).

sary to reduce the sample size considerably due to hardware limitations, the time unit was redefined as a two-week period and a random 30% sample from these observations was selected. This gave a sample of 2,452 observations for the present analysis.

Results

As noted above, I take the average wage rate as a measure of the respondent's resources. In a search theory interpretation one should then assume that the reservation wage is a linear function of this quantity. The income provided in the spell is measured by the unemployment compensation received. With the conception of search as a job shift, using search theory, one should then expect that in the open employment sector the rate of reemployment would be positively related to the wage rate and negatively related to the amount of compensation received.

Changes in the aspiration level are assumed to depend on the time already spent searching, so that an increase in the rate of reemployment will be observed. This should be more pronounced the more likely it is that the respondent is located in the open sector. It seems plausible to assume that inexperienced workers are more likely to be located in the open sector and to be engaging in search while unemployed. Hence, I expect that younger workers have more positive time dependency than experienced respondents. Similarly, minority workers can be assumed to be more common in the open sector, so that the same interaction will be observed for race.

Results of the complementary log-log estimation of various models are shown in Table 5.3. The results conform closely to the predictions. First, note that the model that does not include the interaction terms show no significant effect of experience. The model that includes the interaction terms changes the estimates of the effect of both race and experience considerably, making the main effect of experience highly significant and more than doubling the effect of race.[5] Both the interactions with time are significant. Whites have more negative time dependency than blacks and inexperienced workers have more positive time dependency than experienced workers. Thus, young blacks have the most positive time dependency, while experienced whites have the most negative.

The effect of amount of unemployment compensation is significantly negative. The more compensation received, the longer the spell, if respondents receive any compensation at all. It is of considerable interest to note that the dummy variable measuring being covered by unemploy-

5. Experience is dichotomized as it can be shown that the effect is clearly non-linear.

Table 5.3. Complementary Log-Log Estimation of Models for Rate of Reemployment

	Model 1		Model 2	
	B	S.E.	B	S.E.
Constant	−2.033	.247	−2.179	.412
CHUN	.392	.216	.394	.218
CHNP	−.127	.063	−.130	.064
HAHE	.031	.013	.034	.013
MFTW	.031	.153	−.786	.347
MWHI	.591	.161	1.372	.393
LOGT	−.480	.077	−.453	.179
LOGT*MFTW			.421	.163
LOGT*MWHI			−.375	.172
−2*log-likelihood	1,232.4		1,217.1	
	Model 3		Model4	
	B	S.E.	B	S.E.
Constant	−2.116	.508	−2.167	.409
CHUN	.394	.218	.110	.221
CHNP	−.130	.064	−.046	.062
HAHE	.033	.013	.027	.013
MFTW	−.776	.346	−.746	.343
MWHI	1.360	.394	1.460	.390
LOGT	−.530	.406	−.484	.176
LOGT*MFTW	.417	.163	.417	.161
LOGT*MWHI	−.369	.173	−.389	.169
LOGT*LOGT	.019	.088		
NBF			1.713	.316
−2*log-likelihood	1,217.0		1,195.5	
N = 2,266				

Note: For definition of variables, see Table 5.1.

ment compensation appears to have a positive effect on the rate of re-employment while the amount of coverage has a negative effect. Thus workers with low levels of compensation may have a higher rate of reemployment than those that do not receive any compensation at all. This complicated relation between compensation and rates of reemployment suggests why there appears to be continuing controversy about the impact on compensation on duration of unemployment (Atkinson, Gomulka, and Micklewright 1984).

The effect of the average wage rate received in employment is positive, as predicted when this variable is interpreted as a measure of the respondents' resources. Whites and experienced workers have much higher rates of reemployment than blacks and inexperienced workers. Thus the frequent finding that young or black workers have short spells is largely a result of the positive time dependency. If these workers were in the same employment sectors as whites and experienced workers their spells would be considerably longer.

The third model in Table 5.3 shows the effect of adding a squared term in log$t$ to the model. As noted above, one might expect that the time dependency becomes positive after very long spells. This prediction is not borne out—the effect is insignificant, indicating no pronounced curvilinearity.

The fourth model now adds the measure of having lost unemployment benefits. As expected there is a significant positive effect on the rate of reemployment.

It is interesting to directly identify the spells most likely to occur in the closed sector, where dependency on measured characteristics is hypothesized to be less. PSID asks if the respondents return to the same employer after the spell. These spells are then likely to be layoffs in the closed sector. This information can be used to estimate a competing risk model for the two outcomes of the spell: returning to the same employer versus taking a job with a different employer. The results of estimating the Model 1 of Table 5.3 for these two outcomes are presented in the first panel of Table 5.4. As predicted, few variables show a significant effect on reemployment rates for those who should be more likely to be in the closed sector. Only experience and time have significant effects. As predicted, there is more negative time dependency for these spells. Those spells not resulting in return to the same employer, in contrast, have no significant time dependence and a strong effect of race. In particular, it

Table 5.4. Models for Rates of Reemployment for Spells Ending in Return to Same Employer and Spells Ending in Employment with Different Employer

	Same Employer		Different Employer	
	B	S.E.	B	S.E.
Constant	− 1.603	.487	− 5.370	.783
CHUN	.532	.303	.390	.322
CHNP	− .076	.078	− .253	.114
HAHE	.032	.018	.028	.021
MFTW	− 1.268	.463	.841	.600
MWHI	0.621	.482	2.428	.680
LOGT	− 1.069	.257	.509	.287
LOGT*MFTW	.415	.250	− .065	.242
LOGT*MWHI	− .036	.261	− .732	.256
− 2*log-likelihood	686.9		744.21	
N = 2,262				

Note: For definition of variables, see Table 5.1.

Table 5.5. Models for Rates of Reemployment for Spells in the Closed and Open Sector

	Closed Sector		Open Sector	
	B	S.E.	B	S.E.
Constant	− 1.308	.933	− 2.425	.594
MFTW	− .831	.826	− .361	.488
MWHI	.834	.966	1.893	.551
LOGT	− .785	.484	− .493	.273
LOGT*MFTW	.628	.419	.398	.243
LOGT*MWHI	− .134	.492	− .455	.243
− 2*log-likelihood	223.55		602.63	
N =	376		1,311	

Note: Closed sector in this table is defined as spells covered by unemployment compensation of more than $3.00. Open is defined as not covered by unemployment compensation. For definition of variables, see Table 5.1.

should be noted that the effects of unemployment compensation and wage rates are substantially smaller. This presumably shows that search is less likely to govern the unemployment spell in this more closed sector. However, the second panel of Table 5.4 also shows that the effect of experience is also absent in the more open sector where layoff is not indicated. Presumably, in the more open sector, experience does not discriminate among different employment processes.

Return to the same employer, of course, could also take place in the open sector. Another definition of the closed sector can be obtained by grouping together spells covered by unemployment compensation for those in. Conversely, those spells where compensation was not received are classified as the more irregular or open sector. Since we cannot here use amount of compensation as a variable, only experience and race are included as independent variables. The results are presented in Table 5.5. In the more regular, closed sector, none of the independent variables have an effect. In the more open, irregular sector, race shows very strong effects, while, as with return to the same employer, experience makes little difference. Note also that the rates of reemployment are very much higher in the closed sector than in the open sector.

Conclusion

This paper has shown that unemployment processes are quite heterogeneous according to employment sector. Using indirect indicators to identify sectors, it is demonstrated that in the more closed employment sector of the labor market, the duration of unemployment processes is not greatly influenced by individual characteristics, including the unemployment compensation received, and that remaining heterogeneity results in apparent negative time dependency. In the more open sector, the unemployment process is more dependent on individual decision making, as predicted by search theory. In particular, individual change over the unemployment process results in positive time dependency for those most likely to be located in the open sector, inexperienced workers and minorities.

Of particular policy interest is the quite complicated mechanism detected for how unemployment compensation influences duration of unemployment. Increased compensation does increase unemployment spells, as predicted by search theory. However, those covered by compensation appear to be more likely to be located in the closed sector, where unemployment spells tend to be shorter and, in fact, less dependent on individual characteristics, including the amount of compensation. Without disaggregation, the effects of unemployment compensation will, therefore, depend on the distribution of spells among sectors, and results from different samples will be inconsistent with each other—as the controversy about this amply shows.

The next step is, of course, to rely on direct rather than indirect measures of unemployment sectors. This is done in ongoing research where the life cycle variation in these processes also occupies attention.

6 *Reinhard Hujer and Hilmar Schneider*

Unemployment Duration as a Function of Individual Characteristics and Economic Trends

Introduction

Although unemployment has been one of the most urgent problems of economic and social policy for over a decade, the existing variety of theoretical approaches is confusing and insufficiently put to empirical test (Buttler 1984). Accordingly, the adequate political measures to be taken evoke controversy. The following paper does not claim to be able to do away with these deficiencies. However, it does point to aspects which have been somewhat neglected in previous discussions.

The ongoing period of high unemployment in the Federal Republic of Germany developed in two marked shifts, closely related to the oil price shocks that occurred at the end of 1973 and again over a prolonged period from 1978 to 1981. On both occasions, the crisis led to a period of flat growth because growing productivity could not compensate for the increasing prices of resources.[1] Unfortunately, the data presented in this

This research was supported by the German Science Foundation and the University of Frankfurt. The authors are members of the Sonderforschungsbereich 3, Microanalytic Foundations of Social and Economic Policy.

1. Monatsberichte der Deutschen Bundesbank, April 1978, pp. 22f.; Monatsberichte der Deutschen Bundesbank, April 1981, pp. 13f.; Friedrich and Ronning 1985.

paper only cover the period from 1970 to 1979. Therefore, the following statements are restricted to consequences of the first oil crisis.

In 1974 and 1975 the unemployment rate increased rapidly. The total volume of annual working hours decreased as well. At the same time the working population declined, although this trend later reversed because of a decreased effective working time; that is, the average annual amount of hours worked. The actual increase in unemployment during 1974 and 1975 would have been even greater if the number of persons able to work (i.e., the number of persons between 15 and 65) had not stagnated at the same time.

When analyzing unemployment stock, a growth of unemployment figures can have two causes: A relative growth of inflow or an increase of the mean unemployment duration (Egle 1984). Nevertheless, most of the empirical models concerned with unemployment are restricted to analysis of stock itself (ibid.). Among the few exceptions for Western Germany are the studies of Freiburghaus (1978) and Lempert-Helm (1985). Bailey and Parikh (1985) conclude in a recent study for Great Britain that the increase of unemployment during the seventies was mainly the result of an increase of mean unemployment duration. However, all of these studies are based on aggregate data. The lack of individual data concerning unemployment duration is one of the most important limitations of these studies.

Although the paper of Büchtemann and Brasche (1985) is based on individual data, it is more descriptive than based on explicit behavioral models. In addition to the data presented here concerning the seventies, data from the Socio-economic Panel (see Hujer and Schneider, 1986) should help redress the lack of a model-based analysis.

One of the questions that may be answered with our analysis is whether the overall ascertained increase of unemployment duration should be classified as real or spurious. A real increase would be present if it took place on the aggregate level as well as on the individual level. A spurious increase would result if the individual-specific unemployment duration remained constant throughout the observation period while the probability of inflows to unemployment increased for persons with higher individual-specific unemployment duration. When the former holds true, one should see a significant influence of labor market indicators. This may not happen in the latter case.

Beyond this, individual data allow a differentiation between inflows and outflows to and from unemployment by different prior and destination states. This possibility is represented here by two submodels that separate outflows from unemployment into two destination states: return to occupation, and withdrawal from the labor force. Of course, the analysis of stocks and flows touches only the surface of the problem. Microeconomic approaches try to come to a more profound explanation of the labor market (Helberger 1982). The present paper will take advantage of at least parts of such a theoretical background.

Job search theorists (Lippman and McCall 1976b) argue that the decision of an unemployed person to take up employment depends on two major components. First, a job searcher individually fixes his optimal reservation wage. The reservation wage is inversely related to search and opportunity costs. The second component is the wage that is actually offered for a job. A positive decision to occupy a job will take place when the offered wage exceeds the reservation wage.

It follows from these arguments that a decline in opportunity costs, induced primarily by an increase in unemployment compensation, increases search duration. An increase in the level of unemployment results. Job search theory thus led to a discussion of whether the level of unemployment compensation could be used to control the level of unemployment.

Although the assumptions differ, advocates of contract theory come to similar conclusions regarding the level of unemployment compensation and its influence on the level of employment. From their point of view, unemployment may increase because firms temporarily dismiss employees during periods of capacity underutilization (Feldstein 1975). The lower the related losses for the two contracting parties (i.e., employer and employee), the sooner such behaviour occurs. The applicability of this approach, however, is restricted due to the fact that temporary layoffs constitute only a small part of West German unemployment.

Empirically, the effect of the level of unemployment benefits has been analysed most extensively in the United States (see Hamermesh 1977 for a summary of then current results). A more recent study of the United States by Moffitt (1985) is methodologically similar to our work. His results largely confirm the conclusions of job search theory and contract theory. However, one has to take into account that job offers that call for a decision on the part of the job searcher may occur only rarely during an employment crisis. A reduction of unemployment compensation will therefore have little effect upon unemployment duration, while it will surely increase the problems of the unemployed.

Finally, human capital theorists argue that unemployment may be explained by discrepancies between individual skills and qualification requirements of labor demand (Helberger 1982). Although this argument may hold true outside of economic recessions, it seems to be too simplistic otherwise. It does not appropriately reflect that even high qualifications may not prevent unemployment during a recession.

In general, a problem of these microeconomic labor market theories is their failure adequately to consider global developments in labor demand. It is our objective to overcome this disadvantage by formulating models that incorporate global labor demand as well as individual labor supply components.

Modeling Transitions from Unemployment via the Hazard Rate Approach

Hazard rate models are used to analyze individual changes between discrete states over time as a stochastic process (Andreβ 1985; Arminger 1984; Blossfeld, Hamerle, and Mayer 1986; Cox and Oakes 1984; Diekmann and Mitter 1984b; Heckman and Singer 1986; Kalbfleisch and Prentice 1980; Lawless 1982; Tuma and Hannan 1984). We will treat transitions from unemployment to employment and transitions from unemployment to withdrawal from the labor force as a continuous-time, discrete-state Markov process. The hazard rate $r_{iab}(t)$ of individual i at time t gives an artificial measure for the instantaneous propensity of individual i to leave from an original state a to a destination state b at time t. t is called process time and starts counting from zero each time a change occurs. We assume that the instantaneous transition rate $r_{iab}(t)$ can be explained by a set of measured covariates in the following manner:

$$r_{iab}(t) = \exp\left[\beta_{0ab} + x_i(t)\beta_{ab}\right] \qquad (6.1)$$

where $x_i(t)$ denotes a row vector of the set of covariates of individual i at time t and β_{ab} denotes a column vector of a corresponding set of parameters. β_{0ab} symbolizes a regression constant. The model in equation 6.1 corresponds to an exponential distribution of the random variable t (for a given combination of the values of the covariates). It is therefore called an exponential model. Equation 6.1 implies that any changes in r over t are covariate-induced. Conditions under which this implication is appropriate within the context of transitions from unemployment can, for example, be found in Tuma and Robins (1980). As we are primarily interested in measuring certain covariate effects, we have forgone models that incorporate endogenous time variation of r.

Estimation of our model is accomplished via the maximum-likelihood method. The likelihood function is given by:

$$L_{ab} = \prod_i r_{iab}(t_i)^{c_{iab}} \exp\left[-\int_0^{t_i} r_{iab(\tau)}d\tau\right] \qquad (6.2)$$

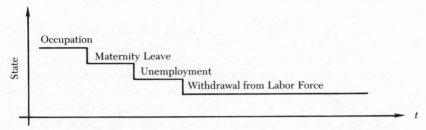

Figure 6.1. Hypothetical Transition from Employment to Withdrawal from the Labor Force

Here, t_i denotes the observed duration of individual i in state a, c_{iab} represents an indicator variable that takes a value of one if individual i changes from a to b at t_i. Otherwise, c_{iab} is always zero.

Formulation of equation 6.2 implies two assumptions. First, it requires independence between individuals. The second implication is called the Markov assumption, which says that transitions to a destination state b are only dependent upon the immediately preceeding state a, not on earlier states. This assumption may at times be problematic. Figure 6.1 gives an example where motherhood produces a transition from occupation to out of the labor force with an intermediate state of unemployment. As will be seen later, we allow for such violations of the Markov assumption by explicitly modeling earlier events, such as childbearing.

The Database

The present analysis is based on individual data from the Lebenslagen-Studie (LeLa) of the Sonderforschungsbereich 3. The main survey was carried out between October 1980 and April 1981. The parent population consisted of the total of all German citizens aged 15 to 60 living in private households in the Federal Republic of Germany and West Berlin. The survey sample was drawn at random, stratified by community size. As a special feature of the sample design, the spouses of married target persons were interviewed as well. The total sample comprises 9,535 completed interviews.

In addition to the survey data, a subsample of 4,165 cases contains data from the officially registered social insurance accounts. The latter were made available by the social insurance offices with the consent of the survey participants. These data allow a retrospective time location of unemployment spells. The data are valid because they form the basis for the calculation of pension claims. The period of 1970–1979 contains a total of 851 spells, of which 509 are transitions to employment, 293 are transitions out of the labor force, while the rest are right-censored (i.e., for these subjects no transition from unemployment was observed during the period in question).

The social insurance account sample is not fully representative for the economically active population of Western Germany, but this should not seriously affect multivariate modeling, as long as there is no misspecification (Hausman 1978). The most relevant deficiencies are that foreigners and retiring people are underrepresented. Foreigners averaged about 7% of the overall population during the observation period, but were only drawn into the sample as the spouse of a German target person. For the same reason the sample is retrospectively biased, because persons who reached age 60 during the 1970s were not directly addressed by the sample design. As an important consequence, transitions from unemployment to pension cannot be observed. It is known from other studies that unemployment sometimes takes the function of premature retirement (Büchtemann and Infratest Sozialforschung 1983).

There are also a number of informational restrictions within the data: Regional information was not available; for the same reason we had to forgo effects of occupational training. A differentiation by industrial sectors would have been possible but seemed inappropriate due to the restricted sample size.

The following summary illustrates the character of the data. Because of the selectivity described and the problems of representation, differences between our data and the officially available data are to be expected. In Figure 6.2, spell durations generated from the sample are compared with

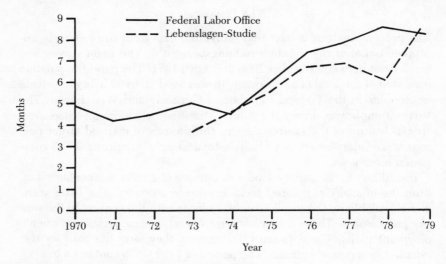

Figure 6.2. Comparison of Mean Unemployment Duration

the official statistics of the Federal Labor Office (Bundesanstalt für Arbeit). The official data were generated by calculating the average of the previous spell durations for the whole unemployment stock in September of each year.

This procedure leads to an underestimation of the true spell duration. To enable a comparison the procedure was replicated with the Lebenslagen data.[2] The trend of the officially computed unemployment duration rises between 1974 and 1976. Afterwards the trend stabilizes at a level around eight months. In this pattern, we find the above-mentioned structural shift following the oil crisis, although lagged one year when compared with other labor market indicators. The observed lag must primarily be ascribed to the computational method used by the Federal Labor Office.

A frequency distribution of the number of spells experienced by the unemployed (see Table 6.1) shows that over two-thirds experienced only one spell throughout the observation period. A relatively small number of persons experience the majority (about 56%) of spells. This agrees with the results of Büchtemann and Brasche (1985) for the nine-year period between 1973 and 1982.

Beyond dating unemployment spells, the data allow estimation of unemployment compensation. Instead of actual income data, we had monthly information about the amount of social credit points at our disposal. These are used to evaluate pension claims but may also be used to infer personal monthly gross income. The following equation holds approximately:

$$\frac{\text{personal monthly}}{\text{gross income}} = \frac{\text{total annual}}{\text{gross income}} \times \frac{\text{social credit points}}{100} \quad (6.3)$$

Table 6.1. Unemployed by Number of Spells, 1970–1979

Number of Spells	N	Percentage of Cases (total = 558)	Percentage of Spells (total = 851)
1	379	67.92	44.56
2	116	20.79	27.26
3	37	6.63	13.04
4	13	2.33	6.11
5	4	0.72	2.35
6	6	1.08	4.23
7	3	0.54	2.47

2. The curve for the Lebenslagen data starts at 1973, as too few cases were available in earlier years.

This makes it possible to take the number of social credit points as a rough indicator of the real amount of unemployment compensation, although evaluation of the latter is based on the last personal monthly net income. Due to the absence of additional information we used the assumption of a constant relationship between gross and net income.

The German Unemployment Insurance System is predominantly financed through contributions of employed persons, excluding civil servants. Eligibility for benefits begins when an employee has contributed for a minimum period within a legally fixed time frame.[3] In the event of unemployment such persons are first entitled to *Arbeitslosengeld*, (unemployment compensation). The maximum claim duration for Arbeitslosengeld commonly comprised 12 months during the seventies. This applied to persons who had been employed for at least twenty-four months within the last three years before unemployment. The level of Arbeitslosengeld amounts to about two-thirds of the last personal monthly net income. After expiration of entitlement to Arbeitslosengeld an unemployed person is next entitled to *Arbeitslosenhilfe*, (reduced unemployment benefits). Its maximum duration is not legally restricted, but is determined with a measure of discretion by the respective local Labor Office. The level of Arbeitslosenhilfe depends not merely upon the last personal monthly net income earned, but also takes other sources of income into account, in particular the income of spouses. Thus, Arbeitslosenhilfe may average less than half of the last personal monthly net income. In practice, for the majority of married women, benefit claims expire with the time limit for Arbeitslosengeld.

Results

The modeling process took two principal steps. First, we constructed a base-line exponential model on the basis of all available individual variables (see Table 6.2). A significance test of the null hypothesis for single parameters was used to select variables for inclusion into the model. The next step consisted of one-by-one inclusions of the available labor market indicators (see Table 6.3). A simultaneous inclusion of two or more labor market indicators could not be accomplished because of strong multicollinearities. The effects of the inclusion of additional variables on the base-line model can be ignored; thus these changes are not presented separately.

The two tables each contain two submodels according to the presently

3. For details on this point see the Arbeitsförderungsgesetz from June 25, 1969, and subsequent changes.

Table 6.2. Base-line Exponential Models for Leaving Unemployment

Variable Name	Return to Employment		Leaving the Labor Force	
	α	Δχ²	α	Δχ²
Constant	0.0651*		0.1507*	
Sex (1 = man, 0 = woman)	1.7370*	34.25	—	
Middle educational degree (1 = Realschule, 0 = other)	—		0.6334*	7.77
High educational degree (1 = [Fach-]Abitur, 0 = other)	0.6315†	6.64	0.4649*	12.27
Employment status before spell (1 = blue collar worker, 0 = other)	1.2670†	6.13	0.6418*	10.18
Employment status before spell (1 = white collar worker, 0 = other)	—		0.6562*	8.81
Age (1 = 50 years or older, 0 = younger than 50 years)	0.7067†	7.26	0.5004*	12.76
Pregnancy before spell (1 = within last 12 months, 0 = other)	0.4093*	18.20	—	
Entitlement to Arbeitslosen-geld (1 = entitled, 0 = not entitled)	1.6250*	20.37	0.5973*	15.12
Time limit of entitlement (1 = last two months of entitlement period reached, 0 = other)	—		4.1520*	45.09
Log-likelihood	−1525.791		−1034.169	
Global χ²	137.092		90.818	
Degrees of freedom	6		7	
PED	0.100		0.094	

Note: A dash indicates that the corresponding effect was not significant at the .05 level and therefore has been excluded.
*Significance level of .01.
†Significance level of .05.

differentiated destination states. The column "α" gives the change factor in the hazard rate when the corresponding variable changes by one unit. The column "Δχ²" indicates the reduction of the global χ² value if the variable is excluded from the model. The decrease of the global χ² value is therefore a measure of the relative influence of a parameter. To evaluate the model fit we use the so-called PED measure (proportion of explained deviance), which was proposed by Arminger (1986). The PED measure may be interpreted as a coefficient of determination. It takes on values in the range between 0 and 1.

Table 6.3. Extended Base-line Models for the Influence of Labor Market Indicators upon the Hazard Rate for Leaving Unemployment

Variable Name	Return to Employment		Leaving the Labor Force	
	α	Δχ²	α	Δχ²
Annual unemployment rate	0.8781*	13.28	1.0460	0.74
Annual number of vacancies (thousands)	1.0010*	11.28	0.9998	0.18
Annual number of unemployed per vacancy	0.9701*	10.22	1.0440	0.96
Annual number of employees excluding civil servants (millions)	1.0920	0.34	0.8041	1.20
Annual number of economically active persons (millions)	1.0001	0.30	0.9996	1.80
Annual number of persons capable of gainful activity— PCGA (millions)	0.9997*	7.46	1.0001	0.07
Total volume of annual number of working hours (billions)	1.0001*	13.42	0.9999	1.04
Annual effective working time (hours)	1.0040*	13.57	0.9988	0.52
Annual working time per PCGA (hours)	1.0050*	14.20	0.9983	0.83

Note: To avoid multi-collinearities, labor market indicators were subsequently included in the baseline model.

*Siginificance level of .01.

The Model of Return to Employment

First of all, the results will be reported for the base-line model of the return to employment. Here, men have a 1.7-fold higher rate than women. The coefficient verifies well-known disadvantages of women in employment. Surprisingly, we find a negative relation between the level of education and the transition rate. The rate for persons with degrees granting entry to a university or senior technical college is only about 60% of the rate for the remaining population. The explanation for this finding must be speculative. Employees with higher degrees may have problems finding an appropriate entry level. A correlation between education and sex may also be responsible. The result, however, corresponds with the employment status coefficients for blue collar workers, who have on the average relatively lower educational degrees than persons with other employment statuses. Blue collar workers show a 1.3-fold higher rate than the rest. The age effect ($\alpha = 0.7067$) for persons aged fifty or older confirms the reemployment problems of older unemployed persons. The variable age had to be included into the model as a set of dummy variables because exploratory analysis showed the relationship between rate and age to be nonlinear in the logarithms. Age less than 50 does not include significantly different subgroups.

Women who had had a child within the 12 months before unemployment show a significantly lower rate than the remaining population. This may be due to true reemployment problems. For example, young mothers who want to return to employment may be primarily interested in part-time jobs, which are relatively rare. Job search theory also suggests that material and, more importantly, immaterial search benefits to young mothers are higher than for other persons, implying delayed resumption of employment. Material search benefits arise, for instance, from saved expenditures for child care. Immaterial search benefits result mainly from the sociological fact that the growing employment of women has not lead to an equivalent adaptation of traditional sex roles. Full-time jobs mean a considerable burden for young mothers who do not have the assistance of an extended family. The state of unemployment may exonerate women from such problems. These two causes for the reduced rate of young mothers are consistent, since the interest in part-time jobs may be viewed as an optimum search plan.

The effect of Arbeitslosengeld is particularly interesting, for it indicates that persons with an existing claim to compensation have a clearly increased rate compared to other persons or periods without a claim. At first sight, this finding appears counter-intuitive. According to the arguments of job search theory one would have expected that people without any benefit claims would be most urgently forced to an early termination of unemployment. This is not the case in our finding. According to human capital theory the present result could be explained by the circumstance that persons entitled to benefit claims have more labor force experience at their disposal than others. In contrast, the majority of the population of unentitled persons consists of entry-level employees or people with a long interruption of their labor force participation. The coefficient for the level of unemployment compensation did not turn out to be significant when added to the model. The coefficient has therefore been left out of the table. In alternative specifications we replaced the dummy variable for entitlement to unemployment compensation by the level of unemployment compensation. The results again showed a highly significant positive effect, which means that the transition rate from unemployment to employment increases with an increasing level of unemployment compensation. The effect becomes insignificant, but still positive, when the sample is restricted to those who are entitled to unemployment compensation.

Due to the better fit, we have given preference to the dummy variable specification in table 6.2.

Finally, we controlled the effect of compensation by a dummy variable, which was set to unity when the end of the time limit for unemployment compensation had been reached, and to zero otherwise. This tests whether people tend to leave unemployment immediately before a threatening cut in compensation. The corresponding effect did not prove to be significant. This indicates to some extent that individuals have limited control over a return to employment. Such difficulties are closely related to global labor market developments, as the following results will show.

A look at the coefficients for the labor market indicators in Table 6.3 shows the expected results. Increasing tightness of the labor market correlates positively with unemployment duration. For example, an increase in the annual unemployment rate by 1% leads to a decrease of the estimated rate by a factor of 0.88. The number of employees, excluding civil servants, as well as the number of economically active persons, do not fit the model variables very well. Both indicators show a decrease after 1973 and an increase after 1977, while unemployment duration increased continuously over the whole observation period. It is obvious that the observable increase of employment indicates a relaxation of the labor market which had been counterbalanced at the same time by a disproportionate increase in the population capable of gainful activity or a decrease in the total number of hours worked.

The Model of Withdrawal from the Labor Force

Transitions from unemployment to out of the labor force fall into two distinct categories. First, such transitions may be the result of discouragement. If the job search is unsuccessful over a long period, people become resigned and withdraw from the labor market. In general, discouragement time should be negatively correlated with the degree of global unemployment. This situation has to be clearly separated from the second category, where registered unemployment is not an indicator for job search. At certain stages of the life course, people may wish to quit their present job and at least temporarily leave the labor market. This usually happens when people approach retirement age or when women decide to devote themselves to child care.

Nonetheless, people will have incentive for becoming registered as unemployed to the extent that they have acquired claims for unemployment compensation from earlier contributions to unemployment insurance. Obviously, such registration is only intended to take advantage of existing compensation claims. It may furthermore be concluded that in this case unemployment duration can be almost fully explained by the duration of entitlement to unemployment compensation and will be independent of labor market developments. Indeed, tables 6.2 and 6.3 show that the process of returning to employment is essentially different from the process that leads to withdrawal from the labor force. In contrast to the preceeding case, the dominant role in leaving the labor force is played by institutional regulations concerning claims for unemployment compensation.

We find that entitled persons have a relatively low rate of leaving the labor force as long as a claim for unemployment compensation exists. Upon reaching the time limit of their claims, the transition rate for this population rises to a level more than four times higher than other periods. Beyond this, both effects produce considerable contributions to the global χ^2 value within the submodel. Excluding the parameter for reaching the time limit of entitlement would reduce the submodel's global χ^2 value by half. Accordingly, not a single labor market indicator has a significant influence within the submodel. Taken together, the lack of significance of labor market effects and the dominance of effects concerning institutional regulation of unemployment support lead to a unique interpretation of the transitions out of the labor force: they are the result of a personal decision preceding unemployment rather than a consequence of unsuccessful job search due to decreased labor demand. Therefore registration as "unemployed" with the Labor Exchange ends with the termination of eligibility for unemployment compensation.

This can be illustrated by some additional figures. Nearly 70% of the transitions that occur at the end of the entitlement period lead out of the labor force, while the overall ratio between transitions out of the labor force and transitions to unemployment is about 3:5. It should be mentioned that the proportion of young mothers with benefit claims who withdraw amounts to about 56%. From this we conclude that child care is a strong but not sufficient reason to leave the labor market. However, among young mothers who are entitled to unemployment compensation and who leave unemployment when the time limit for compensation expires, the number leaving the labor force exceeds the number of transitions to employment by almost seven times.

Summary

Our analysis shows that the transition from unemployment to employment differs fundamentally from the transition out of the labor force after unemployment. This is expressed in the result that leaving the labor force is primarily influenced by institutional regulations of unemployment compensation, while the process of return to employment is dominated by other factors. When they reach the time limit of their claim for compensation, the transition out of the labor force for persons entitled to benefit claims exceeds by four times the rate during other periods. Beyond that, labor market indicators do not have any influence on leaving the labor force, while on the other hand the transition rate from unemployment to employment decreases with increased tightness in the labor market. Bottlenecks in the labor market may prevent persons who are searching for a job from getting one. The timing of withdrawing from unemployment out of the labor force is scarcely influenced by labor market difficulties.

Job search theory often proposes to use the level of unemployment compensation as a regulatory tool to cure unemployment. Our results, however, cast doubts on the effectiveness of such measures. There is no evidence that a lowering of unemployment compensation would help to alleviate the problems of return to employment, although it would surely increase the problems of the unemployed. Even those people who intend to leave the labor force and who become registered only to take advantage of existing benefit claims may not be expected to respond to the level of compensation; nor will unemployment duration be affected, since the decisive effect for this group seems to be the time limit of compensation.

The estimates for the return to employment are impaired to some extent by the fact that the chosen labor market indicators do not produce the strongest effects within the submodel. From our point of view, this is hardly a sufficient justification for viewing unemployment primarily as an individual problem. One must consider that the German labor market situation is quite different over regions and occupational branches. Due to data limitations we were forced to restrict ourselves to global labor market indicators. These are only poor measures for the specific labor market situation, which is relevant for a single individual searching a job. A substantial improvement of the relative explanatory power of the labor market situation, as well as an improvement of the whole model fit, could surely be obtained when using more differentiated variables.

In this context, it seems remarkable that estimations using labor market indicators calculated on a monthly basis did not lead to significant coefficients. Seasonal fluctuations of the labor market indicators apparently do not have the same effect as long-term changes. The range of seasonal fluctuations within a single year often surpasses the range of mean changes between subsequent years. As a result, one of the remaining tasks will be to produce better-fitting indicators for structural problems on the labor market.

II

MIGRATION, FERTILITY, AND MARRIAGE

7 *Michael Wagner*

Education and Migration

The Problem

This chapter presents a theoretical and empirical analysis of three aspects of the relation between education and migration: the regional variation in level of education, the relation between level of education and geographic mobility, and the need to determine whether the effects of education can still be documented if the influence of different variables important to migration analysis is controlled for.

(1) In the Federal Republic of Germany, the level of education varies regionally. The percentage of highly skilled persons in the total population increases with community size and population density (Mammey 1979, Birg 1985). There are two explanations for this geographic difference in educational levels:

(a) The education selectivity of migration leads highly skilled persons to congregate in metropolitan areas.

(b) Individuals raised in large cities receive a better education than individuals raised in rural regions.

In research on migration, there is a tradition behind the thesis that the regional distribution of the population in terms of educational level is determined by migration characterized by education selectivity. The state of affairs has been described in Germany with terms like *Landflucht* (rural exodus), *Auslesewirkungen* (selection), and *Siebungsvorgängen* (filter process), terms that frequently imply value judgements (Heberle 1936, Albrecht 1972, Horstmann 1976).

The second argument rests on the assumption that metropolitan areas are better equipped with educational facilities than rural areas. Pointing to specific examples of parents' high aspirations for their childrens' education merely shifts the problem to the question of why the educational level of parents living in large cities is especially high. In the Federal Republic of Germany, the assumption that local educational infrastructure has a significant influence on participation in the educational system led to political measures aimed at reducing regional disparities in secondary education. In the 1960s, for example, the problem of students having to travel long distances to and from school received a great deal of attention (Geipel 1965).

(2) As documented in many studies, the level of education clearly has an influence on the degree of geographic mobility. For the Federal Republic of Germany, this relation has been shown by Hofbauer and Nagel (1973), Schreiber (1975), and Marel (1980). Evidence for it has also been cited in demographic studies in the United States (Bogue and Hagood 1953, Suval and Hamilton 1964, Friedlander and Roshier 1966, Morrison 1972, Long 1973, Shyrock and Nam 1986), Great Britain (Kiernan 1979), and France (Courgeau 1984, 1985).

The study by Sandefur and Scott (1981), based on retrospective longitudinal data from 1969, has been the only one to come to a negative result on the education selectivity of geographic mobility. The variable of education had no significant influence even on rates of interstate migration in the United States. The authors attributed this inconsistency to the research findings then available, arguing that cross-sectional data overrate the effect of education on geographic mobility. This argument is unconvincing, however, since Kiernan (1979) used longitudinal data to document the influence of education on geographic mobility.

The research results are not uniform on some key issues. First, it is not clear whether the migration rates of education groups also differ in intraregional migration (Quigley and Weinberg 1977). Second, there are few, if any, empirical analyses in which the education selectivity of migration is considered as a function of features of the region of origin or of the destination region. It has not been empirically substantiated that migration from rural areas to cities involves disproportionately great numbers of highly skilled people. A focal assumption of the present study, however, is that the degree of urbanization in a region greatly influences the educational level of people migrating toward or away from it.

Moreover, the results of the aforementioned studies are difficult to compare. Geographical moves are classified by distance in a variety of ways. Classifications based on administrative boundaries are often indiscriminate and imprecise. Furthermore, studies measure education differently. In some studies education is operationalized in terms of the type of educational certificate, diploma, or degree held by the individual; others use duration of formal schooling (Albrecht 1972).

(3) For a theoretical analysis of the relations between educational level and geographic mobility, it is essential to know whether effects of education can be documented even if one takes account of the individual characteristics that are closely associated with education. Lansing and Mueller (1967), for instance, reported that the effect of education vanishes if one controls for the influence of professional status. Moreover, it is uncertain whether the influence of education varies with age. Long (1973) showed that education selectivity in migration in the United States declines with age, indicating that education appears to have only a brief influence on geographic mobility, as in the early phases of a person's occupational career. Working with longitudinal data representative for France, however, Courgeau (1984) documented that the effect of education persists if one statistically controls for age.

Research on migration has hitherto attempted to explain the education selectivity of migration from four perspectives: regional disparities either in the field of education or in the labor market (Lansing and Mueller 1967, Albrecht 1972, Hofbauer and Nagel 1973); the degree to which local ties vary with the level of education (Musgrove 1963); dissimilar levels of information (Grubel and Scott 1967, Shaw 1975); and value patterns (Suval and Hamilton 1964). These viewpoints are outlined and discussed in the following pages.

Theoretical Approaches

Regional Disparities in Educational Facilities and the Labor Market

Regional disparities in the field of education, particularly that of vocational training, determine the scale and direction of migration that serves the purpose of completing a specific kind of training. Apart from the classical small university towns, most public and private facilities for professional training are located in metropolitan areas (Derenbach 1984). Geographical moves motivated by training are unlikely to be numerous, though. The scanty financial resources of people in training, a low level of information, and the necessary early separation from home tend to discourage such changes of residence. As Peisert (1967) documented, re-

gional disparities in the Federal Republic's institutions of secondary education were reduced in the 1960s and 1970s. The number of locations
offering medium high school education (Realschule) and college-
preparatory education (Gymnasium) climbed from 3,000 to 5,100 between 1960 and 1980. The average size of the area served by a given
school shrank from over 32 square miles (84 square kilometers) to just
under 19 square miles (49 square kilometers) (Bundesminister für Raumordnung, Bauwesen und Städtebau 1982). However, the government has
less influence on the siting of firms that offer opportunities for industrial
training. Huge regional differences in the supply of vocational training are
still evident in the 1980s (Derenbach 1984, Bundesminister für Raumordnung, Bauwesen und Städtebau 1986). Even though regional disparities
have been reduced in the education and training system, it is unclear
whether migration motivated by training has declined. Conceivably, all
that has happened through reduction of regional disparities in education
and training is that the number of people in the education system has
increased.

According to a second thesis, it is primarily persons with a high level of
education who enter regionally extended labor markets (Lansing and
Mueller 1967, Albrecht 1972, Hofbauer and Nagel 1973). The higher the
qualification level of occupational positions, the further those positions
are located from each other, because (a) the number of jobs for highly
skilled people is relatively low, (b) these jobs are concentrated in metropolitan areas, and (c) the distribution of such areas is relatively even across
the populated areas of the Federal Republic of Germany.

For a number of reasons, it appears plausible that jobs for highly skilled
people are concentrated in cities. For one thing, firms of the tertiary sector are sited primarily in metropolitan areas (Bundesminister für Raumordnung, Bauwesen und Städtebau 1978), and a large percentage of the
people with a high level of education work in that sector of the economy
(Blossfeld 1985b). Moreover, occupational differentiation in metropolitan
areas is greater than in rural regions. For specialized activities in particular, however, the most qualified persons are those with a high level of
education. Finally, large cities represent centers of economic and political
power. Because of agglomeration economies—for example, a well-
developed infrastructure of transport and communications—firms with
high-status positions demanding highly skilled people are concentrated in
metropolitan areas.

Local and Social Ties

It has been shown many times in migration research that the probability
of moving to a new residence declines with the strength of local ties. The

next question is whether highly educated people have fewer local ties than less skilled people and are therefore geographically more mobile. One reason for asking this question is the finding that the probability of leaving one's place of origin to seek training elsewhere increases with the level of education. In a 1973–1974 study of secondary students in Ellwangen, West Germany, who had passed their final examinations and had thereby qualified for entrance to the university, 83.6% of the 1,228 students interviewed responded that they "had left immediately after their final examinations," with most of them heading for the nearest university town (Niedzwetzki 1979). It should be added that local ties are also reduced by geographic mobility upon entry into professional life, something that facilitates further migration in the course of one's occupational career. Since people with a high level of education have invested a great deal in their training, it would cost them dearly if they were to change professions. If no commensurate job opportunities are available in the place of residence, a change of profession is unlikely; migration, on the other hand, can guarantee the returns on the educational investment. Extended occupational and professional training commits a person to a certain career pattern. He or she must adapt to the regional variations in employment opportunities.

Level of Information and Value Patterns

The effects of education on geographic mobility are interpreted in two other hypotheses that draw on concepts from action theory. Shaw (1975), as well as Grubel and Scott (1967), hold the opinion that the level of information about alternative places and opportunities increases with the level of education. By contrast, Suval and Hamilton (1964) conjecture that acceptance of middle-class values such as achievement and devotion to duty increases with the level of education. Migration, particularly over long distances, is accepted if it serves one's professional career.

As transmitters of knowledge and values, schools have a key function. Musgrove (1963) shows that this fact can also have regional consequences for individuals. He argues that it is even a goal of school education to provide children with opportunities that will make "the family . . . an irrelevance: the child's life chances should be independent of his geographical and kinship connexions." According to Musgrove, it is mainly the secondary schools that prepare children for a professional life that will entail changes of residence in keeping with economic demands. Referring to the British school system, he observed: "Today selection for a grammar-school education is selection for a probably migratory future. The modern grammar-school is an agency for collecting local talent from its region and redeploying it nationally and even internationally" (Musgrove 1963: 88f.).

The influence that the levels of information, values, and attitudes have on regional mobility results primarily from a type of socialization that creates the subjective conditions for ensuring the geographic allocation of employed persons in an economic system with regional disparities.

Data Base and Methods

The data used in this section were collected by Karl Ulrich Mayer from October 1981 through February 1983 as part of the West German Life History Study (GLHS). The population of the retrospective, nationally representative survey consisted of West German or West Berlin women and men in private households, born in the years 1929–1931, 1939–1941, or 1949–1951. The sample of 2,171 respondents, stratified according to sex and birth cohort, was drawn from a compilation of 13,974 lists of private households in 404 voting districts. The methodology upon which the study was based has been described in several reports (Wiedenbeck 1982, Mayer and Brückner 1989). It is noteworthy that the geographic representativeness of the respondents proved to match well with micro-census data in terms of distribution by federal state (Bundesland) and community size (Blossfeld 1987). The survey focused on the retrospective collection of information on key spheres of life along a temporal continuum, dealing primarily with family and residential history, training history, and occupational career.

Each change of residence reported by the respondents was recorded as migration. To distinguish between local and interregional migration, a threshold of 50 kilometers was chosen, the assumption being that changes of residence within that distance still allow for daily commuting to the place of work. Information on community size was based on figures provided by the respondents. Residential areas were classified as hamlet, village, town, intermediate-size city, and large city. The highest general educational certificate, diploma, or degree to have been received by each respondent was used as the measure of that person's level of education on a scale ranging from (a) Volksschule (through grade 9, basic high school education) at most, (b) Mittlere Reife or Realschule (through grade 10, medium high school education), and (c) Abitur or Gymnasium (through grade 13, with qualification to enter a university or technical college).

Multivariate analyses of the education selectivity of migration are being conducted with the aid of dynamic rate models in which the dependent variable is the rate (hazard or transition rate) of changes of residence. The rate is specified as a function of individual characteristics (such as sex and level of education). The question of which factors influence the direction of changes of residence (rural to urban or vice versa) is of special interest.

Periods of residence constitute the analytic units. If the period ended not with a move but with interviewing, the answer was recorded as a censored observation. I have used Cox's (1972, 1975) proportional hazard regression model:

$$r(t \mid x) = r_0(t) \exp(x'\beta). \tag{7.1}$$

In this model, $r(t \mid x)$ is the transition rate; $r_0(t)$ is a basic time-varying transition rate that is unspecified but that is the same for all individuals; x' is a vector of covariates; β is the vector of respective regression coefficients; and t is the duration of residence (in this context, months of residency). The statistical foundations of this procedure are described in detail by Tuma and Hannan (1984) and Blossfeld, Hamerle, and Mayer (1986).

Empirical Results

Educationally Selective Migration from Rural to Urban Areas or an Effect of Infrastructure?

At this point I would like to turn to the theses about the sizable percentage of better-educated persons in large cities. On one hand, it was asserted that this regionally unequal distribution is a result of educationally selective migration from rural to urban areas; on the other hand, metropolitan areas were said to have superior educational facilities. Figures 7.1 and 7.2, which illustrate the patterns for two educational groups and three birth cohorts, show the age-related percentage of respondents living in intermediate-size or large cities.

One of the first findings concerns the regional origin of the respondents in the study's various educational groups. It is very clear that those people with a comparatively high level of education were more likely to have been reared in large cities than were people with a low level of education. Moreover, the percentage of persons who had at least completed a Realschule and who lived in intermediate-size or large cities increased much more sharply up to about age 25 than was the case with those persons who had completed a Volksschule only. Hence, both of the hypotheses cited at the outset are supported. Up to the third decade of life, there was an educationally selective migration from rural to urban areas. On the other hand, the highly skilled people come largely from regions with a relatively good range of educational facilities and programs.

Differences between the birth cohorts were most striking among highly skilled respondents up to the age of twenty years. Among the respondents

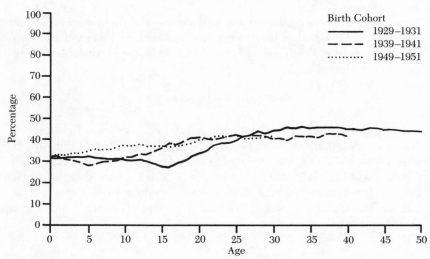

Figure 7.1. Persons with Few Years of Education (Volksschule or less) Living in Large or Intermediate-Size Cities

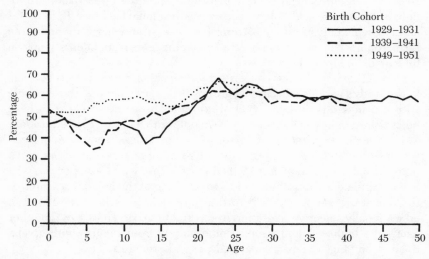

Figure 7.2. Persons with Many Years of Education (Realschule or Abitur) Living in Large or Intermediate-Size Cities

born between 1930 and 1940, the impact of the Second World War in particular is unmistakable. It is worth noting that respondents who (eventually) had a higher education were more likely to leave the cities during the war than those respondents who completed Volksschule only. Presumably, the varying financial resources of parents and the government resettlement programs, which removed children to the countryside and which differed according to the type of school involved, had a bearing on this finding.

Only among respondents who had completed from ten to thirteen years of schooling did the percentage of city dwellers shrink again at 25 years of age. It cannot be determined whether this change reflected migration back to the rural areas of origin or migration to communities on the outskirts of large cities.

The percentage of country dwellers in all three birth cohorts declined after their members turned 16 or 17 years of age. Some of the migration to the cities is bound to be linked to training; what remains unclear is the extent to which such migration was undertaken and whether it entailed significant, cohort-specific differences, stemming perhaps from a decentralization of educational and training facilities. Table 7.1 shows the distribution of migration motivated by education according to birth cohorts.

Besides migrants younger than 15, there is a slight increase in educationally motivated migration across the sequence of the three birth cohorts. Moves usually took place at the end of the second decade of the respondent's life, but with increasing frequency in subsequent age groups as well. It is thus clear that most of this migration was intended to facilitate vocational training, not general secondary education. Because of the brevity of their education, women migrated for training earlier than men

Table 7.1. Education-Related Migration by Age, Birth Cohort, and Sex

Age in Years	Birth Cohort			Men	Women
	1929–1931	1939–1941	1949–1951		
0–14	6.6%	5.2%	3.3%	5.3%	4.7%
15–19	7.6	9.9	10.5	7.5	11.2
20–24	6.4	8.4	10.0	11.1	5.4
25 or more	2.1	2.9	4.0	4.1	1.8
Number of persons	707	728	733	1,087	1,081

Note: A migration was considered to have been educationally motivated if "school," "training," "study," "apprenticeship," "boarding school," "further training," or "master craftsman's examination" was given as the reason for moving. The values reflect the number of training-related moves per 100 persons in the respective subgroup.

did. Participation in the educational and training system clearly increased, especially among women, across the sequence of birth cohorts (47.3% of the women in the study's eldest cohort began vocational training as compared to 65.8% in the 1939–1941 cohort and 83.1% in the most recent one), but there is no comparable trend in the migration motivated by training. Despite a possible reduction of regional disparities in the educational and training system, a notably high number of moves still take place for training purposes. Presumably, the 1949–1951 birth cohort in particular was affected by the sharp downturn in industrial training capacity between 1970 and 1975 (Derenbach 1984). Since the course of this decline probably differed between regions, such differences could be a reason for the slight increase in training-related migration between the second cohort and the most recent one. There were, and are, population groups handicapped by a meager educational infrastructure. No conclusions about changes in these regional disparities can be drawn from the data above since no figures are available on educational aspirations, the housing market, financial conditions, or other important factors that can lead to educationally motivated migration.

In the theoretical part of this article, it was posited that persons from rural regions migrate especially often for purposes of training because of regional disparities in the educational system. In general, this view cannot be supported by the available data. Table 7.2, which shows the percentage of training-related migration for every one hundred persons from places grouped into four size categories, reveals no relationship. Persons from towns were most prone to migrate for training purposes at 33%, a rate that declined as the size of the place of origin increased. In that sense,

Table 7.2. Education-Related Migration through Age 30 by Birth Cohort and Regional Origin

| Birth Cohort | Size of First Place of Residence | | | |
	Village	Town	Intermediate-Size City	Large City
1929–1931	13.3%	34.1%	30.7%	27.0%
	(330)*	(132)	(88)	(152)
1939–1941	23.8%	25.4%	37.8%	25.3%
	(332)	(126)	(82)	(186)
1949–1951	22.4%	38.7%	27.0%	24.6%
	(299)	(150)	(111)	(171)
Total	19.8%	33.1%	31.3%	25.5%
	(961)	(408)	(281)	(509)

*The values in parentheses are the number of persons per subgroup on which the percentage is based.

the aforementioned thesis is confirmed. But those persons whose first place of residence was a village undertook fewer training-related moves than did persons from towns and intermediate-size cities. If one assumes that infrastructural educational facilities are worst in village communities, then the number of moves motivated by education would necessarily tend to be greatest among village dwellers. Since that is not the case, one can presume that young people from villages are tied largely to their local communities, have modest educational aspirations, or have less information about educational facilities in other places. Only detailed analyses would be able to show which of these explanations applies.

No clear cohort trends were found even when regions of origin are differentiated. The single interesting result was that respondents of the 1929–1931 birth cohort who grew up in villages invested little in their training in terms of migration. That finding can be attributed to the Second World War, when vocational training was inconceivable in large cities.

Various Educational Groups and Regional Mobility: Specific to Age and Birth Cohort

Table 7.3 shows age-specific migration rates by the cohort affiliation of respondents with differing levels of education. In almost all age brackets the persons with a higher level of education were geographically more mobile than their less educated counterparts. In fact, some of the rates were twice as high. Among the 25- to 29-year-olds of the second birth cohort, there were 55 moves per 100 respondents with only a basic high school education (Volksschule or less), while in the group of better educated respondents (Realschule or Abitur) the rate was 102. The only exception to this pattern was the 15- to 20-year-olds in the second and third birth cohorts. This finding has to do with the fact that, unlike the respondents in the second educational group, those who did not progress beyond basic high school were no longer in the school system, a circumstance that promoted their mobility in general. Another noteworthy point is that age selectivity of migration persisted even when the data were arranged according to educational groups. In both groups the 20- to 24-year-olds were the most mobile. People changed their residences less frequently as they grew older. There was no evidence that the educational selectivity of migration declined with age, however. The ratio of the migration rates remained rather stable across the age groups. Accordingly, the effect that education has on geographic mobility can also be said to extend beyond the early phases of a person's biography.

A comparison of cohorts reveals that respondents of the 1939–1941 cohort who had more than a basic high school education were especially

Table 7.3. Age-Specific Migration Rates per 100 Persons by Birth Cohort and Level of Education

| | Birth Cohort | | | | | |
| | 1929–1931 | | 1939–1941 | | 1949–1951 | |
Age	Volksschule Only	Realschule or Gymnasium	Volksschule Only	Realschule or Gymnasium	Volksschule Only	Realschule or Gymnasium
15–19	68.6%	86.9%	56.1%	51.3%	49.8%	47.4%
20–24	73.0	100.8	82.4	126.0	89.3	112.1
25–29	59.1	96.1	55.0	102.6	56.5	87.1
30–34	35.3	48.5	32.7	59.1	—	—
35–39	22.5	35.4	20.1	35.7	—	—
40–44	17.3	23.1	—	—	—	—
45–49	10.7	14.6	—	—	—	—
Number of persons	577	130	574	154	494	239

mobile in all age groups. The differences in the migration rates of the educational groups were relatively large, too, with the educational selectivity of geographical mobility being highest for the respondents born around 1940 and lowest for the 1949–1951 cohort. One can assume that there was an especially great demand for highly skilled labor at the beginning of the 1960s, particularly in the cities, meaning individuals born around 1940, being at the beginning of their job career, could increase their income through occupationally oriented migration. In addition, the 1960s were marked by the rise in the number of industrial sites (Derenbach 1984). Although the demand for moderately skilled labor can often be satisfied "on site," that is less frequently the case for highly skilled labor.

The Effect of the Level of Education on Local and
Interregional Migration

The fact that the rates of migration vary among educational groups has been made clear thus far. I now wish to address the question of the extent to which geographic mobility depends on educational level. Beyond that, educational selectivity might be a phenomenon associated only with certain types of migration. Moreover, there is the issue of *why* the level of education has an effect on geographic mobility. A few theses about this issue have already been reviewed and will now be compared with empirical results.

It is clear from Table 7.4, which relates only to the survey's employed respondents, that the extent of education's influence on geographic mobility depends on whether one has figured in the effects of other factors, especially age, professional status, and local ties. As far as local migration is concerned, it is understandable why past research produced contradictory results: the relation between education and local migration does not become apparent until it is studied in terms of age. Even local migration tends to involve persons with a relatively high level of education.

The level of education nevertheless has a perceptibly stronger effect on interregional migration than on local migration. A disproportionate number of highly skilled respondents participated in long-distance migration flows. Looking at the final line in Table 7.4, one sees that the chances of moving to another dwelling a short distance away were 16% higher among respondents with a tenth-grade education than their lesser educated counterparts ([exp(0.15) − 1] × 100% = 16%). Respondents who had qualified to enter the university had a rate of local migration that was 51% higher than that of respondents with only a basic high school education. The corresponding rates for interregional migration were 46% and 166%.

Obviously, part of the relation between education and interregional mi-

Table 7.4. Effects of Educational Level on Rates of Local and Interregional Migration

Control Variables	Local Migration		Interregional Migration	
	Realschule	Gymnasium	Realschule	Gymnasium
None	0.07	0.12	0.36*	0.77*
COHO	0.05	0.12	0.37*	0.77*
COHO, SEX	0.04	0.13	0.36*	0.79*
COHO, SEX, AGE	0.15†	0.40*	0.61*	1.32*
COHO, SEX, AGE, OCC	0.17†	0.48*	0.48*	1.21*
COHO, SEX, AGE, OCC, LT	0.15†	0.41*	0.38*	0.98*
Number of periods of residence	1,696		619	
Number of censored observations	2,012		3,091	

Note: The data base is all periods of residence that begin when the respondent was employed. The reference group consisted of the respondents with basic high school education (Volksschule) only.

Legend:
COHO   Birth cohorts: 1929–1931 (0/1), 1939–1941 (0/1), 1949–1951 (0/1)
SEX   0 = men, 1 = women
AGE   Age when period of residence began; five age classes, each coded 0/1
OCC   Occupational status, categorized as blue collar, white collar, civil servant, or self-employed; each category coded with 0/1
LT   Local ties: 0 = person does not live in place of birth, 1 = person lives in place of birth
   *Level of significance is 1%.
   †Level of significance is 5%.

gration is explained by the occupational status of the respondents, but the effect of education was strong nonetheless. The same is true for local ties; they reduced the effect of education but did not neutralize it completely. In that sense, it is correct to hypothesize that highly skilled persons move great distances either because they take jobs in the labor market that require such migration or because previous moves have left them with few close local ties. These factors reduce the effect of education only to a small extent, however.

Education Selectivity of Migration Depending on the Degree of Urbanization of Origin and Destination Regions

As a final step, I would like to examine whether formal education effects the direction of migration. Based on the classification system described on page 134, Table 7.5 shows that the size of origin and destination region is a significant criterion in accurately establishing regional differences in the population's educational level.

Table 7.5. Effects of Educational Level on the Distance and Direction of Migration

Level of Education	Local Migration				Interregional Migration			
	R/U*	R/R	U/R	U/U	R/U	R/R	U/R	U/U
	Without Control Variables							
Realschule								
	0.03	0.17	0.08	−0.04	0.56†	−0.40	0.04	0.71**
Gymnasium								
	0.32	−0.11	0.46	0.08	1.15**	0.24	0.79**	0.82**
	Controlled for Cohort Affiliation, Sex, Age, Occupational Status, and Local Ties							
Realschule								
	0.10	0.28†	−0.01	0.03	0.62†	−0.24	0.02	0.64**
Gymnasium								
	0.35	−0.16	0.63	0.45**	1.41**	0.62	0.95**	1.01**
Number of periods of residences	113	682	118	781	137	145	132	193
Number of censored observations	1,706	1,137	1,753	1,091	1,682	1,674	1,739	1,678

*R = Rural (hamlet, village, town); U = Urban (intermediate-size or large city); Region of origin/destination region.
†5% level of significance.
**1% level of significance.

Without going into detail about the variations in educational effects that arise when additional factors are introduced, one sees clearly that interregional migration from rural to urban regions had the highest degree of educational selectivity. It should not be overlooked, however, that a countercurrent flow did exist, albeit a weak one. After all, among the respondents who moved from the city to the country, there was a disproportionately high number only of persons qualified to enter the university, not of persons with less education.

The attractiveness of urban regions for highly skilled persons is also expressed by the educational selectivity of long–distance migration between large cities. One can infer from this that the decisive reason for the educational level's effect on migration is not the size of the region of origin as much as it is the size of the destination region. Long-distance migration between rural regions, for example, involved respondents with lower education about as often as it involved respondents with higher education. In short, there was no educational selectivity with respect to such migration.

The level of education was found to have little, if any, effect on local migration. Respondents who migrated from rural to urban regions did not differ in terms of their schooling. Within rural regions, there was a weak, nonlinear relation in that only persons with a medium high school education (Realschule) were distinguished from persons in the lowest educational group, although not from people qualified to enter the university. As for changes of residence within cities, educational selectivity was minor, and school education played no role in moves to areas surrounding the city.

Conclusions

The level of education is a determinant of geographic mobility, one that takes on significance even when age, occupational status, and local ties are considered in the analysis.

The concentration of highly skilled persons in large cities is the result of two factors. First, it stems from an educationally selective migration from rural to urban areas, a movement whose impact on the social structure of the destination region is not offset by a corresponding migration flow in the opposite direction. Second, it comes from the high percentage of individuals with more than a basic high school education born in large cities.

The number of people in the educational system has risen enormously, but migration rates motivated by training has increased only slightly. Quantitatively, though, these moves cannot be ignored, and the calculation of the training costs involved must include not only losses of income but also monetary and nonmonetary migration costs. Persons raised in cities of intermediate size are best able to bear these costs. Further research is needed on the questions of why people living in villages enter upon training-related migration more rarely than do people from towns and intermediate-size cities. Because of the low level of training-related migration among people living in large cities, there is a bell-shaped relation that cannot be explained solely in terms of regional disparities in the educational and training system.

Regionally, the labor market of highly skilled people extends very far, but that is not its only characteristic. It also is located in metropolitan areas. This is an important condition that causes different migration rates among educational groups and might also be the reason why an extended occupational and professional training is available principally in large cities.

The educational selectivity of interregional migration can definitely be documented, but it depends on the size of the destination region. Whether of rural or urban origin, the migration flows into the cities are the ones with disproportionately great numbers of highly skilled persons. Hence, educationally selective migration has a primary effect on the social structure of rural regions. This fact, in turn, is bound to have a significant effect on industrial siting. Because the supply of skilled, employed people seems to be limited in rural regions, many firms do not settle there. A rise in the educational level of the rural population will at first be more likely to increase out-migration than to improve the local economy.

Evidently, changes of residence among highly skilled people is an important subordinate process in the geographic allocation of factors of production. That is the reason for social rules and norms whose function is to ensure sufficient geographic mobility of human capital. That purpose entails communication systems (such as employment ads in newspapers) that make it possible to recruit labor from other regions, governmental moving allowances (such as aid to Berlin and tax deductions), and an ideology based on the view that modern human beings should always be geographically mobile.

8 *Nancy Brandon Tuma and Johannes Huinink*

Postwar Fertility Patterns in the Federal Republic of Germany

Since the late nineteenth century, the overall level of fertility has tended to decline in Germany, as it has in all industrialized nations. But since the mid-1960s, the decline has been striking: the net reproduction rate in the Federal Republic of Germany was only 0.605 in 1984, 0.603 for native Germans and 0.659 for the foreign population, which is mainly of Turkish and Southern European origin (Statistisches Bundesamt 1986).[1] One can easily understand why such figures have led to the popularization in West Germany of the question of whether Germans are "becoming extinct" and to renewed discussion of various pro-natalist policies.

Our goal is neither to recommend population policies nor to forecast the consequences of recent fertility trends. Instead, we consider fertility

The authors thank Karl Ulrich Mayer for his generous support and encouragement, and Andrew L. Creighton and Kathryn A. Tuma for their excellent research assistance. Peter Blossfeld and Georgios Papastefanou provided helpful advice at several key points. Support for the research was provided by the Max-Planck-Institut für Bildungsforschung and the Stanford Center for the Study of Families, Children and Youth.

1. The latter figure is even more surprising than that for native Germans because it is so much lower than the rate for these populations in their native lands. Fertility is also low in the German Democratic Republic (GDR). In 1984 the total fertility rate was 1773.5 in the GDR (Staatliche Zentralverwaltung für Statistik 1986) as compared to 1289.5 in the Federal Republic (Statistisches Bundesamt 1986).

patterns of native Germans since World War II in some detail and discuss the relationship of these patterns to various factors that may have promoted them.

The data we analyze come from the 1981–1982 German Life History Survey (GLHS), a retrospective survey of native German men and women, which we describe more fully below. These data provide an opportunity to examine basic patterns of fertility in finer detail than aggregate data permit. We can study the impact of social structural variables by comparing fertility patterns of different subgroups.

We confine our analyses here to the seemingly simple methods of event history analysis that are *not* multivariate. However, we do control several important explanatory variables (in particular, gender, parity, and cohort) by stratifying the sample. This approach is similar to the common demographic analyses of aggregate data. Most previous demographic studies of fertility patterns in West Germany have been based on aggregate data, including some that have used refined methods of cohort analysis to study age- and cohort-specific birth rates (see, e.g., Dinkel 1983; Birg et al. 1984; Hoepflinger 1987; and Huinink 1989). The main shortcoming of these other studies, which is largely due to the inherent limitations of official statistics, is their inability to examine heterogeneity in fertility patterns within the German population (due to gender, parity, background, and other variables). In contrast to studies based on official statistics, we examine fertility patterns of men as well as women, and for second and third births, as well as the first birth. In addition, we consider the dependence of fertility patterns on educational level and vocational training for one subgroup whose overall fertility patterns have a surprising form.

We use only simple descriptive analyses, not dynamic models that treat individual fertility behavior as the outcome of a set of interdependent choices in different life domains (e.g., Marini 1985; Michael and Tuma 1985; Rindfuss et al. 1984; Strohmeier 1985; Huinink 1987). Analyses such as ours, a refined version of the classic demographic descriptions, can be a powerful tool in investigating family formation processes in particular and life histories in general. The second aim of the paper is, therefore, to demonstrate the empirical and theoretical potential of such exploratory approaches to analysis of life history data.

We begin with a short description of the sample used in our analyses. We then present the main numerical and graphical results, which show the potential value of this analytical strategy. We conclude with an extensive summary of the findings.

Description of the Sample

The Data

Analyses of individual dynamics of fertility require a fairly unusual form of data: longitudinal data on the fertility of a sample of people with known attributes. The data we analyze were gathered in the 1981–1982 German Life History Survey sponsored by Sonderforschungsbereich 3 and the Max-Planck-Institut für Bildungsforschung under the leadership of Karl Ulrich Mayer (Mayer 1979).[2] The respondents were selected through a sampling plan that was designed to give a representative picture of native Germans living in the Federal Republic of Germany in 1981–1982 who had been born in one of three periods: 1929–1931, 1939–1941, and 1949–1951.[3] We refer to these as the 1930, 1940, and 1950 cohorts for short. The total sample size is 2,171, roughly half men and half women.

Each respondent was personally interviewed using a questionnaire that focused especially on the individual's previous life history. It collected detailed information on both parents and siblings of respondents, and on their schooling, vocational training, employment, residential history, marital history, and fertility history. Limited information on the current spouse was also collected for respondents who were married at the time of the interview.

These data give the dates of many life events (usually to the nearest month and year), and not just a picture of the respondents at specific ages or in specific years. That is, the data provide event histories for several major life domains. By focusing on three cohorts, these data let one study change over time in the behavioral patterns of West Germans in the post-war era.

These data are not without limitations, of course. Two are worth stressing. First, the sample is much smaller than is ideal when investigating changes across cohorts and differences between men and women. Second, the sample excludes nonnative Germans, who compose roughly 8% of the population of West Germany, and who mainly come from countries

2. A very small number of respondents were interviewed in early 1983. Designating this as the 1981–1982 study gives the best picture of its timing for the majority of the respondents.

3. The respondents were selected through a sampling plan based on the "ADM" sampling design, which involves three steps: (1) a stratified sampling of voting districts in the Federal Republic of Germany, in which the probability of selection is proportional to the number of households in the district; (2) random sampling of households in the voting districts chosen; and (3) random sampling of exactly one respondent per household who was born in the desired years from all households that have at least one member in the desired cohorts. For further information, see Mayer and Brückner (1989) or Wiedenbeck (1982).

of higher fertility. Because of the omission of nonnative Germans, these data cannot be used to compare native and nonnative Germans; moreover, care must be taken in extrapolating from these data to the Federal Republic of Germany as a whole.

Number of Children Born to Respondents

Table 8.1 reports the number of children born to the GLHS respondents before the interview by sex and cohort. The top panel reports the number who have had *exactly* each number of children by the interview, as well as the mean (see also Table 8.3); the bottom panel gives the number who have had *at least* a given number of children (i.e., the number who have ever been at risk of having the next higher number of children).

The entries under the exact count correspond to completed fertility for the 1930 cohort, whose members were over 50 years old at the interview. Since relatively few children are born to women after age 40 (and also, it appears, to men of that age), the entries probably underestimate completed fertility for the 1940 cohort only slightly (by under 0.02 children). But those in the youngest cohort ranged from 30 to 33 years old at the interview and can be expected to have roughly 0.25 additional children

Table 8.1. Counts of Respondents' Children by Sex and Cohort

Number of Births	Men			Women		
	1930	1940	1950	1930	1940	1950
			Exact Count			
0	45	58	154	38	39	86
1	79	85	101	77	82	106
2	110	175	94	126	137	136
3	64	42	16	60	62	30
4	28	15	0	38	23	6
5	8	4	0	10	8	3
6	9	3	0	3	2	0
7	3	3	0	5	0	1
8	3	0	0	2	2	0
Mean	2.13	1.76	0.92	2.17	1.98	1.39
			Cumulative Count			
1	304	317	211	321	316	282
2	225	232	110	244	234	176
3	115	67	16	118	97	40
4	51	25	0	58	35	10
5	23	10	0	20	12	4
6	15	6	0	10	4	1
7	6	3	0	7	2	1
8	3	0	0	2	2	0

on average before completing their fertility.[4] The entries in the top panel therefore are not good indicators of completed fertility for the 1950 cohort. Still, these figures suggest that completed fertility has declined across the three cohorts.

It is interesting that the maximum number of children born to any respondent is eight, and that 3.2% of respondents have five or more children. In contrast, 15% of the respondents came from families with five or more children and 3% from families with eight or more. Thus, not only has average family size shrunk considerably across the generations, but large families have also become much rarer.

The cumulative-count portion of Table 8.1 shows that, however much one might like to study birth rates at higher parities, it is not possible with these data. The number of births of order four or more is simply too few to support such an analysis. Therefore, we concentrate on the first birth, the transition from the first birth to the second, and the transition from the second birth to the third. Moreover, results pertaining to the last transition must be viewed with some skepticism due to the relatively small number of third births, especially for the 1950 cohort.

Comparisons with Official Statistics

We compare selected summary statistics based on these data with corresponding estimates based on official statistics obtained from Birg et al. (1984). Such comparisons help in assessing the degree to which the fertility of GLHS respondents is representative of the fertility of the larger West German population. These comparisons are limited to women born in 1939–1941 and 1949–1951 because birth rates are not published for men or for women born in 1929–1931.

In making these comparisons, one must keep in mind two basic differences. First, the GLHS sample is limited to native Germans whereas the official statistics are based on all permanent German residents. Second, estimates based on the GLHS sample refer to the first child ever born, ignoring marital status. The official statistics count the first birth in the *current* marriage. Thus, they exclude births outside marriage. Moreover, the first birth within a marriage may not be the first *ever* for women who have been married previously. The estimates presented here attempt to correct for the unusual definition of first birth and the restriction to marriages;[5] still, an *estimation* procedure is required with the official statis-

---

4. These estimates are based on age-specific birth rates of the cohorts (Birg et al. 1984; Statistisches Bundesamt 1983–1986). For the 1950 cohort, it was necessary to estimate the age-specific birth rates of those over 35.

5. The estimates reported by Birg et al. (1984) are adjusted for births outside marriage, but they only suggest strategies for correcting for bias introduced by the fact that official statistics report the first birth in the current marriage.

Table 8.2. Proportion of Women with Fewer than N Births by Age and Cohort

	N = 1		N = 2		N = 3	
	1940	1950	1940	1950	1940	1950
Age 20						
GLHS	.836	.791	.966	.981	.997	1.000
Official	.840	.758	.975	.961	.998	.997
Age 25						
GLHS	.381	.473	.731	.791	.929	.970
Official	.374	.434	.749	.789	.936	.962
Age 30						
GLHS	.172	.253	.441	.552	.822	.890
Official	.181	.293	.484	.589	.821	.904
Age 35						
GLHS	.118	—	.385	—	.751	—
Official	.118	—	.391	—	.762	—

Note: A dash indicates no information.

tics. Hence, one should not be too surprised if the two sets of figures differ somewhat, quite aside from sampling fluctuations.

Table 8.2 reports the proportion of women who have not yet had a first, second, or third child, respectively, by selected ages for the 1940 and 1950 cohorts as estimated from the 1981–1982 GLHS and from the official statistics. All differences are less than .01 for the first birth to women in the 1940 cohort. Differences for the first birth to the 1950 cohort are somewhat greater (typically around .04), but the estimates are not consistently larger or smaller for one source than for the other. The similarity of the estimates from the two sources is also clearly apparent in the case of the second and third births. No difference exceeds .043, and on average it is much less, only .016. Overall there are no systematic or large differences casting doubt on the representativeness of the 1981–1982 GLHS for studying German fertility.

Other Characteristics of the Sample

Before discussing fertility of the GLHS respondents, we review a few of the characteristics that may be related to their fertility. Means of selected variables are given in Table 8.3

We report the person's education and participation in vocational training because these variables are excellent predictors of future life chances and may also be associated with family-related values. (For example, individuals are likely to be more family-oriented and to have more children if they have less education.) There is a marked shift across the cohorts to higher levels of education and, for women, more vocational training. Still, women tend to be less educated than men, even in the youngest cohort, and they are much less likely than men to have had vocational training.

Table 8.3. Means of Selected Covariates by Sex and Cohort

	Men			Women		
	1930	1940	1950	1930	1040	1950
Respondent's education						
No *Abschluss*	.116	.079	.059	.102	.063	.059
Abschluss	.686	.703	.525	.699	.659	.597
mittlere Reife	.116	.130	.194	.142	.194	.213
Abitur	.082	.088	.222	.057	.084	.131
Vocational training	.604	.742	.689	.280	.457	.588
Age of spouse − age of respondent (in years)	−2.83	−2.49	−2.83	3.21	3.23	3.14
Number of children						
Respondent	2.13	1.76	0.92	2.17	1.98	1.39
Respondent's parents	3.62	3.27	3.01	3.70	3.32	3.16
Number of cases	347	375	365	361	355	368

Note: With regard to educational level, "no *Abschluss*" means some elementary school but without a degree, *Abschluss* means elementary school with a degree (about nine years), *mittlere Reife* is roughly equivalent to some high school (about ten years), and *Abitur* means graduation from a gymnasium (at least thirteen years).

Over time the structure of respondents' parental homes has changed substantially. In particular, the average family size of respondents' parents declines across the cohorts. If a person's fertility is partly imitative of his or her parents', then we expect those with more siblings to tend to have more children. Hence we expect some decline in respondents' fertility across the three cohorts. The inter-cohort trend in respondents' average number of children does parallel that of their parents, but is markedly lower.

Table 8.3 also reports the mean age difference between the respondent and his/her spouse for those who were married at the time of the interview. It is about three years for all three cohorts.

Results

First Birth

First we examine in more detail the proportion who are still childless as a function of the respondent's age, sex, and cohort. To those interested in reasons for the decline in *overall* fertility in West Germany, timing of the first birth may seem to be of little interest because fertility decline is usually regarded as the result of a sharp decrease in the number of people having *many* children. But postponement of the birth of the first child can be a factor in this decline. First, it has been suggested (Dinkel 1983; Birg

Table 8.4. First, Second, and Third Quartiles of the Timing of Selected Birth Intervals by Sex and Cohort

	Men			Women		
	1930	1940	1950	1930	1940	1950
	Age at First Birth (in years)					
25%	24.8	24.4	25.5	22.3	21.5	20.8
50%	28.1	27.2	29.9	25.8	23.8	24.8
75%	32.6	31.5	—	29.4	27.8	30.8
	Duration between First and Second Births (in years)					
25%	2.2	2.2	2.3	2.0	2.2	2.6
50%	4.3	3.9	4.2	4.1	4.1	4.5
75%	16.8	12.0	—	13.2	15.2	10.6

Note: A dash indicates no information.

et al. 1984; Huinink 1989) that childlessness is becoming more common among recent German cohorts, and study of the timing of the first birth can help to assess this. In addition, postponement of the first birth among those who do eventually have at least one child shortens the period during which a person is at risk of having additional children, and thus can reduce total fertility indirectly.

The top panel of Table 8.4 shows the first, second, and third quartiles of the age at first birth by sex and cohort. These estimates come from Kaplan-Meier (1958) estimates of the survivor functions for the first birth of men and women in the three cohorts; the point estimates (with 95% pointwise confidence intervals) are displayed graphically in Figures 8.A1 through 8.A3 in the appendix. For women, the first quartile of age at first birth occurs at the lowest age for the 1950 cohort and at the highest age for the 1930 cohort. The latter may seem surprising. We think that hardships in the period after World War II led those in the 1930 cohort to delay family formation. Men in the 1930 cohort also tended to remain childless longer than men in the 1940 cohort, but not as long as men in the 1950 cohort.

The difference between the first and third quartiles, a measure of spread in the distribution of age at first birth, is smallest for the 1940 cohort and largest for the 1950 cohort of women (and, most likely, for the 1950 cohort of men, too).[6] Thus, the timing of the first birth varies least in the 1940 cohort, somewhat more in the 1930 cohort, and still more in the

6. By age 32.4 years, 37% of the men in the 1950 cohort are still childless. Unless 12% of the men in this cohort had their first child between ages 32.4 and 33.4 (which seems extremely improbable), the inter-quartile range for men will turn out to be largest for those in the 1950 cohort.

1950 cohort. Estimates based on the official statistics show that the spread of the age at first birth declined from older cohorts to the 1946 cohort, when variation in this timing reached a minimum, and then began to increase again. Thus, external evidence suggests that this pattern is not a peculiarity of the GLHS sample.

It is easy to understand why those in the 1930 cohort, who postponed their first birth during a period of national recovery, tended to have their first child in a relatively narrow age range. It is less obvious why age at first birth varies relatively little in the 1940 cohort. Most members of this cohort had their first child during the early 1960s, a period of economic expansion, an improving standard of living, and relaxation of traditional norms of sexual behavior. The latter may have encouraged members of the 1940 cohort to have children at an earlier age. Moreover, the favorable economic conditions may have reduced variation in the timing of the first child, just as unfavorable conditions in the postwar period did for the 1930 cohort. That is, very favorable as well as very unfavorable societal conditions may dampen variation in the timing of births that occurs due to heterogeneity in personal attributes. Hence, the greater variation in the timing of the first birth in the 1950 cohort suggests that individual characteristics may explain entry into parenthood for the 1950 cohort more than for the others.

Another change over time in fertility patterns that can be seen in the top panel of Table 8.4 pertains to the differences between men and women in the timing of the first birth. As expected, for each cohort men tend to have their first child at an older age than do women. In addition, the difference between men and women in age at first birth has increased over time. For each quartile of the distribution of age at first birth, the male-female difference is least for the 1930 cohort (where it ranges from 2.3 to 3.2 years) and greatest for the 1950 cohort (where it ranges from 4.7 to 5.1 years).

This finding may seem somewhat surprising since the fraction of married women who are employed began to rise slowly but steadily after 1967–1968,[7] and because the ideology of women's liberation (i.e., sex role equality) received much attention in West Germany during the 1970s when the 1950 cohort was, for the most part, having a first child. Yet, this period emphasizing women's economic contributions and equality between the sexes reveals increased *in*equality in a major sex-linked behav-

7. The percentage of married women who were employed fluctuated very little between 1959 and 1967, but began to rise, slowly but steadily, beginning in 1968 (Statistisches Bundesamt, various years, 1962–1982). For example, the percentage of women married rose from 52% in 1968 to 63% in 1982 for those aged 20–25, and from 41% to 53% for those aged 30–40.

ior—birth of the first child. Moreover, since the ideology of sex role equality has tended to encourage women's activities outside the home more than men's activities in the home (Davis 1984), at first glance one might expect this ideology to affect women's fertility behavior more than men's.

In fact, the large male-female difference in the timing of the first birth in the 1950 cohort may reflect the changes in norms and women's behavior that began in the late 1960s. On average German women marry men roughly three years older than themselves (see Table 8.3), and this age difference seems to be relatively constant over time. Hence, men in the 1950 cohort are married on average to women in the 1953 cohort. One might expect the new norms and the trend toward greater female labor force participation to affect wives of the men in the 1950 cohort even more than the women in that cohort. That is, when there is a growing tendency to delay the first birth, as began in West Germany in the late 1960s, the male-female difference in the timing of the first birth tends to increase for men and women in a given birth cohort, as well as for women in slightly different birth cohorts. Thus, the finding that the male-female difference in age at first birth is greater for the 1950 cohort than for the other cohorts is congruent with the spread of new norms about sex roles and, concomitantly, with women's growing participation in work outside the home, which began in the late 1960s.

Another way to study differences between men and women in different cohorts with respect to the birth of the first child is to compare their age-specific birth rates.[8] Plots of the Nelson-Aalen[9] estimates of the rate of first birth (smoothed over a year) versus age are displayed by cohort for men and women in Figures 8.1 and 8.2, respectively.

Figure 8.2 suggests that the first-birth rates of women in the 1930 and 1940 cohorts were fairly similar at ages under 22 years. The main difference between these two groups is that the first-birth rate for women between 22 and 25 years is markedly higher in the 1940 cohort than in the 1930 cohort. Women in the 1930 cohort eventually "catch up" by a higher first-birth rate between ages 25 and 35 years than women in the 1940 cohort.

The first-birth rate of women in the 1950 cohort is noticeably different from that of women in the other two cohorts. There is a marked bimodality in the distribution of the first-birth rate, with one peak occurring about

8. Examination of log survivor plots is often recommended to see whether rates vary over time. Here we have strong reason to expect age variation a priori, so this step is not very informative. In any case, plots of the rates versus age are easier to decipher.

9. This estimator was first proposed by Nelson (1972); later, Aalen (1978) gave it a firmer statistical foundation. It has therefore come to be called by the names of both men.

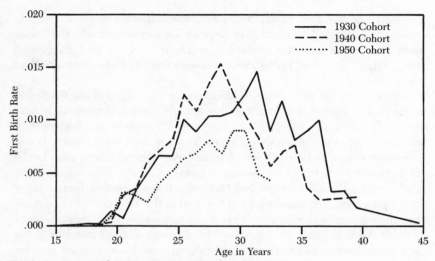

Figure 8.1. First-Birth Rate versus Age: Men by Cohort

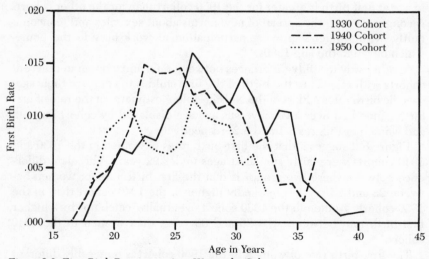

Figure 8.2. First-Birth Rate versus Age: Women by Cohort

age 21 and another about age 26. A roughly similar pattern can also be seen in the official statistics for slightly younger cohorts (see Birg et al. 1984), so it is probably not a peculiarity of the GLHS sample.

There are at least two possible explanations for this bimodality. First, it may result from observing a mixture of two (or more) groups with rather strikingly different norms concerning when to begin family formation. According to this explanation, one group is similar to the 1940 cohort of women and tends to begin family formation early; another group postpones the birth of the first child. The first group may adhere to more traditional values about women's roles, whereas the second may be more accepting of modern values and more interested in women's enhanced opportunities for employment. Variables that might differentiate fairly well between these two postulated groups are education and vocational training. We expect women to fall largely in the first group if they have relatively little schooling and training, and in the second group if they are relatively well schooled and trained.

Second, the bimodality may reflect a pure "period" effect. The marked drop in the birth rates between ages 22 and 25 for the 1950 cohort of women occurs around 1972–1975. In 1973–1974, oil prices rose sharply in Western Europe, causing a period of economic uncertainty and decline relative to the boom in the late 1960s. These economic and social changes in German society may have caused many young women in the 1950 cohort to postpone family formation for a few years.

To try to assess the first explanation of the bimodal pattern, we estimated the first-birth rate of women in the 1950 cohort whose highest educational degree did and did not exceed the "Hauptschulabschluss" (the degree from an elementary school), which corresponds to about nine years of completed schooling (see Figure 8.3). Bimodality is clearly appar-

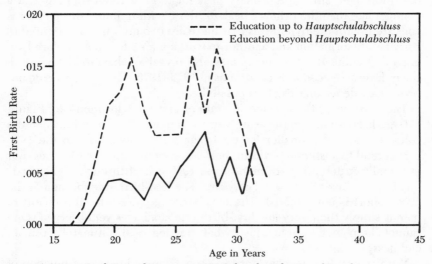

Figure 8.3. First-Birth Rate of Women in 1950 Cohort by Educational Level

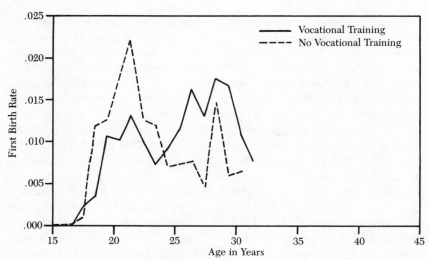

Figure 8.4. First-Birth Rate of Women in 1950 Cohort with No More than *Hauptschulabschluss*, by Training

ent for the less educated group of women (levels 1 and 2) but not for the more educated women (levels 3 and 4), for whom the rate of first birth has a single peak in the late twenties. Next we estimated the first-birth rate of less educated women with and without a vocational training degree (see Figure 8.4). Although bimodality is still apparent, it is less than in Figure 8.3. Moreover, since the primary peak for those without training is at a younger age than the primary peak for those with training, this picture is consistent with the hypothesis that there are two groups, one oriented to early family formation and another to working for a few years before having a first child. But the curves may also reveal a behavioral response to the unfavorable economic conditions in 1973–1975. These analyses do not provide evidence on this other possibility.

The patterns of the age-specific rate of first birth for men (see Figure 8.1) are fairly similar to those for women, though differences between the cohorts tend to be smaller for men than for women. Men in the 1930 cohort tend to postpone births in their late twenties and early thirties, but eventually "catch up" with men in the 1940 cohort through higher first-birth rates at ages 33 through 38 years. The first-birth rate for men in the 1950 cohort is not bimodal. The most striking pattern for this cohort of men is simply their very low first-birth rate at all ages yet observed. One cannot help but wonder just what fraction will ultimately remain childless.

With regard to this, consider the proportion childless as a function of age (see the top panel of Table 8.5). It is striking that nearly half of the men in the 1950 cohort are still childless by age 30. Contrast this figure with the figures for men in the 1930 and 1940 cohorts (.384 and .301, respectively), and also with those for women in the 1930, 1940, and 1950 cohorts (.236, .180, and .266, respectively). Although men are biologically capable of producing children for many more years than women, Figures 8.1 and 8.2 indicate that, for the older cohorts, men over 35 years of age have only slightly higher birth rates than women, and that birth rates are very low for both sexes after age 35. This suggests that men in the 1950 cohort will either break this pattern and have much higher birth rates in their thirties (and perhaps at older ages) than men in previous cohorts, *or* will remain childless throughout their lives to a truly

Table 8.5. Proportion with Fewer than N Children by Age (in years), Sex, and Cohort

	Age				
	20	25	30	35	40
N = 1					
Men					
1930	.968	.739	.384	.186	.132
1940	.984	.699	.301	.181	.155
1950	.984	.792	.496	—	—
Women					
1930	.910	.551	.236	.116	.105
1940	.864	.402	.180	.121	.110
1950	.820	.489	.266	—	—
N = 2					
Men					
1930	.997	.962	.703	.455	.372
1940	.997	.920	.640	.445	.389
1950	.997	.958	.772	—	—
Women					
1930	.994	.850	.548	.377	.324
1940	.986	.780	.467	.369	.341
1950	.989	.809	.562	—	—
N = 3					
Men					
1930	.997	.988	.914	.778	.700
1940	.997	.987	.925	.861	.821
1950	.997	.994	.978	—	—
Women					
1930	.997	.931	.875	.726	.676
1940	.997	.941	.828	.755	.727
1950	.997	.984	.905	—	—

amazing degree. Since the proportion of childless women in the 1950 cohort at any given age does not differ from that of women in the older cohorts to such a considerable extent, these men may largely be postponing rather than permanently avoiding fatherhood. On the other hand, since men tend to marry women about three years younger, their high degree of childlessness may reflect the greater tendency of women in still younger cohorts to engage in market work rather than house work and to choose careers over children. New data are needed to answer this question.

With the GLHS data, the proportion ultimately childless can be estimated only for the 1930 and 1940 cohorts. An indicator of this quantity is the proportion childless at age 40 (see "N = 1" in Table 8.5). Since the confidence interval at this age is fairly wide, one must be cautious about comparing the point estimates. Still, the proportion childless at age 40 is remarkably similar for the 1930 and 1940 cohorts for a given sex, though about 3–4% more men than women seem to be childless at this age. One forecast predicts that 18% of the 1950 cohort of women will be childless ultimately (Huinink 1987). This could be too high since the proportion of childless women in the 1930 cohort dropped from .236 at age 30 to .105 at age 40. Note that the proportion of childless women at age 30 is .266 for the 1950 cohort, which is only .03 higher than for the 1930 cohort. Only new data can show to what extent it is becoming more common to remain childless over the life span.

Second Birth

The Kaplan-Meier estimated probability that men and women have not yet had a second child is given as a function of age for the 1930, 1940, and 1950 cohorts in the middle panel of Table 8.5. Several patterns noted in the case of the first birth are again apparent, but not all. Again the 1940 cohort is noteworthy for tending to have a second child at a younger age and in a smaller range of ages than the other two cohorts, especially the 1950 cohort. As in the case of the first child, having a second child tends to occur several years later for men than women, and the male-female difference in age at the child's birth increases across the cohorts. Finally, the relatively small fraction of men and women having a second child between ages 35 and 40 indicates a marked decline in the birth rate after age 35.

The proportion who ultimately have at least two children can be approximated from the proportion at age 40 for the 1930 and 1940 cohorts. For women, this figure is .676 and .659, respectively; for men, .628 and .611. The inter-cohort differences for individuals of the same sex are too small to be taken seriously given the width of the 95% confidence intervals. The male-female difference in a given cohort is probably genuine, but it seems to reflect mainly men's late start in child-fathering rather than ultimate differences in achieved parenthood. In sum, for the two older cohorts, roughly one-third have one or fewer children. Since we reported above that about 11% in these cohorts remain childless, about 22% (33% − 11%) have exactly one child. In contrast, about 15% of the respondents come from one-child families.

Since members of the 1950 cohort were in their early thirties at the time of the interview, one cannot accurately estimate the fraction that will ultimately have more than one child. Note, however, that the proportion of 30-year old women with at least two children is similar for the 1930 and 1950 cohorts, .452 and .438, respectively. The proportion of 30-year-old men with at least two children is much smaller (.228) in the 1950 cohort, but it does not differ strikingly from that for the other two cohorts of men, in contrast to the case of the first birth. Since men in the 1950 cohort are childless to a much greater extent than men in the other cohorts at any age yet observed, a similar proportion with two children implies that most men in the 1950 cohort who have one child go on to have two. This points to another form of heterogeneity in the 1950 cohort that is similar to that for women: one group remains childless (or delays child-bearing until ages beyond those observed) and a second group has rather traditional fertility patterns.

Third Birth

As we noted earlier, the occurrence of a third birth is relatively uncommon in these data, especially in the 1950 cohort. Consequently, one cannot say much at all about the third birth for that cohort, and only a little about it for the other two cohorts.

The bottom panel of Table 8.5 gives the Kaplan-Meier estimated probability of not yet having a third child by age, sex, and cohort. The greatest difference between the 1930 and 1940 cohorts is in the proportion having a third child by age 40, which falls from .300 to .179 in the case of men, and from .324 to .273 in the case of women. Recall that members of the 1930 cohort tended to have their first and second children at older ages than members of the 1940 cohort. Yet by age 40, the overall fertility of those in the 1930 cohort has not only caught up with that of the 1940 cohort, but exceeded it. This finding illustrates that *postponement* of the first birth need not lower *completed* fertility.

Birth Spacing

The probability of having a second or third child by a given age depends on the timing of previous births. For example, the rise in the male-female

Table 8.6. Proportion with Fewer Than N Children by Duration since Previous Birth (in years), Sex, and Cohort

	Duration			
	2	5	10	15
N = 2				
Men				
1930	.773	.444	.298	.274
1940	.797	.380	.272	—
1950	.799	.424	.262	—
Women				
1930	.760	.411	.274	.246
1940	.781	.402	.270	.253
1950	.831	.469	.259	—
N = 3				
Men				
1930	.862	.622	.496	—
1940	.882	.788	.705	—
1950	.931	.744	—	—
Women				
1930	.848	.663	.540	.519
1940	.858	.685	.607	—
1950	.910	.752	.606	—

Note: A dash indicates no information.

difference in the age at the second birth across the cohorts may result primarily from the increasing male-female difference in the age at first birth. An examination of the spacing of births after the first helps to clarify such issues.

The top panel of Table 8.6 reports Kaplan-Meier (1958) estimates of the probability of not yet having a second child for given durations since the first child by sex and cohort. The differences between men and women in a given cohort are very small, as are the differences between the cohorts. The overall impression is one of much greater similarity in the spacing between the first and second births than in the timing of the first birth. Women in the 1950 cohort tend to delay the birth of the second child slightly longer than women in the other two cohorts, but this is the only noticeable difference among the groups.

The bottom panel of Table 8.4 gives the first, second, and third quartiles of the duration from the first to the second birth. Twenty-five percent have a second birth within a little over two years after the first birth, and 50 percent have a second birth within 3.9–4.5 years. Again, there are no especially noteworthy differences between men and women or between the different cohorts in this pattern.

Figures 8.5 and 8.6 show plots of Nelson-Aalen estimates of the rate of transition from birth one to birth two as a function of the duration since birth one by cohort for men and women, respectively. For both sexes in all three cohorts, the rate is identically zero under a half year, and it is also very low in the second half year, undoubtedly for biological reasons.

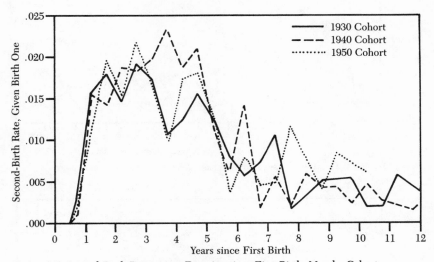

Figure 8.5. Second-Birth Rate versus Duration since First Birth: Men by Cohort

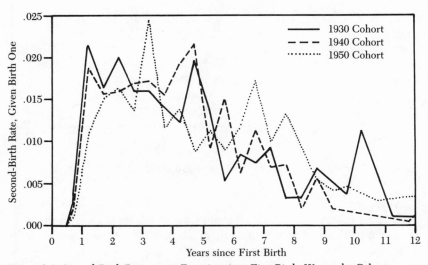

Figure 8.6. Second-Birth Rate versus Duration since First Birth: Women by Cohort

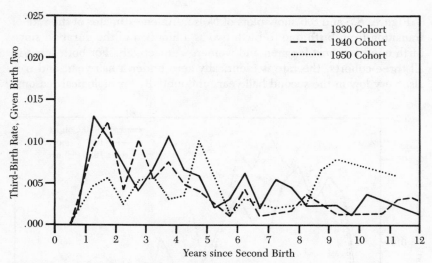

Figure 8.7. Third-Birth Rate versus Duration since Second Birth: Men by Cohort

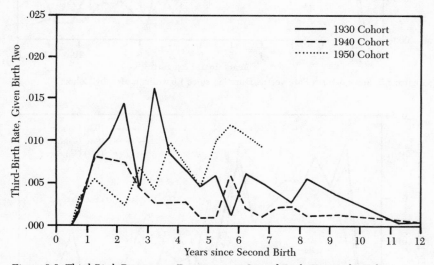

Figure 8.8. Third-Birth Rate versus Duration since Second Birth: Women by Cohort

Between one and five years after the first birth, the second-birth rate tends to be relatively high for all groups, although its shape and the timing of the peak varies. Women (and, to a lesser extent, men) in the 1950 cohort have a noticeably lower second-birth rate between 1.0–1.5 years after the first child than do the other groups; this probably results from the widespread adoption of effective contraceptive methods by married couples in the 1970s in order to space births as well as to avoid unwanted births. Indeed, a spacing of about three years appears especially popular. Between five and ten years after the first birth, the second-birth rate declines but remains significant. In fact, the Kaplan-Meier estimates of the proportion without a second child falls on average by about .15 between 5 and 10 years after the first child's birth (see the top panel of Table 8.6), which indicates that the spacing between the first and second births is quite long in a substantial fraction of cases.

As we mentioned before, due to the rarity of third births in the data, one can only gain a general impression of the transition from the second to the third birth. The middle panel of Table 8.6 gives the Kaplan-Meier estimated probability of not yet having a third child among those with a second child for selected durations by sex and cohort. Male-female differences are small; cohort differences are larger. As one expects, the more recent the cohort, the smaller the proportion who have had a third birth after any given duration since the second birth. The greater frequency of at least three children among the 1930 cohort than among the other cohorts is especially apparent.

Nelson-Aalen estimates of the rate of transition from the second to the third birth are shown in Figures 8.7 and 8.8 by cohort for men and women, respectively. For any given duration since the second birth, these rates tend to be much lower than the rate of transition from the first to the second birth (compare Figures 8.5 and 8.6). Moreover, they are much less peaked. The low level and flatness of the third-birth rate for the 1950 cohort of women is especially evident, suggesting that third births are often unintended and unplanned in this cohort.

Variation across the cohorts seems quite clear for men: in the first three years after the second birth, which is when the majority of third children are born, the third-birth rate tends to fall from the 1930 to 1940 to 1950 cohort. The pattern for women is similar, although the differences between the 1930 and 1940 cohorts are less marked than for men.

Summary

Analyses of the 2,171 individuals interviewed in the 1981–1982 German Life History Survey reported in this paper are designed to provide an overall picture of fertility patterns of native West Germans in the years since World War II. We have therefore focused on describing basic patterns and on comparing these for men and women across the three cohorts for which data were gathered: 1930 (those born in 1929–1931), 1940 (1939–1941), and 1950 (1949–1951). Multivariate analyses of these data will be reported in subsequent papers. The main conclusions of the research reported in this paper are as follows.

First, completed family size falls as one moves from the 1930 to the 1950 cohort. This appears to be mainly due to a significant decrease in the fraction having at least three children. There is no strong suggestion that childlessness is becoming much more common, except possibly in the 1950 cohort of men. They were in their early thirties at the time of the interview, however, and have many remaining years in which they could father children.

Second, the rate of transition from the second birth to the third is quite low and relatively flat for both men and women in all three cohorts. The low level suggests that a third child is rarely intended; the flatness suggests that the third child is usually not planned. Although this rate is low in all three cohorts, it still tends to decline across the cohorts, suggesting that the desire for three or more children has declined in recent years.

Third, spacing between the first and second births is remarkably similar for men and women in all cohorts. The only deviation from this pattern of overall similarity is a reduction in the likelihood of a very short spacing (under 18 months) in the 1950 cohort, which suggests that members of this cohort use contraceptives for birth spacing as well as birth avoidance. In all three cohorts a spacing of about three years is especially common, suggesting that this spacing is preferred when another child is planned.

Fourth, the tendency to postpone the birth of the first child is especially noticeable for men relative to women, and for the 1930 and 1950 cohorts relative to the 1940 cohort. The difference between men and women presumably reflects traditional norms about mate selection. We suggested that the 1930 cohort tended to postpone births during the postwar period, when they were of an age at which they might normally have been expected to have a first child, while recovering from the hardships resulting from World War II. We think that the 1950 cohort tended to postpone the first birth for very different reasons, in particular because of the increasing opportunities for women to engage in market work and perhaps also because of economic uncertainty and decline in the mid-1970s.

Fifth, even though members of the 1930 cohort tended to postpone their first birth, they also exhibit a marked tendency to "catch up" at older ages. Despite a late start at child-bearing, members of the 1930 cohort still seem to have the highest completed fertility. Thus, fertility of the 1930 cohort shows that postponement of the first birth need not mean permanent avoidance of parenthood.

Sixth, variation in the timing of the first birth is greatest in the 1950 cohort. There seems to be more variation in fertility to be explained by individual differences for this cohort than for the older ones. We suggested that there may be relatively little variation in this timing for the 1930 cohort because most delayed child-bearing during the postwar recovery and for the 1940 cohort because relaxation of sexual norms and favorable economic conditions encouraged most people to begin child-bearing early. Thus, either very favorable or very unfavorable general social and economic conditions can produce a social situation that dampens the effects of individual attributes on fertility.

Seventh, the rate of first birth for women in the 1950 cohort as a function of age is clearly bimodal. This seems to be partly due to heterogeneity across social groups in the fundamental shape of the birth rate pattern. It may also be partly a period effect due to the adverse economic conditions in 1973–1975. We suggest that the heterogeneity may result from a mixture of two groups, one whose views of women's roles are more traditional and who chose to have children at relatively young ages, and another whose views are more modern and oriented to women working outside the home, which leads to postponement of the first child. We found that the level of completed education and whether a woman has a vocational training degree discriminate among fertility patterns and substantially reduce the extent of bimodality in the first-birth rate of women in the 1950 cohort.

Finally, we wish to call attention to the methodological value of exploratory, descriptive analyses of the type reported here. It has become common for analysts of event history data to estimate complex multivariate models that assume that hazard (or transition) rates are unimodal and/or proportional. The rate of first birth for women born in 1950 is clearly bimodal, not unimodal, in the aggregate. Moreover, though this rate appears to be unimodal for more educated women in the 1950 cohort, it may not be so for less educated women. In addition, even if further stratification of the sample by measured covariates does yield subgroups in which the first-birth rate is unimodal, the age at which this mode occurs definitely seems to depend on individual characteristics. Consequently, a hazard rate model that assumed proportional effects of covariates would not be valid. Thus these exploratory analyses have given valuable suggestions about the classes of multivariate hazard rate models that can plausibly be considered in subsequent analyses of fertility in the Federal Republic of Germany.

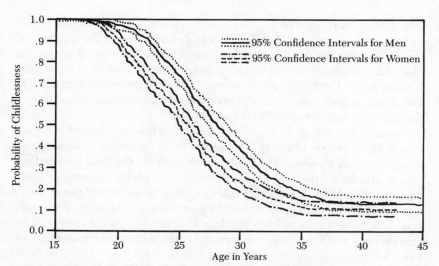

Figure 8.A1. Survivor Plot: First Birth: Men and Women, 1930 Cohort

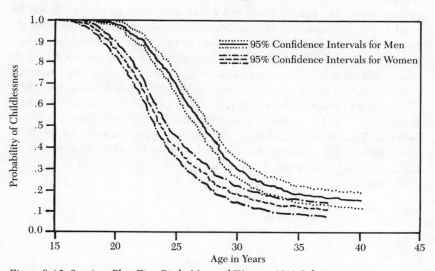

Figure 8.A2. Survivor Plot: First Birth: Men and Women, 1940 Cohort

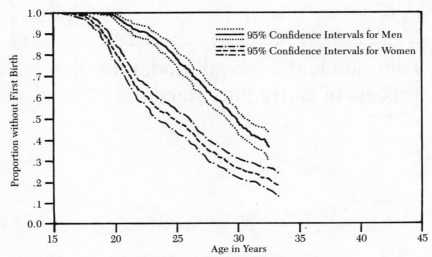

Figure 8.A3. Survivor Plot: First Birth: Men and Women, 1950 Cohort

9 *Andreas Diekmann*

Diffusion and Survival Models for the Process of Entry into Marriage

Introduction

Estimates of the age-dependent hazard rate for entry into first marriage consistently reveal a nonmonotonic, bell-shaped pattern for different nations, cohorts, and socioeconomic groups (e.g., Espenshade 1983; Sørensen and Sørensen 1986; Papastefanou 1987). This "marriage bell" (see Figure 9.1) corresponds to a unimodal frequency distribution (see Figure 9.2), and to a typical S-shaped cumulative distribution of age at marriage and an S-shaped survival curve (see Figure 9.3).[1]

The law-like property of the marriage process is well known in social demography. One of the first to identify this regularity was Adolphe Quetelet. He argued that the observed frequency distribution shows that there exists a perfect law governing the marriage process (Quetelet 1914).

I am very much indebted to Carol Cassidy, Glenn Carroll, Eckehart Köhler, Peter Mitter, Annemette Sørensen, Aage Sørensen, and Rolf Ziegler for helpful comments. This research was supported by the German Research Association (Deutsche Forschungsgemeinschaft), Sonderforschungsbereich 333, Project B4. This article was first published in *Journal of Mathematical Sociology* 14:31–44. Reprinted by friendly permission of the publishers. ©1987 Gordon and Breach Science Publishers Inc.

1. See, for example, Elandt-Johnson and Johnson (1980) for life-table estimation techniques.

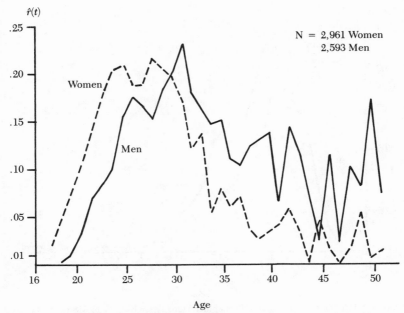

Figure 9.1. Life-Table Estimation of Hazard Rate for Entry into Marriage, by Sex

A consistently observed regularity gives rise to questions about the mechanisms generating the observed pattern. Three types of formal models explaining the observations can be distinguished.

The first type of model can be called a *latent state model*. Age at marriage, or, equivalently, the time span from minimum legal marriage age until marriage, is conceived as the sum of random variables referring to duration of the two latent states "not in search of a mate" and "in search of a mate". For example, Coale and McNeil (1972) assume that the waiting time until entering the search state is normally distributed and that search time prior to transition to marriage consists of the sum of exponentially distributed waiting times. A similar line of reasoning is adopted in the model of Mitter (1987).

A second type of model can be classified as an *unobserved heterogeneity model*. In the case of rational search behavior under imperfect information, the standard model of economic search theory (Lippmann and McCall 1976a; see McKenna 1985 for a survey) predicts an increasing hazard rate for acceptance of a marriage offer. If the individual hazard rate increases linearly with age, and if the degree of increase (the slope) varies in the population according to the gamma distribution (unobserved het-

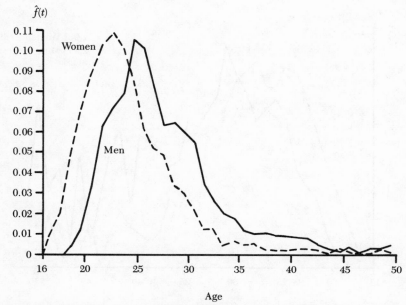

Figure 9.2. Life-Table Estimation of Probability Density for Entry into Marriage, by Sex

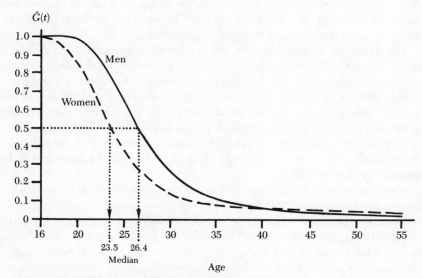

Figure 9.3. Life-Table Estimation of Survivor Function, by Sex

erogeneity), a nonmonotonic aggregated population hazard rate for entry into marriage can be derived (Diekmann 1987).

The conceptualization of the marriage process as a process of social diffusion gives rise to a third class of models. *Diffusion models,* as proposed by Hernes (1972), are based on the assumption of "contagion," imitation or some kind of social pressure to marry, exerted by the married persons in a cohort on the unmarried cohort members.

In this chapter we restrict our discussion to the third class of models of the marriage process, the diffusion models. There is a simple connection between diffusion and survival models.[2] As will be shown in the following section, the Hernes diffusion model can be analyzed in terms of survival and reliability theory. On the other hand, the log-logistic model, which is well known in survival theory, can be derived from assumptions of diffusion theory. The following mathematical analysis provides for an extension of the Hernes model and a deeper understanding of the log-logistic model. In the concluding section, the alternative versions of diffusion models are tested using German and U.S. data on the marriage process. The nonmonotonic sickle hazard rate (Diekmann and Mitter 1983, 1984a) is also included in this comparison as a possible third candidate for the description of the observed marriage pattern.

Diffusion Models of the Marriage Process

The Hernes Model

Hernes (1972) successfully applied the following model to the cumulative distributions of age at marriage of U.S. birth cohorts:

$$\frac{dF(t)}{dt} = s(t) \, F(t) \, [1 - F(t)], \tag{9.1}$$

where

$$s(t) = m \exp[-c(t-1)], \qquad t \geq 1; \, m,c > 0. \tag{9.2}$$

Here, $F(t)$ is the proportion of a cohort first married at age $t + t_0$ (t_0 is the minimum legal marriage age), $s(t)$ is a decreasing function of time, and m, c are parameters estimated by empirical data. The model is similar to

2. For different survival models see, for example, the textbooks of Elandt-Johnson and Johnson (1980) and Nelson (1982).

previous diffusion of innovation models (Coleman, Katz, and Menzel 1957; Hamblin, Jacobsen, and Miller 1973).

Although $F(t)$ is a cumulative probability distribution with density $f(t) = dF(t)/dt$, it should be noted that $F(t)$ may be defective; namely,

$$\lim_{t \to \infty} F(t) \le 1, \tag{9.3}$$

which is in fact the case for the Hernes model and for the sickle model, which will be developed below.

In the Hernes model the increase in the proportion first married per unit of time and per candidate for a marriage—$dF(t) / \{dt[1 - F(t)]\}$—is the product of two terms: the increasing social pressure $F(t)$ inducing imitation or "infection," and a decreasing chance of marriage $s(t)$ dependent on age. As argued by Hernes (1972), $s(t)$ may be interpreted as a function expressing the decay of the marriage potential of an unmarried candidate. Alternatively, $s(t)$ can be interpreted as the decreasing chance of having contacts with a potential marriage candidate of the opposite sex because $1 - F(t)$ also decreases with age so that search costs increase.[3]

Hernes (1972) did not deal with hazard rate models but derived from differential equations (9.1) and (9.2) the solution for the cumulative distribution $F(t)$ and fitted it to empirical data. However, there is a simple correspondence between diffusion models of the above type and hazard rate models. Define the survival function as $G(t) = 1 - F(t)$ and the hazard rate as:

$$r(t) = \lim_{\Delta t \to 0} \frac{\Pr(t + \Delta t > T \ge t \mid T \ge t)}{\Delta t} = \frac{f(t)}{G(t)} \tag{9.4}$$

then it follows from equation 9.1 that

$$r(t) = s(t) F(t) \tag{9.5}$$

3. As argued by R. Ziegler (personal communication), the opportunity structure of the random chance of contacts between unmarried persons could be explicitly modeled in equation (9.1) by multiplying the right side by $[1 - F(t)]$. Then $F(t)$ would represent the social pressure and $[1 - F(t)][1 - F(t)]$ the chance of contacts between unmarried members of the population. This model involves a nonmonotonic hazard rate (see below) even when $s(t)$ is constant. In this case, however, the rate assumes its maximum independently of the value of the constant when $F(t) = .5$. The model is identical to the Floyd model described in Mahajan and Peterson (1985, 30). There is no explicit solution to this model, but it has the nice property that a transformation of $F(t)$ can be formulated as a linear function of t.

The solutions for the survival function $G(t) = 1 - F(t)$ and the hazard-rate function $r(t)$ can be derived by solving differential equation 9.1 and applying formula 9.5, yielding the result:

$$G(t) = \frac{1}{1 + ka^{b^{t-1}}} \quad t \geq 1 \tag{9.6}$$

$$r(t) = \frac{\ln a \ln b \, b^{t-1}}{1 + (ka^{b^{t-1}})^{-1}} \tag{9.7}$$

where

$$k = \frac{1 - G(1)}{G(1)} e^{m/c}$$
$$a = e^{-m/c} \tag{9.8}$$
$$b = e^{-c}$$

and $G(1)$ is the initial proportion married after one time unit has elapsed.

The "immune" proportion of the population (Hernes 1972) and the median waiting time can easily be derived from equation 9.6:

$$G(\infty) = \frac{1}{1 + k} \tag{9.9}$$

$$T^* = \frac{1}{\ln b} \ln \left(- \frac{\ln k}{\ln a} \right) + 1. \tag{9.10}$$

Hernes (1972) estimated the three model parameters by applying a fitting technique proposed by Prescott (1922) for the estimation of Gompertz distributions. We also make use of this quick and simple estimation technique in our empirical test of the models. However, it should be noted that, in principle, maximum-likelihood estimates techniques for censored data would yield estimates with optimal statistical properties (Nelson, 1982). The likelihood function to be maximized with respect to parameters a, b, and k takes the form

$$L = \prod_{i=1}^{N} r(k, a, b, t_i)^{d_i} G(k, a, b, t_i), \tag{9.11}$$

where d_i is a status variable indicating that a case is censored; that is, that $d_i = 1$ for a person married at t_i and $d_i = 0$ otherwise.

The Log-Logistic Model

As an alternative to the specifications in equation 9.2 for the decreasing function $s(t)$, we choose the following function:

$$s(t) = \frac{p}{t} , \tag{9.12}$$

where $t \geq 0$, and where p is a parameter estimated by empirical data. Hence, the differential equation for the diffusion process takes the form

$$\frac{dF(t)}{dt} = \frac{p}{t} F(t) [1 - F(t)]. \tag{9.13}$$

In this case it follows from equations 9.12, 9.13, and the relation $F(t) = 1 - G(t)$, that

$$G(t) = \frac{1}{1 + (\lambda t)^p} , \tag{9.14}$$

where the additional parameter λ results as a constant of integration. Because $r(t) = s(t) [1 - G(t)]$—see equation 9.5—the model yields the following hazard function:

$$r(t) = \frac{p\lambda (\lambda t)^{p-1}}{1 + (\lambda t)^p} . \tag{9.15}$$

Equations 9.14 and 9.15 represent the log-logistic hazard rate model, with the nonmonotonic hazard function 9.15 in case of $p > 1$. The widely used log-logistic model is, therefore, not only a descriptive model but derivable from differential equation 9.1 by specifying $s(t) = p/t$.

The Sickle Model

Although not derivable from a simple diffusion model,[4] the sickle function proposed by Diekmann and Mitter (1983) is included in this comparison

---

4. Relation (9.5) is, of course, also true for the logistic distribution where $s(t)$ is constant, which leads to a monotonically increasing hazard rate. I am indebted to Peter Mitter, who directed my attention to his derivation of the monotonic property of the hazard rate of the logistic model starting with the differential equation of the logistic process. His hint stimulated me to study in general the relationship between the diffusion and survival models and the consequences of this relationship for a variety of models. The proportionality characteristic of the logistic model (i.e., the proportional relation between the hazard rate and the

because the sickle model also assumes a nonmonotonic (sickle-shaped) hazard function which might be appropriate for a description of the observed nonmonotonic pattern of the age-dependent marriage rate. This model was applied before to occupational mobility and deviance data and with good success to the nonmonotonic divorce risk of marriage cohorts (Diekmann and Mitter 1983, 1984a). The hazard function of the two-parameter sickle model takes the form

$$r(t) = ct \exp(-t/\lambda), \tag{9.16}$$

where the parameter λ is interpretable as the time until the maximal rate.

The model leads to the following survival function (Diekmann and Mitter 1983):

$$G(t) = \exp\{-\lambda c[\lambda - (t + \lambda) \exp(-t/\lambda)]\} \tag{9.17}$$

with the property

$$G(\infty) = \exp(-c\lambda^2) \tag{9.18}$$

As in the Hernes model and unlike in the log-logistic model, the sickle model has a defective distribution, in that it allows for a proportion of "immune" cases in the population (Hernes 1972). This property is sometimes desirable, particularly for the analysis of divorce data, where a large proportion of the married population does not experience an event.

Empirical Test of the Models

Both variants of the diffusion model, the sickle model and the exponential model with constant rate, were tested using data from the German National Social Survey. The sample contains about 6,000 households interviewed in 1982 and 1984.[5] Time until marriage is defined as age at first

---

cumulative distribution function) is further mentioned in Elandt-Johnson and Johnson (1980, 64). Surprisingly, no hint can be found in textboks on survival analysis that the log-logistic model (a standard model in survival analysis which is not to be confused with the logistic model) can be derived in a simple manner from a diffusion equation (see equations 9.12 through 9.15). However, just before correcting the proofs of this article, I became aware of the article of Keeley (1979) who connected differential equation 9.13 to the log-logistic distribution. In his analysis of marriage data Keeley did not refer to survival analysis but instead used regression techniques for estimation of covariate effects on model parameters.

5. The German National Survey ("Allgemeine Bevölkerungsumfrage der Sozialwissenschaften"—ALLBUS) is a random sample of households. Data are weighted by a variable correcting for different household size. Reanalysis without weighting yields no substantial differences. An additional more detailed analysis of the unweighted data broken down by sex

Table 9.1. Estimated Parameters of Survival Models for the Process of Entry into Marriage

Model	$r(t)$ and $G(t)$	Parameter	
		Men	Women
Exponential model	$r = a \quad G = e^{-at}$	$\hat{a} = 0.0882$	$\hat{a} = 0.0933$
Sickle model	$r = ct\,e^{-t/\lambda}$ $G = \exp\{-\lambda c(\lambda - (t+\lambda)\exp(-t/\lambda))\}$	$\hat{\lambda} = 17.061$ $\hat{c} = 0.025441$	$\hat{\lambda} = 10.157$ $\hat{c} = 0.03901$
Log-logistic model	$r = \dfrac{\lambda p(\lambda t)^{p-1}}{1 + (\lambda t)^p}$ $G = \dfrac{1}{1 + (\lambda t)^p}$	$\hat{\lambda} = 0.1165$ $\hat{p} = 3.006$	$\hat{\lambda} = 0.1302$ $\hat{p} = 2.735$
Hernes model	$r = \dfrac{\ln a \ln b\, b^{t-1}}{1 + (ka^{b^{t-1}})^{-1}}$ $G = \dfrac{1}{1 + ka^{b^{t-1}}}$	$\hat{a} = 0.0002096$ $\hat{b} = 0.91298$ $\hat{k} = 57.788$	$\hat{a} = 0.0005223$ $\hat{b} = 0.8711$ $\hat{k} = 21.609$

Note: All models assume $t \geq 0$ except the Hernes model, which assumes $t \geq 1$.

marriage, determined by a retrospective question, minus minimum legal marriage age (which in Germany was sixteen for women and eighteen for men until equalization by law in the mid-seventies). Persons who were never married by the time of interview were treated as censored. Censored data were taken into account by estimating the survival function by life-table methods and by maximum-likelihood estimation of model parameters. The three parameters of the Hernes model are estimated from the life-table values of the survival function by the method suggested by Prescott (1922; see Hernes 1972). Parameters of the log-logistic, sickle, and exponential distributions are estimated by the maximum-likelihood method using formula 9.11 with the appropriate hazard rate function and survival function of the respective model.[6]

Estimated parameters for women and men are contained in Table 9.1.

---

and birth cohorts yields the same pattern of performance of the three models (1. Hernes, 2. Log-logistic, 3. Sickle) for all ten cohorts included in the analysis.

The data used in this article were made available by the "Zentralarchiv für empirische Sozialforschung", Universität Köln. The ALLBUS is a project funded by the Deutsche Forschungsgemeinschaft. Project leaders are: M. Rainer Lepsius (1980–1982), Walter Müller (1984), Franz Urban Pappi (1984), Erwin K. Scheuch (1980–1984), and Rolf Ziegler (1980–1984). The ALLBUS project is organized in cooperation with the Zentrum für Umfragen, Methoden und Analysen (ZUMA). Neither the aforementioned persons nor institutes are responsible for the data analysis or interpretation of results in this article.

6. I would like to thank Gilg Seeber for estimating the parameters of the log-logistic model for the German and U.S. data using a GLIM-Macro.

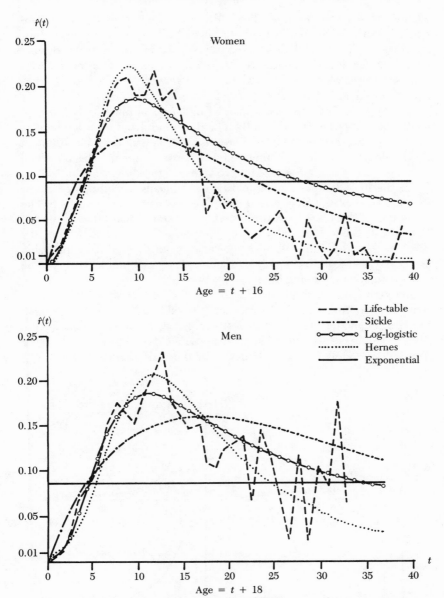

Figure 9.4. Comparison of Models' Parametric Hazard Rate Functions with Life-Table Estimations

Figure 9.4 displays observed life-table values for the hazard rate compared with the predicted hazard rate functions of the parametric models, and Figures 9.5 and 9.6 show the observed and predicted survival functions for women and for men, respectively. The exponential model with constant rate allows only for modeling the average marriage rate (Figure 9.4). Consequently, the first part of the survival function is strongly underestimated and the second part of the survival function is overestimated (see Figures 9.5 and 9.6). On the other hand, the log-logistic model and the Hernes model yield quite good fits with the data, although the log-logistic hazard function somewhat overestimates the observed marriage rate of women where t > 15 years (Figure 9.5).

For the male sample the log-logistic model leads to better predictions than the Hernes model, as can be seen from inspection of Figure 9.6. The sickle model does not do as well as either variant of the diffusion model. In contrast, the sickle model is highly superior to the log-logistic model (Diekmann and Mitter 1984a) in the analysis of divorce data, probably because of its incorporation of "immunity." The sickle model seems to be less adequate in modeling the marriage process.

Computation of a simple goodness-of-fit measure confirms the conclusions reached from graphical inspection (see Table 9.2). It can be seen that the Hernes model yields the lowest average absolute deviation for the female sample, while the log-logistic model yields the best fit of the four parametric models for the male data. For the male sample, surprisingly,

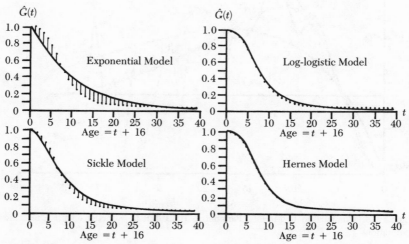

Figure 9.5. Comparison of Models' Parametric Survival Functions with Life-Table Estimations for Women

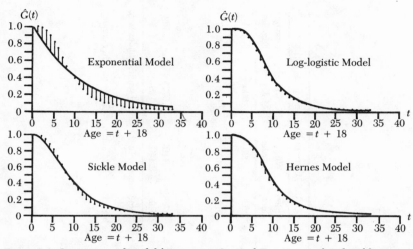

Figure 9.6. Comparison of Models' Parametric Survival Functions with Life-Table Estimations for Men

the two-parameter log-logistic model leads to better predictions than the three-parameter Hernes model. Is this an accident? Is the good fit of the log-logistic model caused by idiosyncratic data?

Table 9.2. Goodness of Fit of the Four Survival Models (German data)

	Exponential Model	Sickle Model	Log-logistic Model	Hernes Model
Women	0.076	0.030	0.017	0.004
Men	0.086	0.024	0.007	0.015

Note: Goodness-of-fit measure = $(1/33) \Sigma \mid G_{\text{life-table}} - \hat{G}_{\text{model prediction}} \mid$

In order to investigate this issue the log-logistic model was tested using the marriage data of the nine birth cohorts reported in Hernes (1972). Estimated parameters of the log-logistic model and goodness-of-fit measures for the log-logistic and the Hernes models are contained in Table 9.3. The marriage process for seven out of nine cohorts is better approximated by the Hernes model than by the log-logistic model. The average prediction error for the observation period amounts to 0.6% for the Hernes model and 1.2% for the log-logistic model.

Conclusions

The confrontation of different survival models with empirical data of the marriage process leads to the result that the Hernes model complies quite

Table 9.3. Goodness of Fit of Hernes Model and Log-Logistic Model (U.S. data)

	White Females Born 1920–1924 (U.S.)	U.S. Citizens 35 Years of Age in 1960				U.S. Citizens 75 Years of Age in 1960			
		White Males	White Females	Nonwhite Males	Nonwhite Females	White Males	White Females	Nonwhite Males	Nonwhite Females
Hernes model	.004	.005	.006	.005	.006	.003	.006	.009	.011
Log-logistic model	.019	.018	.015	.010	.013	.012	.011	.006	.007
Parameter of log-logistic model (MLE)									
$\hat{\lambda}$	.1208	.1011	.1402	.0945	.1442	.0768	.1101	.0778	.1309
$\hat{\rho}$	2.783	3.523	2.787	2.571	2.012	2.810	2.146	2.129	1.675

Note: For parameter estimation of log-logistic model, minimum age at marriage is $t_0 = 14$ for all nine cohorts. In the case of white females born 1920–1924, observations are from age 15 to 38. For all other cohorts, observations are from age 14 to 34.

Goodness-of-fit measure $= (1/n) \sum | C_{\text{life-table}} - \hat{C}_{\text{model prediction}} |$ where $n = 24$ for white females born 1920–1924 and $n = 21$ for all other cohorts. See Hernes (1972) for a more detailed description of the data.

well with the observations while the log-logistic model yields a middling approximation to the data. However, it should be noted that the two-parameter log-logistic model is a more parsimonious parameterization than the three-parameter Hernes model. Both models are not merely descriptions of observed data but also have considerable theoretical appeal. The hazard rate functions and survival functions can be derived from differential equations of social diffusion processes.

In general there is a simple relation between diffusion models expressed in terms of equation 9.1 and hazard rate models. This provides the opportunity to estimate and test a variety of diffusion models (see Mahajan and Peterson 1985 for an overview) using standard methods of survival analysis. The models of the marriage process discussed in this chapter may be useful for predicting and analyzing age-at-marriage data (see Sørensen 1986 for an application of the log-logistic model). However, as mentioned in the beginning of this chapter, other types of models should also be considered for analyzing the process of entry into marriage.

10 *Lawrence L. Wu*

Simple Graphical Goodness-of-Fit Tests for Hazard Rate Models

Introduction

Social scientists have increasingly used event history models to examine life course events such as birth, death, marriage, divorce, migration, and labor force entries and exits. When transition rates for these outcomes have strong time dependencies, researchers often invoke some tractable time-dependent parameterization, where time may represent age, duration, or historical period. Although this strategy can be reasonable, it is often wise to check the parametric assumptions, especially since available theory typically provides little or no guidance for choosing one parameterization over another.

This paper discusses a general method for assessing the fit of parametric models by comparing nonparametric estimates against the predictions from parametric models. In particular, this method provides a simple graphical procedure for identifying systematic departures of the data from

This paper was written at the Department of Sociology and Office of Population Research at Princeton University, with support from a faculty research grant from Princeton University and from a grant to the Institute for Research on Poverty by the National Institute of Child Health and Human Development (HD 19473). I wish to thank Johannes J. Huinink, German Rodriguez, James Trussell, and Nancy Brandon Tuma for helpful comments on earlier versions of this paper. The conclusions expressed in this paper do not reflect opinions or policies of funding agencies or the Institute for Research on Poverty.

the assumptions of parametric models. I describe a class of transformations for survivor plots proposed by Lawless (1982) that provides goodness-of-fit tests for parametric hazard rate models and use these methods to test the fit of four parametric models to data on the transition to first marriage for women in the United States.

I begin with a brief overview of terms and review the common Kaplan-Meier estimator for the survivor function. I then describe the transformed survivor plot and derive specific tests for several common parametric models. I conclude by illustrating the procedure using retrospective data on age at first marriage from the June 1980 Current Population Survey (U.S. Bureau of the Census, 1983).

Basic Terms

For concreteness, consider statistical definitions for individual-level event history data, where, for simplicity, I restrict attention to a single, nonrepeatable transition. Let T_i^e be an independent and continuous positive random variable representing the time of event for person i, where $i = 1, \ldots, I$. We observe (or gather retrospective information) for person i during the survey period $[\tau_{0i}, \tau_i]$, where the τ_{0i} represents the time at the start of the survey period, and τ_i represents the censoring time; for example, the relevant time at the last survey date for which information exists. Because not all individuals experience the event during the survey period, the data consist of a final time $T_i = \min(T_i^e, \tau_i)$, representing the time of event or the censoring time, and a censoring indicator c_i equal to one if the data for person i are censored and zero otherwise. A standard assumption is that the event and censoring times, T_i^e and τ_i, are independent.

The survivor probability, $G_i(t)$, has a simple definition—it is the probability that person i has not had the event by time t:

$$G_i(t) = \Pr\,(T_i^e \geq t). \tag{10.1}$$

The hazard rate is defined as the limit of the probability of the event for person i at time t given that the event has not yet occurred:

$$r_i(t) = \lim_{\varepsilon \downarrow 0} \frac{\Pr\,(T_i^e < t + \varepsilon \mid T_i^e \geq t)}{\varepsilon}, \tag{10.2}$$

where the limit is taken for positive ε. The survivor probability and hazard rate are closely related, as follows:

$$G_i(t) = \exp\left[-\int_{\tau_{0i}}^{t} r_i(s)\, ds\right]. \tag{10.3}$$

The Kaplan-Meier estimator (Kaplan and Meier 1958) provides a non-parametric estimator for the survivor probability; more precisely, it is the maximum-likelihood estimator of the survivor probability for homogeneous populations when minimal assumptions are made about the distribution of event and censoring times. Let $N(t)$ denote the number of individuals who have the event at time t and let $R(t)$ denote the number of individuals at risk of the event just before t

$$R(t) = \{i: T_i \geq t\}. \tag{10.4}$$

The Kaplan-Meier estimator for $G(t)$ is defined by

$$\hat{G}(t) = \prod_{\{R(s):\ s<t\}} \left[1 - \frac{N(s)}{R(s)}\right], \tag{10.5}$$

with variance

$$\text{Var } \hat{G}(t) = \hat{G}^2(t) \sum_{\{R(s):\ s<t\}} \frac{N(s)}{R(s)[R(s) - N(s)]}, \tag{10.6}$$

where the product and sum are taken over the set of individuals at risk just before t. Two-sided pointwise $1 - \alpha$ confidence intervals can be obtained as follows

$$\hat{G}(t) \pm z_{\alpha/2} [\text{Var } \hat{G}(t)]^{1/2}. \tag{10.7}$$

Transformed Survivor Plots for Assessing Goodness of Fit

This section outlines a simple but general plotting procedure suggested by Lawless (1982) that allows one to compare nonparametric and parametric survivor estimates. I apply this procedure to several existing parametric hazard models used in event history analyses: the exponential or constant rate, Weibull, Gompertz, Makeham, log-logistic, log-Gaussian (lognormal), Coale-McNeil, and Hernes models. The first three models assume a monotonic function for time dependence and have been used widely in analyses of outcomes ranging from marital instability to organizational death. The last four models assume a nonmonotonic function for time dependence and have been used for life course outcomes such as first marriage.

The basic procedure is extremely straightforward. It consists of specifying an appropriate transformation for the survivor probabilities under a parametric model. The resulting transformed survivor plot is similar to the quantile-quantile plot, for example, the normal probability plot used to check if the error term in a linear regression follows a Gaussian distribution. Like the quantile-quantile plot, the transformed survivor plot should resemble a straight line if the parametric model holds; conversely, systematic departures from linearity can help to identify where the parametric model fails to fit the data. One advantage of the transformed survivor plot is that confidence intervals for the survivor function can be used to obtain confidence intervals for the transformed survivor plot; this allows investigators to assess the significance of observed departures from linearity. Another advantage is that one can typically obtain plots without explicit parameter estimates for the parametric model, although if estimated parameters are available, they can be used to obtain a more precise test.

Tests based on transformed survivor plots compare favorably with other methods for assessing goodness of fit. The most common procedure is an informal one that proceeds in much the same spirit as the transformed survivor procedure; see, for example, Tuma and Michael (1986) and Diekmann (1987), who compare nonparametric survivor estimates against parametric survivor estimates. However, unlike the transformed survivor plot, these procedures require maximum-likelihood estimates for parameters in the parametric model; also, systematic departures are more easily detected using the transformed survivor plot than by inspecting the untransformed survivor estimates. Rodriguez and Trussell (1980) describe a statistic based on the censored sample analog of a Kolmogorov-Smirnov test, but note that no distributional results are known for this statistic; hence, they correctly caution that this statistic cannot be used to test goodness of fit formally. Tests based on χ^2 statistics have been proposed by Hjort (1984), but unlike the tests proposed in this paper, they require maximum-likelihood estimates for model parameters and prespecification of time intervals in which to assess observed and expected values of the test statistic.

The following discussion provides a general statistical framework for the transformed survivor plot. Most parametric event history models can be expressed by some monotonic transformation $Y = v(T)$ of the observed times T, where the random variable Y is assumed independently and identically distributed with parametric distribution $F(y)$. Then we have

$$1 - F(y) = G(y) = G[v(t)] = G(t), \qquad (10.8)$$

where $y = v(t)$. That is, since y is a monotonic function of t, we can write the survivor probability G as a function either of y or t. Consider the function $Q(x)$ defined by

$$Q(x) = G^{-1}(x), \tag{10.9}$$

that is, let $Q(x)$ denote the inverse of the parametric survivor function G such that $Q[G(y)] = y$. We now have a general graphical test, since

$$Q[G(y)] = Q[G(t)] = v(t) \tag{10.10}$$

Thus, a plot of $Q[\hat{G}(t)]$ versus $v(t)$ should be close to a straight line if the parametric family $F(y)$ is a reasonable one for the data, where $\hat{G}(t)$ denotes the Kaplan-Meier estimator. Note that because $G(t)$ is strictly monotonic, $Q(x)$ is also strictly monotonic; hence, the confidence intervals for $G(t)$ in equation 10.7 can be used to obtain conservative confidence intervals for $Q[G(t)]$

$$Q\{\hat{G}(t) \pm z_{\alpha/2} [\text{Var } \hat{G}(t)]^{1/2}\}. \tag{10.11}$$

Table 10.1 presents $G(t)$, $r(t)$, and $Q(x)$ for eight common models for a time-dependent hazard rate. Derivations for $Q(x)$ in Table 10.1 for the exponential (or constant rate), Weibull, and log-Gaussian specifications are given in Lawless (1982, sec. 2.4). Derivations for the log-logistic, Hernes, and Coale-McNeil models form the remainder of this section.

Log-Logistic Model

The log-logistic is a standard parametric model for a nonmonotonic hazard and has been used in simulation analyses of migration by Baydar, Tuma, and Wu (1987) and empirical analyses of first marriage by Sørensen and Sørensen (1986), Papastefanou (1987), and Diekmann (1987). In plots of parametric and nonparametric survivor estimates presented by Diekmann, the log-logistic model appears to give a good fit to marriage data for cohorts of German men but a rather poor fit to cohorts of German women.

A standard formulation for the log-logistic hazard rate supposes that $Y = \log T$ has a logistic distribution with location parameter μ and scale parameter σ, where

$$F(y) = \frac{\exp[(y - \mu)/\sigma]}{\sigma\{1 + \exp[(y - \mu)/\sigma]\}^2} \tag{10.12}$$

The survivor probability (see, e.g., Cox and Oakes 1984) is

$$G(t) = \frac{1}{1 + t^{1/\sigma}e^{-\mu/\sigma}} \tag{10.13}$$

Table 10.1. Expressions for $G(t)$, $r(t)$, $Q(x)$, and Plotting Abscissa

Model	$G(t)$	$r(t)$	$Q(x)$	Abscissa
Exponential	$\exp(-\lambda t)$	λ	$\log x$	t
Weibull	$\exp[-(\lambda t)^{\beta}]$	$\beta\lambda(\lambda t)^{\beta-1}$	$\log(-\log x)$	$\log t$
Log-logistic	$\dfrac{1}{1 + t^{1/\sigma}e^{-\mu/\sigma}}$	$\dfrac{t^{(1-\sigma)/\sigma}\exp(-\mu/\sigma)}{\sigma G(t)}$	$\log(x^{-1} - 1)$	$\log t$
Log-Gaussian	$1 - \Phi\!\left[\dfrac{\log t - \mu}{\sigma}\right]$	$\dfrac{\exp[-(\log t - \mu)/2\sigma^2]}{\sigma t\sqrt{2\pi}\,G(t)}$	$\Phi^{-1}(1 - x)$	$\log t$
Coale-McNeil	$1 - \sigma\{1 - I[e^{-\lambda(t-\mu)};\ \beta/\lambda]\}$	$\dfrac{\lambda\exp\{-\beta(t-\mu) - \exp[-\lambda(t - \mu)]\}}{\Gamma(\beta/\lambda)G(t)}$	$\log I^{-1}[1 - (1 - x)/\sigma;\ \beta/\lambda]$	t
Hermes	$\dfrac{1}{1 + \sigma^{-1}\exp(-\beta\lambda^t)}$	$-\sigma\beta\lambda^t\log\lambda\,\exp(\beta\lambda^t)G(t)$	$\log[-\log\sigma - \log(x^{-1} - 1)]$	t

Note: Parameters λ, β, μ, and σ are assumed to be strictly positive. In addition: for the Hermes model, $0 < \lambda < 1$; for the Coale-McNeil model, the parameter $\beta/\lambda = .604$. $\Phi(x)$ denotes the standard Gaussian cumulative function, $I(x;\ p)$ denotes the incomplete gamma integral with parameter p, and $\Gamma(x)$ denotes the gamma function.

189

Let $Q(x)$ be

$$Q(x) = \log\!\left(\frac{1}{x} - 1\right). \tag{10.14}$$

Then substituting equation 10.13 into equation 10.14 yields

$$Q[G(t)] = (\log t - \mu)/\sigma. \tag{10.15}$$

Hence, a plot of $Q[\hat{G}(t)]$ against $\log t$ should be close to linear if the observed event times conform to the log-logistic model. Note that explicit estimates of μ and σ are not required to obtain the transformed survivor plot.

Hernes Model

Another unimodal parametric model for the hazard rate is given by Hernes (1972), who proposes a diffusion model for first marriage probabilities. Hernes posits two competing processes to explain observed marriage patterns—social pressures to marry as one's peers marry and decreasing social attractiveness as individuals age. Using a slightly modified Hernes model, Gilks and Hobcraft (1981) obtain a good fit for data from England and Wales. In plots of parametric and nonparametric survivor estimates in Diekmann (1987), the Hernes model appears to provide good fits to cohorts of German women but poor fits to cohorts of German men, while the log-logistic model provides good fits to cohorts of German men but poor fits to cohorts of German women.

The Hernes model has a distribution function with three parameters:

$$F(t) = \frac{1}{1 + \sigma \exp(\beta\lambda^t)}, \tag{10.16}$$

with survivor function corresponding to

$$G(t) = \frac{1}{1 + \sigma^{-1} \exp(-\beta\lambda^t)}, \tag{10.17}$$

where β and σ are positive constants and $0 < \lambda < 1$. Let Q be given by

$$Q(x) = \log[-\log \sigma - \log(x^{-1} - 1)] \tag{10.18}$$

Then evaluating $Q[G(t)]$ yields

$$Q[G(t)] = \log \beta + t \log \lambda \tag{10.19}$$

Note that Q is a function of x and σ; thus, obtaining the transformed survivor plot for the Hernes model requires an estimate of σ. Given such an estimate, plotting $Q[\hat{G}(t)]$ versus t should result in a linear function if the data conform to the Hernes model.

Estimates for σ can be obtained by the method of maximum-likelihood; however, a rough estimate for σ can be obtained by noting that $0 < \lambda < 1$, from which it follows that

$$\lim_{t \to \infty} G(t) = G(t_\infty) = \lim_{t \to \infty} \frac{1}{1 + \sigma^{-1} \exp(-\beta\lambda^t)} = \frac{1}{1 + \sigma^{-1}} \quad (10.20)$$

Thus,

$$\sigma = \lim_{t \to \infty} \frac{G(t)}{1 - G(t)} \quad (10.21)$$

Note that equation 10.21 implies that the Hernes model yields a defective distribution for the age at first marriage.

Coale-McNeil Model

The Coale-McNeil marriage model (Coale and McNeil, 1972) has been used by several investigators in analyzing marriage rates (Coale and McNeil 1972; Hoem et al. 1980; Rodriguez and Trussel 1980; Gilks and Hobcraft 1981; Trussell and Bloom 1983). Formally, Coale and McNeil proposed to model the density of first marriage times by the convolution of an infinite number of independent exponentially distributed waiting times and one Gaussian waiting time, which can be approximated well by the simpler convolution of two exponential waiting times and one Gaussian waiting time. This yields a closed-form expression for the density, but not for the hazard or survivor functions.

Following Rodriguez and Trussell (1980), the Coale-McNeil density is given by

$$f_\sigma(t) = \sigma f(t) = \frac{\sigma\lambda}{\Gamma(\beta/\lambda)} \exp\{-\beta(t - \mu) - \exp[-\lambda(t - \mu)]\}, \quad (10.22)$$

with distribution function

$$F_\sigma(t) = \sigma F(t) = \frac{\sigma\lambda}{\Gamma(\beta/\lambda)} \int_{-\infty}^{t} \exp\{-\beta(s - \mu) - \exp[-\lambda(s - \mu)]\} \, ds, \quad (10.23)$$

where $\Gamma(\cdot)$ denotes the gamma function, and $1 - \sigma$ is the proportion who will never experience the event. The parameter β/λ is assumed to be a constant; Coale and McNeil (1972) and Rodriguez and Trussell (1980) somewhat arbitrarily suggest standardizing this parameter to $\beta/\lambda = .604$.

Consider the random variable $X = \exp[-\lambda(T - \mu)]$, or, equivalently, $\log X = -\lambda(T - \mu)$. Then rewriting $F(t)$ as a function of X yields

$$F(t) = \sigma(1 - I\{\exp[-\lambda(t - \mu)]; \beta/\lambda\}), \qquad (10.24)$$

where $I(x, p)$ denotes the incomplete gamma integral with parameter p:

$$I(x, p) = \frac{1}{\Gamma(p)} \int_0^x s^{p-1}e^{-s} \, ds. \qquad (10.25)$$

Then the survivor function under the Coale-McNeil model is given by

$$G(t) = 1 - \sigma(1 - I\{\exp[-\lambda(t - \mu)]; \beta/\lambda\}). \qquad (10.26)$$

Following Rodriguez and Trussell, fix $\beta/\lambda = .604$; then $Q(x)$ is given by

$$Q(x) = \log I^{-1}\left(1 - \frac{1-x}{\sigma}; .604\right). \qquad (10.27)$$

Evaluating $Q[G(t)]$ yields

$$Q[G(t)] = -\lambda(t - \mu). \qquad (10.28)$$

Hence, given an estimate of σ, the plot of $Q[\hat{G}(t)]$ versus t should be close to linear if the Coale-McNeil model holds. The values of $Q(x)$ must be calculated by numerical methods because no closed-form expression exists for the inverse of the incomplete gamma integral.

A set of FORTRAN subroutines that calculate values of $Q[G(t)]$ for the log-logistic, log-Gaussian, Hernes, and Coale-McNeil models are available upon request.

Examples

The data used in the examples below are taken from the Marriage and Fertility Supplement to the June 1980 Current Population Survey (hereafter, June 1980 CPS) gathered by the U.S. Bureau of the Census (1983). This supplement to the June 1980 CPS gathered retrospective marital histories for all respondents aged 15 or older for a sample of more than 71,000 households drawn from the civilian noninstitutional population. From these data, I constructed a subsample of 50,139 first-marriage histories for white women. Additional details for these data are given in Wu (1986).

The examples restrict attention to the simple univariate models for $r(t)$ in Table 10.1 and do not attempt to control for the effects of observed covariates, for example, by using regression-like models for the rate. This restriction was dictated in part because the data available in the June 1980 CPS lack detailed covariate information for individuals and because, as shown by evidence I report elsewhere (Wu 1986), the data routinely violate the assumption of proportionality, which suggests that commonly used proportional hazard models are inappropriate for analyzing first-marriage rates. However, I should emphasize that transformed survivor plots are easily obtained for hazard rate models with covariates, since one can obtain predicted values for $r_i(t)$ and hence predicted values for the survivor probabilities $G_i(t)$ using the relationship in equation 10.3. See Bailey (1983, 1984) and Hjort (1984) for details on asymptotics and obtaining parametric survivor estimates when model parameters are estimated by maximum-likelihood methods.

Figure 10.1 presents estimates of survivor probabilities for the subsample of 50,139 white women in the June 1980 CPS. For these data, we observe that 100%, 99%, 86%, 63%, and 7% of women had not yet married by ages 12, 15, 18, 20, and 40, respectively. Figure 10.1 also includes estimates for two-sided .05 confidence intervals; however, because of the large sample sizes, the curves for the upper and lower confidence intervals are difficult to distinguish from the estimated survivor curve.

To lend some insight into interpreting test values, Figure 10.2 illus-

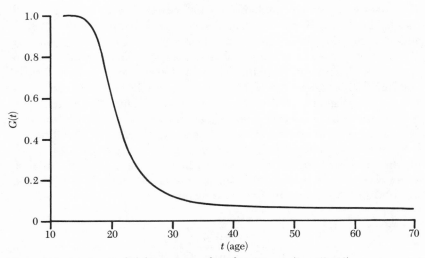

Figure 10.1. Survivor Probabilities versus t for White Women ($I = 50,139$)

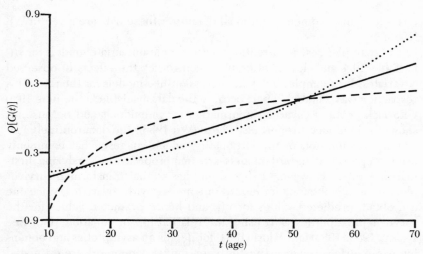

Figure 10.2. Reference Line (solid curve) and $Q[G(t)]$ versus t for Two Hypothetical Models (dotted and dashed curves)

trates two hypothetical plots of $Q[G(t)]$ versus t. Three curves are plotted: a downward bending dashed line, an upward curving dotted line, and a solid line that serves as a baseline reference. Values of $Q[G(t)]$ that lie above the baseline reflect predicted survivor probabilities that are greater than observed survivor probabilities; conversely, values of $Q[G(t)]$ that lie below the baseline reflect predicted survivor probabilities that are lower than observed survivor probabilities. For the dashed curve in Figure 10.2, predicted survivor probabilities are greater than observed probabilities for $14 \leq t \leq 51$ and less than observed probabilities for $12 \leq t < 14$ and $t > 51$. Similarly, predicted marriage probabilities (given by $1 - G[t]$) are greater at early and later ages, and lower at intermediate ages, than observed probabilities. For the dotted curve, predicted survivor probabilities for $14 \leq t \leq 15$ are less, and for $12 \leq t < 14$ and $t > 15$ are greater, than observed survivor probabilities. Thus, the dotted curve reflects predicted marriage probabilities that are lower at early and later ages, and higher at intermediate ages, than the observed probabilities.

Figure 10.3 examines the fit of the log-logistic and log-Gaussian models for the sample of 50,139 white women in the June 1980 CPS. To allow easier comparisons, I have centered and rescaled values of $Q[G(t)]$ in Figure 10.3 and the remaining figures as follows:

$$\frac{Q[G(t)] - Q(1/2)}{Q(15/16) - Q(1/16)} \tag{10.29}$$

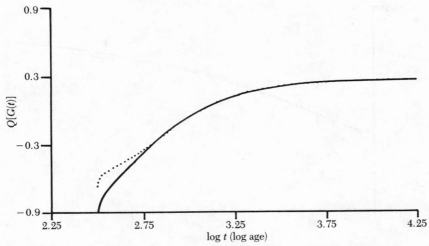

Figure 10.3. $Q[G(t)]$ versus Log t for the Log-Logistic (solid curve) and Log-Gaussian (dotted curve) Models

Thus, the rescaled values of $Q[G(t)]$ equal zero at the median age at first marriage and are rescaled by the range of raw test values that capture the central 7/8 of the distribution of event times. The curves in Figure 10.3 for the log-logistic (solid) and log-Gaussian (dotted) models agree closely for log $t > 2.75$ ($t > 15$). However, both curves exhibit a downward bending pattern for log $t > 3.25$ ($t > 26$). Because both curves exhibit sharp departures from linearity, neither model appears to provide a satisfactory fit.

Figure 10.4 illustrates the fit of the Hernes (solid) and Coale-McNeil (dotted) models. Recall that both the Hernes and Coale-McNeil models require a parameter σ related to the proportions eventually experiencing the event. Not surprisingly, the fit of these models is sensitive to values of σ, especially at later ages. To avoid over-fitting, I estimated σ using the value of $G(t)$ obtained from the lower .05 confidence interval at the last observed event time:

$$\hat{G}(t) - z_{\alpha/2} \, [\text{Var } \hat{G}(t)]^{1/2}. \qquad (10.30)$$

The results in Figure 10.4 suggest that both models provide a better fit to these data than do the log-logistic and log-Gaussian models in Figure 10.3. The curves mimic one another closely and are close to linear for $t \leq 40$. However, for $t > 40$, both curves exhibit a slightly downward bending shape, which suggests that the predicted survivor probabilities are less than the observed survivor probabilities—that is, both models

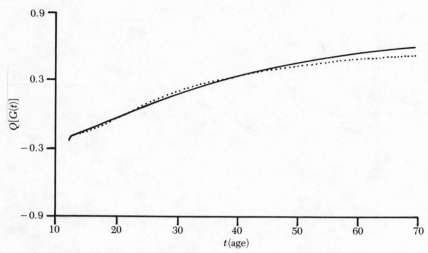

Figure 10.4. $Q[G(t)]$ versus t for the Hernes (solid curve) and Coale-McNeil (dotted curve) Models

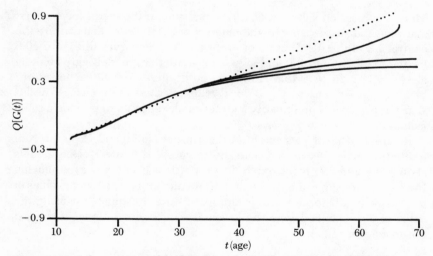

Figure 10.5. Reference Line (dotted curve) and $Q[G(t)]$ with 95% Confidence Intervals (solid curves) versus t for the Coale-McNeil Model

appear to predict that *more* women eventually marry at later ages than these data show.

The estimates in Figure 10.5 allow a closer examination of the fit of the Coale-McNeil model by including upper and lower 95% confidence intervals for the estimates of $Q[G(t)]$. Because of the large sample sizes, the confidence intervals are extremely narrow during the usual marrying ages, but widen slightly at earlier ages and markedly at later ages. For reference, I have plotted a straight line (dotted curve) with slope and intercept estimated by fitting an OLS line to values of $Q[G(t)]$ for $t \leq 40$. Compared to the dotted curve, the model slightly underestimates never-marrying proportions at early ages, slightly overestimates never-marrying proportions at intermediate ages, and significantly underestimates never-marrying proportions at later ages.

The estimates in Figure 10.6 present upper and lower 95% confidence intervals and a straight-line reference for the Hernes model; as in Figure 10.5, the straight line was obtained from OLS estimates for $t \leq 40$. A comparison of Figures 10.5 and 10.6 suggests that the Hernes model provides a noticeably better fit to these data than the Coale-McNeil model, particularly below age 40. However, the straight-line reference lies above the confidence intervals in Figure 10.6 after age 40. Thus, both the Hernes and Coale-McNeil models appear to underestimate observed never-marrying proportions after age 40.

How well does the Hernes model fit for ages less than 40? Figure 10.7 reproduces Figure 10.6 for $12 \leq t < 40$ using an expanded vertical scale. These estimates show that the dotted reference line lies slightly above the plotted confidence intervals at very early ages and below the confidence intervals between ages 18 and 31. Choosing a slightly different criterion for the reference line—say, by estimating the reference line for $18 \leq t < 31$—would allow the reference line to fit the data for some

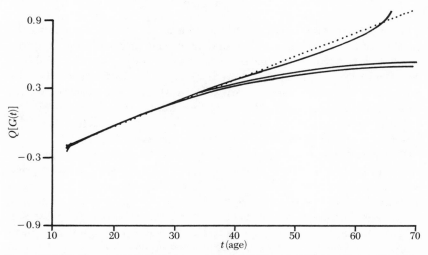

Figure 10.6. Reference Line (dotted curve) and $Q[G(t)]$ with 95% Confidence Intervals (solid curves) versus t for the Hernes Model

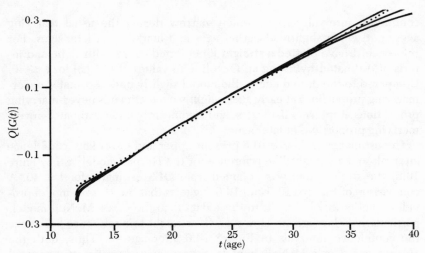

Figure 10.7. Reference Line (dotted curve) and $Q[G(t)]$ with 95% Confidence Intervals (solid curves) versus t for the Hernes Model (for $12 \leq t < 40$)

ranges but would produce larger deviations from the reference line at other ages. Thus even for usual marrying ages, the Hernes model exhibits small but significant departures from the patterns of age dependence in these data.

Discussion

This paper has described a general graphical procedure for assessing the fit of parametric models for survival data by comparing transformations of predicted survivor probabilities with observed survivor probabilities. Systematic departures of model predictions can be easily observed by departures of estimates from linearity. The resulting transformed survivor plots were used to assess the fit of four parametric models—the log-logistic, log-Gaussian, Coale-McNeil, and Hernes models—that have been used in life course analyses of the timing of first marriage.

The results suggest that the four models exhibit small but significant departures from the data at early ages, but much larger, significant, and systematic departures at later ages. A conservative conclusion is that all four models provide roughly adequate fits to the data during usual marrying ages but fail to fit the data at later marrying ages. Both the log-logistic and log-Gaussian models fit the data less well than the Coale-McNeil and Hernes models; the Coale-McNeil model fits these data less well than the Hernes model. The poor performance of the log-logistic and log-Gaussian models stems from the fact that both models imply a *non-*

defective distribution—that is, they imply that all women eventually marry. All models appear to predict higher marriage probabilities at later ages than are observed for U.S. data obtained from the June 1980 Current Population Survey.

The poor fit of the models at later ages suggests two alternative conjectural interpretations: first, that the models misspecify the form of age dependence for the rate of first marriage at later ages, or second, that the models correctly specify the form of age dependence but do not explicitly control for other sources of population heterogeneity that could result in the observed pattern of age dependence at later ages. Clearly, one important aspect of the transformed survivor plots described in this paper is that they can be used to assess both sorts of explanations, since they can be easily applied to different time-dependent parameterizations or to alternative parameterizations for observed (or unobserved) heterogeneity in the hazard rate.

III
METHODOLOGICAL ISSUES

11 *Jan M. Hoem, Bo Rennermalm, and Randi Selmer*

Restriction Biases in the Analysis of Births and Marriages

Introduction

General Problem

In retrospective studies of individual life histories, some or all of the information pertaining to periods prior to the most recent event interval will sometimes be left out. This simplifies data collection and it may improve the reliability of the data actually obtained by reducing misreporting. Unfortunately, failure to collect information on selected life history events may give rise to distortions in the analysis of marriage, childbearing, employment, and other population processes on the individual level, as is evident from contributions scattered throughout the literature.

An example of immediate concern to demographers is the effects of restricting analyses of birth interval components to data on the latest open and latest closed birth interval only. Hobcraft and Rodriguez (1980) and

The authors would like to thank the Danish National Institute of Social Research and Statistics Sweden for providing us with the data for this project. Discussions with Britta Hoem were helpful in the interpretation of our findings. Most of our work with the Danish data was done by Hoem and Selmer while they were affiliated with the Laboratory of Actuarial Mathematics, University of Copenhagen, Denmark. An extended version of this paper appeared in Mayer and Tuma (1987, 555–600).

Page et al. (1980) have demonstrated that such analyses can yield highly misleading results.[1] Much more needs to be known about restriction biases, however, and surprises still seem to be in store. For instance, Rindfuss, Bumpass, and Palmore (1985) recently found that latest-birth-interval restrictions did *not* seriously distort parameter estimates in logistic regressions that they made to examine determinants of birth intervals in Korea.

This paper presents the outcome of an empirical investigation into the extent of selection biases in a retrospective study of nonmarital cohabitation, marriage, and childbearing when information on consensual unions is essentially restricted to the most recent cohabitation and is obtained only for women who are separated, divorced, or married, or who are unmarried but cohabit at interview. Information of this nature has apparently been collected in several surveys. The British General Household Survey is one of them (see, e.g., Brown and Kiernan 1981), and the Danish fertility survey of 1975 is another. Our investigation was induced by problems encountered in the analysis of the latter, which can serve as a good example of its type. The general tenor of the findings presented below is that there certainly are appreciable biases in estimates based on the Danish observational plan, but that the biases need not be serious enough to preclude valid conclusions about general trends and general levels in analyses of the life-table type.

Our Investigation

In the Danish survey, women who were currently married, separated, or divorced when interviewed (4,071 cases) were asked about the latest marriage alone, as well as about any cohabitation with the husband just before that marriage, including the starting date of any consensual union and of the marriage. The 119 women who reported that they were separated or divorced and currently living with a man other than their latest husband were asked also to report the starting date of their current union. Among the 1,103 unmarried respondents, the 428 women who said they were currently cohabiting were asked to state when they started living together with their man. The 66 widowed respondents were not asked any questions about dates of cohabitation or marriage. Information about any other period(s) of cohabitation before the latest marriage or then current consensual union was not collected for any woman. Complete childbearing histories were collected for all respondents.

---

1. Some mathematics explaining this feature can be found in Hoem (1985, sec. 2.3). Allison (1985) recently reviewed items concerning the closely related notion of backward recurrence times.

Various analyses of these data have appeared already; see Hoem and Selmer (1984) and their references. This paper concentrates on marriages and first births to nulliparous unmarried cohabiting women, and presents results from the Danish data below. Our findings indicate a dramatic fall in cohabitational nuptiality over the cohorts involved.

By contrast, the level of cohabitational first-birth rates computed is remarkably stable cross cohorts. (Given the impression of skyrocketing numbers of nonmarital births, one might have expected these rates to increase over cohorts.) A comparison with corresponding rates for married women, reported by Hoem and Selmer (1984), shows that first-birth rates are much lower in consensual unions than in marriage.

Because the cohabitational histories are so incomplete, these results cannot be taken at face value without an assessment of the selectivity effects inherent in the Danish observational plan. Fortunately, subsequent fertility surveys in Norway in 1977 and in Sweden in 1981 offer opportunities for checking on our findings for Danish women. Both of the latter collected complete cohabitational and marital histories for all respondents along with their childbearing histories. If we disregard national differences in matters of detail and discount some national differences in process levels, the surveys demonstrate the same general cohort trends in marriage rates and first-birth rates among cohabiting nulliparous unmarried women in Norway and Sweden as we have found for Denmark. By analogy, this lends credence to our findings for Danish women despite the less fortunate observational plan of the Danish survey.

The trends mentioned for Norway have been reported by Selmer (1984); Hoem and Rennermalm (1985) have presented results concerning the behavior of cohabiting unmarried women in Sweden; and a comparison with corresponding married women can be based on reports by Finnäs (1983) and by Qvist and Rennermalm (1985). Several glimpses of these Scandinavian comparisons are given below, but a detailed documentation is not needed here. Our assessment of the Danish biases does not depend on these analogies, nice as they are, but on the empirical experiment that follows below.

Given access to the anonymous individual data from the Swedish fertility survey of 1981, we have imitated the ascertainment method of the Danish survey by removing from the Swedish data information collected according to the Swedish but not the Danish design, and have compared the outcomes of the corresponding computations with the counterpart outcomes based on the full Swedish data. This has provided estimates of the biases that would have been produced if the Danish observational plan had been used in Sweden. Our general conclusion from this experiment is that for the analysis of marriages and first births to women in consensual unions, the Danish observational plan produces appreciable biases. However, these biases do not mask any trends across cohorts or any differences by age at the start of the consensual union in our Swedish data.

Like most such empirical experiments, our results are strictly tenable for our complete data set only. Its extension to other data sets, including to the restricted Danish one which induced our experiment in the first place, must be based on analogy and on informed judgment. Factors contributing to the biases are discussed at some length in the following section, and we have given them further consideration in a previous mathematical paper (Hoem 1983). Real rates of marriage and of union dissolution for cohabiting women are important contributors to the biases, and any differences in these and other factors will contribute to differences in biases in the Swedish and the Danish population. There will be similar effects of any differences in nonresponse. Evidently, behavior is not identical in the two populations, and the biases in the Danish data are not exactly those estimated in our experiment. Nevertheless, in our judgment the biases operating on our Danish estimates are hardly likely to be so radically different in size or direction from those revealed by our analysis that they seriously affect a comparison between the two countries. We find it even harder to believe that differential biases can give any important distortion of the trends found below in marital and childbearing behavior over our cohorts. Despite their differences, demographic processes in the Danish and Swedish populations must be among the most closely similar anywhere.[2]

In this spirit, a comparison of the outcomes of the two surveys offers the insight that nulliparous Danish women living in a consensual union marry more readily and are much less prone to get a child outside marriage than are their Swedish counterparts in each comparable cohort. By this token, Sweden is a trend setter, for together the two populations are world leaders among industrialized nations in the prevalence of nonmarital cohabitation.

To summarize, this paper has several foci. Its main contribution is the assessment of restriction biases. The outcome of this assessment is that the empirical investigation of the Danish data gives somewhat biased but largely valid results. Because it does, a cursory comparison of the relevant demographic behavior in Denmark and in Sweden is possible.

2. The use of information from populations different from but similar to the study population to supplement incomplete data from the latter is commonplace in demography. Indeed, the whole notion of model life tables and much of the practical use of stable population theory are based on this idea.

Cohabitational Marriages and First Births in Denmark

The Danish Data

The Danish fertility survey of 1975 collected interviews with 5,240 respondents, which corresponded to a response rate of 88%. Selective nonresponse is unlikely to have had an important effect on our results. As we have noted, however, there may be selection biases due to the fact that information was not collected on periods of cohabitation before any latest marriage or current consensual union. This lack of knowledge of a woman's cohabitational status at any time outside of the periods actually recorded precludes any analysis of noncohabitational births and rules out almost all analysis of the formation of consensual unions and of marriages not starting in such unions. This paper shows that it is possible to make a sensible investigation of some of the behavior in consensual unions by means of life-table methods.

The questionnaire left it to the respondent to define whether she was or had been living in a consensual union as described. This approach seems to be common practice, and presumably the situation perceived by the respondent herself is as good an operational definition as any for our purposes. Nevertheless, there must have been some problems with reporting accuracy of a status of such uncertain definition, and which some women may have been reluctant to reveal, although few real problems seem to have arisen in the interview situation. In particular, many women would have found it difficult to pinpoint a starting date or to remember it accurately when interviewed, even though the interviewer asked for only the month and year for this and all other dates of events. The difficulty shows up in the relatively high nonresponse rate for such starting dates (246 cases out of 1,571 recorded nonmarital unions), and also in an inflated number of reported starting dates of either six or twelve months before marriage. Such rounding tendencies are revealed in our study of cohabitational marriage rates, reported below, but they cannot have distorted our main results in that section or elsewhere, for the results do not depend on details of this nature.[3]

As a move toward homogeneity of each population group, and with a view to removing disturbing effects of differential behavior of unmarried women who start the recorded cohabitation with previous children or previous marriages, we have excluded from analysis all consensual unions

3. For a further discussion of the reliability of Scandinavian interview data on cohabitation, see Hoem and Rennermalm (1985). Further information about our data was given by Finnäs and Hoem (1980) and by Hoem and Selmer (1984).

with a starting parity above 0 and a reported starting age of 25 or more. Remaining consensual unions have been classified according to the reported age of the woman at the start of the union: those who started at an age below 20 and those who started at ages 20–24. This is to control for differing behavior according to age at initiation. Similar birth cohort differentials are picked up by grouping our respondents into conventional five-year birth cohorts, from 1926–1930 through 1951–1955. Women who reported premarital cohabitation but gave insufficient information about their starting age in this union were deleted, as were a negligible number of respondents for whom some other vital information was missing or evidently wrong, as well as some respondents born in 1925, 1956, and 1957.

After these various deletions, we have 1,240 women whose records satisfy our present requirements, which are that they should contain sufficient information on a consensual union started at parity 0, before any first recorded marriage, and at an age below 25, for a woman born in 1926– 1955. We should perhaps emphasize that our present analysis deliberately is restricted to the data on these 1,240 women. We do not draw conclusions about population totals or population means valid, say, for all of the Danish population at the time of the survey or at any previous time, as in a standard enumerative survey. Instead, we take the super-populationist stand relevant to life-table analysis. A further discussion of these matters was given by Hoem and Selmer (1984). The deleted records are not relevant for this analysis and are not documented here. Table 11.1 lists the sizes of the groups used here.

Methods of Analysis

Our investigation uses straightforward life-table methods, in this case with two decrements (marriage and first birth). Life-table methods are particularly well suited for the analysis of waiting-time data with heavy censoring, such as ours. Each of the respondents of Table 11.1 has been followed month by month from the beginning of cohabitation, recorded as starting in ordinal month 0 of the union, since dates were only recorded by month and year and ordinal months were computed as differences between calendar months. Respondents have been recorded as decrements from observation at marriage, at first births, or at interview (censoring), timed to happen in the middle of the ordinal month of occurrence. For each ordinal month, an ordinary occurrence/exposure rate has been computed for recorded marriages, as well as another one for first births. As is evident from Table 11.1, some groups simply are too small for analysis by this method, and even for the larger groups, attrition is often so rapid that it is hard to study behavior over longer durations than a couple of years.

Table 11.1. Age of Danish Women at Reported Start of Consensual Union[a]

	19 or Younger			20–24		
Cohort	Number of Respondents	Married before First Birth	Nonmarital First Birth	Number of Respondents	Married before First Birth	Nonmarital First Birth
1926–30	17	16	1	20	18	2
1931–35	28	23	5	28	24	4
1936–40	58	54	4	59	54	3
1941–45	100	82	16	139	120	15
1946–50	147	117	27	261	202	20
1951–55	223	91	33	160	40	12
Total	573			667		

[a]Women with starting parity 0 only.

209

Results on Cohabitational Nuptiality in Denmark

Scandinavia has a long-standing tradition of nonmarital cohabitation (Hyrenius 1941, Trost 1978, Matović 1985), and our data contain a lot of evidence of the recent strong increase of its prevalence. Our computations of marriage rates for nulliparous women by single months of duration of reported consensual unions add color to this picture. Marriage rates computed for Danish women who reported an age of 19 years or younger at the start of cohabitation are a bit lower in each cohort than corresponding rates for those who said their union began at age 20–24 (see Table 11.2). Because the difference seems relatively unimportant, we have combined the two groups in each cohort (column 3).

A plot of the cohabitational marriage rates is typically like that in Figure 11.1, which is for the cohort born 1946–1950. We regard some features of the diagram as reflections of genuine properties of the underlying intensity function, others as artifacts due to reporting errors or the influence of sampling variations. The increase in the marriage rates over the first few months of cohabitation probably reveals a corresponding increase in the intensity function. A similar feature appears generally in our plots of marriage rates for the various groups studied, and it is easily explained in terms of some initial waiting time needed before partners in a newly established union can get around to becoming married.

On the other hand, the peaks at durations of 6 and 12 months in Figure 11.1 are indications of rounding tendencies in the reporting of starting months of cohabitational unions leading to marriage. Evidently, many women in this category have "rounded off" the reported duration of the premarital union to half a year or to a full year. More accurate reporting no doubt would have placed many of these unions at neighboring durations. Because of this, and since we can see no obvious trend in the cohabitational marriage rates over durations above the first few months, we

Table 11.2. Marriage Rates for Danish Nulliparous Women in Consensual Union (duration of 5–23 months)

| Cohort | Starting Age (rate per 1,000 women per month) | | | Partial Marriage Probability for All Starting Ages 24 Years or Younger |
	19 or Younger	20–24	All 24 or Younger	
1926–40	71	88	79	78%
1941–45	67	73	70	74%
1946–50	49	50	50	61%
1951–55	20	22	20	32%

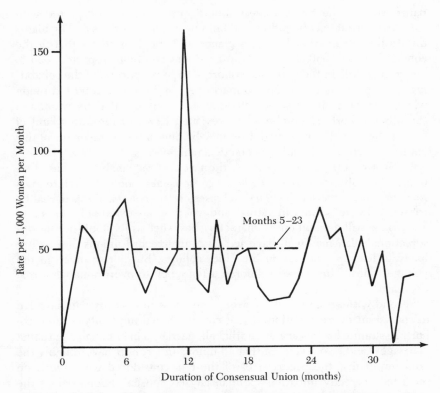

Figure 11.1. Marriage Rates for Nulliparous Cohabiting Danish Women 24 Years Old or Younger (1946–1950 Cohort)

have recombined the data and have computed a common rate for the interval from 5 to 23 months, with results given in Table 11.2. (We could have gone above a duration of 23 months in the data of Figure 11.1, but not in several of the other, smaller groups involved.)

One may possibly get a better feeling for the import of numerical values of rates like those in column 3 of Table 11.2 by transforming them into the domain of probabilities. Column 4 contains the value of $1 - \exp(-19\bar{\eta})$ for each marriage rate $\bar{\eta}$. The transformed value is an estimate of the probability of marrying before the union has lasted two years, for a nulliparous woman who has lived in a consensual union for five months, in the absence of any competing risks (death, union dissolution, first birth). According to Table 11.2, this probability has been about halved between our two youngest cohorts.

The tremendous drop in the cohabitational marriage rate observed, particularly in the two youngest cohorts, needs to be interpreted with some care, for it may be influenced both by reporting errors and by biases due to the observational plan. A glance at Table 11.1 shows that in the cohorts born in 1950 or before, most consensual unions reported lead to marriage, while in the youngest cohort, a large proportion of the cohabiting women had not had time to marry yet, or were in a reported union which might dissolve at some date after the interview. Perhaps women in the other cohorts remembered or revealed fewer of the latter kind of unions. Some of the recorded drop may be due to reporting errors of this nature, which would tend to overstate a real decrease.

Even if reporting were perfect, the fact that our analysis is based on information obtained about the latest consensual union only (before marriage or interview) may have led to biases on two counts. First, in reality, consensual unions differ in nature, and whether one eventually turns into a marriage will depend on its characteristics, such as its stability. Our observational plan may well have led us to overrecord unions of a nature likely to lead to marriage in the older cohorts, but not so much in the younger ones. This would reinforce a tendency to overdramatize a real decrease.

Secondly, the practice of recording the latest union only will have led to consistent overestimation of real cohabitational nuptiality in each cohort. Assuming for this argument that all marriages in our analysis are first marriages, and also assuming that all unions in a cohort have roughly the same nuptiality, the occurrences of the risk considered will have been recorded correctly but time spent in any consensual unions before the ones reported will be missing from the exposures, leading to inflated nuptiality rates. The extent of this upward bias will depend on several factors. For instance, it depends strongly on the level of risk of dissolution of a consensual union. If this risk has increased, say, from older to younger cohorts, corresponding to increasing casualness in cohabitational relations and paralleling increased divorce risks in marriage, then the overestimation will be progressively greater in younger cohorts, *ceteris paribus.* This would tend to mask a real drop, which would be stronger than the one recorded if the effect of all other factors remained the same across cohorts.

This effect would be diluted by the fact that young women just would not have had the same time to experience periods of cohabitation prior to the one recorded at interview as older women would have if the risks of forming dissolving cohabitational unions were the same at each age. If other things were equal, therefore, less exposure time would be missing for the younger women.

Some other aspects of the observational design may have influenced occurrences as well as exposures. Widows should have contributed to occurrences *and* exposures to the extent that they lived in consensual unions before first marriage, but they now contribute nothing to either. Furthermore, we cannot be certain that all recorded marriages are first marriages. A remarried woman will contribute wrong amounts to the exposures and possibly also to the occurrences if after a marriage she enters a recorded consensual union with no prior children and then marries her cohabitant. Her recorded exposure will then come from her recorded cohabitation rather than from whatever time she spent in consensual unions before her first marriage. If she has her first child in the recorded consensual union, she will also contribute to recorded first births, when if anything she should have contributed to first marriages. A woman who has her first child in one consensual union but whose subsequent union we record will similarly contribute nothing to the exposure and also will not contribute to the first-birth occurrences, as she should.

Many of these items may seem trivial, and one might at first assume that the influence of several of them must be negligible. Some of our groups are so small, however, that incorrect recording of data about single women caused by the observational plan turn out to be most influential. The total outcome of the various conflicting effects cannot be assessed accurately from general reasoning alone; external information is needed, and we will present some later. One cannot get sufficient insight from the flawed data themselves. It will not do, for instance, to compute a marriage rate separately for those who actually marry in each cohort, for such a rate will be strongly influenced by other selection biases discussed elsewhere in the literature.

This discussion of potential biases in comparisons between cohorts reveals the possibility that there may be similar biases in the comparison made between the cohabitational nuptiality rates by starting age for each cohort. Just as the older cohorts have had more time to lose exposure in previous consensual unions, women reporting a starting age of 20 to 24 years for their current union may have more unrevealed exposure than those in the same cohort who reported a starting age of 19 years or younger. This may have led us to overestimate the cohabitational nuptiality rates of the older starters more than for younger starters. Our computed rates depend only weakly on reported starting age, but according to this argument, some tendency of older starters to marry more slowly than younger starters may be covered up by differential biases. On the other hand, some of the women for whom we have recorded a later starting age may actually have an unrevealed earlier real debut into cohabitation. Since the corresponding unrevealed exposure is missing in the marriage rates computed for starting ages 15 to 19 years, this would work towards distorting the latter rates upwards. The balance between these competing biases can only be assessed empirically, as we will do below.

Results on First Births to Unmarried Cohabiting Danish Women

As can be seen in Table 11.1, rather few women have reported first births in consensual unions. The risk of such first births must have been quite small. For Danish women in consensual unions of a duration up to 24 months, we have computed rates of 8.8 and 5.2 first births per 1,000 women per month for those who started cohabiting as teenagers or at ages 20–24, respectively. This is for all cohorts taken together. We have been unable to detect any real trend in our rates from older to younger cohorts. Formal significance tests (see Hoem and Selmer 1984) suggest that observable cohort differences may well be due largely to random fluctuations. On the other hand, the tendency of the first-birth rate of members of a cohort who reported a starting age of 19 or younger to be somewhat higher than the corresponding rate for those who said they started at ages 20 to 24 seems to be a significant difference. As in many other contexts, those who report an earlier start appear to have a higher pace of fertility at this stage as well.

The difference discovered here may possibly even underestimate a real difference. Since early periods of cohabitation may have been missed during data collection, so that we cannot be certain whether the starting age recorded is the real age at debut of cohabitation, some of those assigned to the later starting age group may actually belong in the earlier group for age at real start of cohabitation. If the cohabitational fertility of such women is on a par with those whose real cohabitational debut is at ages 20 to 24, then they are classified correctly by our system, and the birth rates computed would reveal real differences (apart from random fluctuations and in the absence of other biases). If fertility depends on real rather than recorded starting age, they would be misclassified by our system, and a correct classification would tend to reveal a greater real difference than the one we observed. Intermediary levels of fertility for this group would also tend to underestimate the difference.

Otherwise, the first-birth rates computed here are subject to much the same kind of biases as those discussed for the marriage rates of women in consensual unions. As noted, there could be some contamination of our sets of presumed premarital unions by unrevealed intermarital unions for divorced women who later married and only got to report the second marriage. Cohabitational first-birth rates have the same problem with the exposures as cohabitational marriage rates have, for the same computed exposures are used for both kinds of rates. In addition, cohabitational first births may be undercounted in the Danish system, because some of those

births occur in consensual unions before the ones we analysed. This will
tend to counteract the upward bias due to the underestimation of exposures. A first-birth rate for consensual unions computed here will tend to
be less of an overestimate of the real rate than is the case for the corresponding marriage rate. In fact, so many first births may be missing that a
computed first-birth rate may be an underestimate of the real thing.
Again, an empirical investigation is needed to see how these conflicting
effects work themselves out in practice.

Because of the interaction of competing risks, constant first birth fertility and falling nuptiality in consensual unions imply an increasing probability of having a first birth in the union during a given period under constant mortality and constant risk of union dissolution. To illustrate this
effect by a "pure" measure, let us disregard the latter two risks in the
usual manner, and let us make calculations as if consensual unions can
only convert into marriages. For a constant first-birth intensity α and a
constant marriage intensity η, the probability of having a first birth during
a period of length z is then

$$\pi(z) = \int_0^z e^{-(\alpha + \eta)t}\alpha \, dt = \frac{\alpha}{\alpha + \eta} (1 - e^{-(\alpha + \eta)z}) \qquad (11.1)$$

If we take the marriage rates in column 3 of Table 11.2 and the above birth
rates for all cohorts combined at face value, then estimates of $\pi(z)$ for each
cohort and each group of starting ages can be computed as in Table 11.3.
We have used $z = 19$ months because Table 11.2 was based on data for a
total of 19 months of union duration. By Table 11.3, for each starting age
group the estimated probability has increased by some 60% between the
oldest cohorts and the youngest one. The final line in Table 11.3 shows

Table 11.3. Estimated Probability $\hat{\pi}(z)$ of a Nonmarital First Birth in a Consensual Union
($z = 19$ months) (%)

Cohort	Age at Start of Cohabitation	
	19 or Younger	20–24
1926–40 (combined)	8.1	4.9
1941–45	8.7	5.3
1946–50	10.1	6.1
1951–55	12.9	7.9
No nuptiality	15.4	9.4

Note: Marriage rates from Table 11.2 by cohort. Birth rates for all cohorts combined. Estimates were made for unions under the competing risks of childbearing and marriage, disregarding mortality and union dissolution.

what the estimate $\hat{\pi}(19)$ would be if there were no cohabitational nuptiality, that is, if $\eta = 0$.

The Extent of Distortion

The Swedish Data

We now turn to our assessment of the biases that the Danish observational design would have produced in the Swedish data. In the aspects of interest here, the nature of the data collected in the Swedish fertility survey of 1981 are much the same as in the Danish survey of 1975, except that in Sweden complete cohabitational and marital histories were collected. The sample was drawn by simple random sampling from each of the five-year cohorts born in Sweden from 1936–1940 through 1956–1960 and registered as resident in the country at the time when the sample was drawn, irrespective of marital status. Interviews were conducted with 4,300 respondents, which corresponded to a response rate of 87%. The demographic behavior of nulliparous unmarried cohabiting women and some other aspects of these data have been analyzed by Hoem and Rennermalm (1985), who also describe the data more fully. For further information about the Swedish data, see Arvidsson, et al. (1982) and Lyberg (1984).

There are some differences between the two data sets, or in our treatment of them. A comparison with pages 207–8 shows that the two surveys have the four cohorts born in 1936–1940, 1941–1945, 1946–1950, and 1951–1955 in common. The Danish data also contain the two previous five-year cohorts born in 1926–1930 and 1931–1935, while the Swedish data have the additional youngest cohort born in 1956–1960. Thus, there is a shift in coverage. It is also possible that the more complete coverage of cohabitational histories in the Swedish questionnaire may have led to greater response reliability than would the corresponding more restricted formulation in the Danish questionnaire. Given the general nature of the results of our bias assessment (presented below), however, it is unlikely that the shift in coverage or, potentially, in response accuracy, can have been important for our interpretation of the experiment. With our group sizes, random variation is frequently a very important element in our bias estimates.

Distortion Results

After selection of eligible respondents and deletion of a few records with irreparably deficient information, we have ended up with the group sizes listed in Table 11.4. At a given duration, let E_s and O_s be the exposures

Table 11.4. Recorded Number of Cohabitations among (apparently) Never-Married Swedish Nulliparous Women

Cohort	By the Swedish Design[a] (at starting age)			By the Danish Design[b] (at starting age)		
	19 or Younger	20–24	All[c]	19 or Younger	20–24	All[c]
1936–40	59	78	189	38	69	154
1941–45	149	255	543	116	217	445
1946–50	227	417	786	157	326	594
1951–55	371	500	941	239	375	675
1956–60	346	200	546	215	165	380
Total	1,152	1,450	3,005	765	1,152	2,248

[a]Using the complete data set.
[b]Application of the Danish observational plan to the Swedish data set.
[c]All respondents regardless of starting age, including ages 25 and over.

and one of the three occurrences (say, the number of marriages) recorded by the Swedish observational plan, and let E_D and O_D be the corresponding exposures and occurrences, respectively, produced by imitating the Danish observational plan on the same individual level data. Then the Danish-type occurrence/exposure rate O_D/E_D has an estimated bias of

$$\hat{b} = \frac{O_D/E_D}{O_S/E_S} - 1. \qquad (11.2)$$

Figures 11.2 and 11.3 contain plots of sequences of distortion factors $100 (1 + \hat{b})$ for selected cohorts. Note that single-month duration intervals have been used for ordinal month 0 to 11, two-month intervals were applied for ordinal months 12 to 23, and twelve-month intervals were used for subsequent ordinal months. The gap at ordinal month 4 in the curve for the cohort born in 1956–1960 in Figure 11.3 is due to the fact that there were no recorded marriages there ($O_S = O_D = 0$), in which case the estimated bias $\hat{b}$ is undefined.

Several features of Figures 11.2 and 11.3 deserve comment. First, a

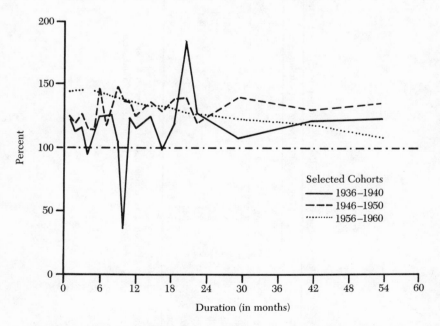

Figure 11.2. Distortion Produced in Marriage Rates by Applying Danish Observational Plan to Swedish Data. All Starting Ages Combined

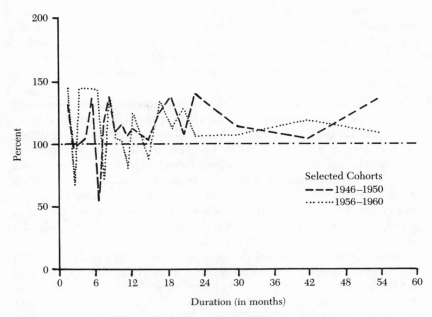

Figure 11.3. Distortion Produced in Rates of First Birth by Applying Danish Observational Plan to Swedish Data. All Starting Ages Combined

negative bias (or equivalently, a distortion factor $1 + \hat{b} < 1$) is possible for marriage rates as well as for first-birth rates. We were alerted to this possibility for first-birth rates by Hoem (1983), but the appearance of negative biases for marriage rates took us by surprise. It is a demonstration that misrecording of data for even only a few women caused by flaws in the observational plan (or otherwise) can have striking effects.

Second, bias estimates for periods of short duration are vulnerable to random effects. This is demonstrated by the peak at ordinal month 21 for the cohort of 1936–1940 in Figure 11.2, as well as by the general raggedness of the bias sequences. The recording or nonrecording of single events may have strong effects. For these reasons, we have combined the data for several ordinal months and have based our bias analysis on computations for longer intervals.

Third, in spite of the nice monotonic appearance of bias curves (as for the cohort of 1956–1960 in Figure 11.2), we have been unable to detect any systematic durational pattern in the biases, even after some careful minor grouping of the ordinal months. Therefore, our main bias analysis has been for the long interval of ordinal months 5 to 23 combined for marriage rates, and ordinal months 1 to 23 combined for first-birth rates. The deletion of the first ordinal month(s) avoids initiation effects of a union. A separate analysis of the biases in first-birth rates for ordinal months 5 to 23 combined gave no further insight and is not reported here. We have seen little point in going beyond a cohabitational duration of two years with our data.

For cohabitational marriage rates of ordinal months 5 to 23 combined, there is little pattern by cohort and by starting age in the estimated biases due to the Danish observational design. It systematically overestimates the tendency to marry, roughly by one-fifth to one-third. Nevertheless, the dramatic fall in marriage rates over cohorts is well represented, as is the greater risk of marriage of women starting cohabitation at ages 20–24 as compared to those who start at age 19 or younger. A compact impression of the trend in marriage formation over cohorts (and of the corresponding biases) results if all starting ages through 24 are combined, as in table 11.5.

For cohabitational first-birth rates of ordinal months 1 to 23 combined, the biases are smaller than for corresponding marriage rates (Table 11.6), and the birth rate biases are negative for our earliest cohort. Otherwise, they tend to be around one-fifth or more for starting ages of 19 or younger, and roughly one-tenth or more for ages 20–24 at the start of cohabitation. The differential bias would tend somewhat to overestimate the fertility differences by age at start of cohabitation. These smaller biases hardly mask the general stability in cohabitational first-birth rates across cohorts or the differential by starting age. In fact, even our single outlier observation—namely, the fall in the first-birth rate for teenage Swedish women living in consensual unions in our youngest cohort—is picked up well by the biased procedure.

Table 11.5. Marriage Rates for Nulliparous Swedish and Danish Women in Consensual Unions, at Durations 5 to 23 Months, All Starting Ages through 24 (per 1,000 women per month)

| Cohort | Swedish Women | | | Danish Women |
	Swedish Plan	Danish Plan	Bias[a]	
1936–40	62.5	73.3	17%	80
1941–45	47.7	57.5	21%	70
1946–50	23.8	31.0	30%	50
1951–55	11.7	15.3	31%	20
1956–60	6.5	8.8	36%	—

Note: Dash indicates no data available.
[a]100 (S/DK − 1).

Table 11.6. First-Birth Rates for Swedish and Danish Women in Consensual Unions

| | Starting Age 19 or Younger | | | | Starting Age 20–24 | | | |
| | Swedish Women | | | | Swedish Women | | | |
Cohort	Swedish Plan	Danish Plan	Bias[a]	Danish Women	Swedish Plan	Danish Plan	Bias[a]	Danish Women
1936–40	25.8	18.6	−28%	5.3	17.3	13.1	−24%	6.3
1941–45	22.5	20.8	−7%	7.6	10.6	11.2	6%	6.1
1946–50	20.9	25.6	27%	10.6	9.6	10.6	10%	2.8
1951–55	16.1	18.0	12%	7.0	9.0	9.8	9%	6.9
1955–60	9.8	11.8	20%	—	12.6	14.0	11%	—
All cohorts[b]	15.9	16.7	5%	8.2	10.1	10.9	8%	5.2

Note: Durations 1 through 23 months combined.
[a]100 (S/DK − 1).
[b]For Sweden, women born in 1936–60. For Denmark, women born 1926–55.

Our general conclusion of this analysis of the biases inherent in the Danish observational plan, therefore, is that the estimated risk levels may be somewhat biased, usually upward, but not enough to mask any trends across cohorts or any differences by age at the start of the consensual union.

This impression is reinforced when we juxtapose diagrams of schedules of duration-specific marriage and first-birth rates of cohabiting women, as in Figures 11.4 and 11.5. Even though a detailed comparison of corresponding curves in each figure will reveal some distortion effects, these are really minor in comparison to the general impressions of duration dependence and cohort trends.

A Comparison of Cohabiting Nulliparous Women in Sweden and Denmark

Tables 11.5 and 11.6 invite a comparison between the behavior in Denmark and Sweden. Table 11.5 (columns 2 and 4) suggests that in each of the cohorts born in 1936 to 1955, noticeably more nulliparous Danish women tended to marry than their Swedish counterparts. Even if we reduce the biased Danish marriage rates of the cohorts born in 1941–1945 and 1946–1950 by an amount intended to remove distortion[4] and bring them into line with the corresponding unbiased Swedish rates in column 1, the corresponding Danish partial marriage probabilities[5] over the nineteen months in question are about 65% and 50%, respectively. Their Swedish counterparts are about 60% and 30%. For the cohort of 1951–1955, the bias-adjusted Danish partial probability is 25% and the Swedish is 20%.

On the other hand, nulliparous Swedish women living in consensual unions have had about twice the first-birth rates of their Danish counterparts (Table 11.6). To see how this interacts with the differential nuptiality, we have also computed estimated partial probabilities $\hat{\pi}(z)$ of having a nonmarital first birth in a consensual union over $z = 19$ months when marriage is a competing risk but mortality and union dissolution are disregarded, as in Table 11.3, for Denmark and Sweden separately (see Table

4. Divide the rate in column 4 of Table 11.5 by the item in column 2 and multiply by the item in column 1. Then the bias in the Danish rate will be removed, provided the proportionate biases are the same in Denmark and Sweden.

5. As in column 4 of Table 11.2, where corresponding *unadjusted* Danish partial probabilities were listed, the figures given here are estimates of the single decrement life-table probability of marrying at some time during the nineteen months in the absence of any competing risks (death, union dissolution, first birth). It is called a *partial* probability because one accounts only for some of the risks actually involved.

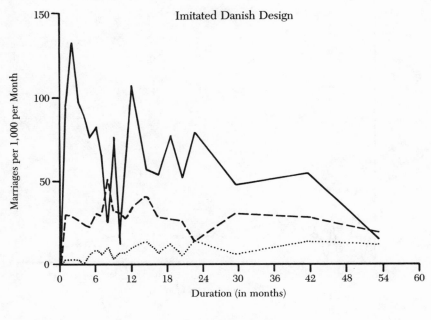

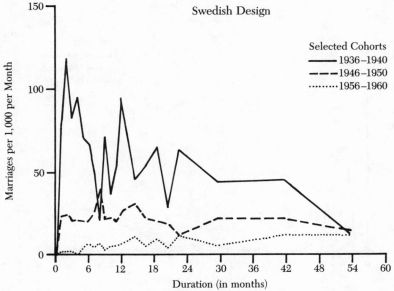

Figure 11.4. First Marriages per 1,000 Cohabitating Swedish Women at Parity 0. All Starting Ages Combined.

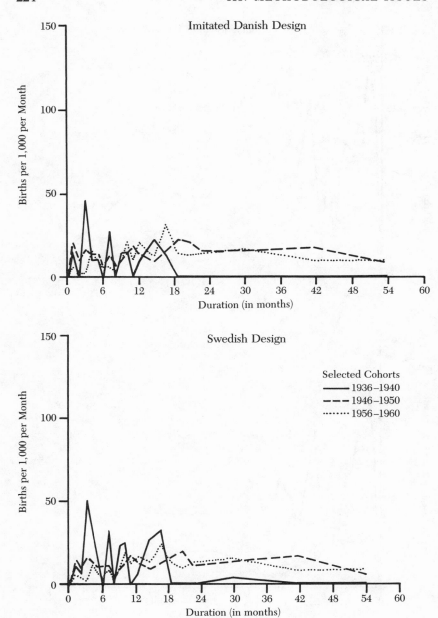

Figure 11.5. First Births per 1,000 Cohabiting, Never-Married Swedish Women.

Table 11.7. Estimated Probability $\hat{\pi}(z)$ of a Nonmarital First Birth in a Consensual Union, for Complete Swedish and Adjusted Danish Data ($z = 19$ months) (%)

Cohort	Starting Age 19 or Younger		Starting Age 20–24	
	Sweden[a]	Denmark[b]	Sweden[a]	Denmark[b]
1936–40[c]	16.4	8.2	9.9	4.7
1941–45	19.0	8.3	11.0	5.4
1946–50	22.1	10.1	13.8	6.2
1951–55	23.9	12.0	15.5	7.5
1955–60	24.8	–	16.1	–
No nuptiality	26.0	13.8	17.5	8.7

Note: Estimates were made for unions under the competing risks of childbearing and marriage, disregarding mortality and union dissolution.

[a]Swedish marriage rates are by cohort and starting age. First-birth rates from Table 11.6, by starting age, for all cohorts born 1936–60 combined.

[b]Danish marriage rates are computed from Danish data and subsequently adjusted for design bias as described in chapter note 4, for each cohort and starting age separately. First-birth rates from Table 11.6, by starting age, for all cohorts born 1926–55 combined, reduced in each case by 0.4 per 1,000 to adjust for design bias.

[c]For Denmark: 1926–40 combined.

11.7). The Danish cohabitational marriage and first-birth rates have been adjusted with the intention of removing design biases. In each column of Table 11.7, the first-birth rate used is the same for each cohort since there are no great differences across cohorts, while the marriage rate is the one pertaining to each cohort. The marriage rate has been set to 0 in the final line of the table to get a "pure" fertility measure. The formula for $\pi(z)$ was given in connection with Table 11.3. A comparison between Tables 11.3 and 11.7 show the negligible effect of the bias adjustment.

In each case, the childbearing probability for a Swedish woman is about twice its Danish counterpart, as were the birth rates themselves. By the standards of industrialized Western countries, Denmark probably has much nonmarital cohabitation (Brown and Kiernan 1981) and a high incidence of cohabitational first births. By comparison to Sweden, however, it evidently was a laggard on both counts in the period we have investigated.

12 *Heinz P. Galler and Ulrich Poetter*

Unobserved Heterogeneity in Models of Unemployment Duration

Introduction

In analyses of unemployment duration data, it is important to discriminate between true negative duration dependence of the exit rate from unemployment, caused, for instance, by dequalification, and spurious negative duration dependence due to unobserved heterogeneity of the observations. Besides the different implications for labor market policy, it is important to separate the impact of unobserved heterogeneity from true duration dependence for statistical reasons. As demonstrated by Heckman and Singer (1984), parameter estimates may be rather sensitive with regard to the assumptions they introduce for the distribution of unobserved heterogeneity in the population. At the same time, findings by Trussell and Richards (1985) indicate that estimates also depend on the specification of duration dependence adopted. This makes model specification a crucial point in empirical analyses of duration data.

In the case of unemployment duration it is rather difficult to derive the structural form of the hazard rate from economic theory. The search model commonly used by economists leads to complex nonlinear relations that cannot be solved analytically without further simplifications. Approximations have to be applied to obtain an operable specification suited for empirical work. However, since different approximations can be applied, the question is how to deal appropriately with true duration dependence and unobserved heterogeneity in simplified models.

Search Models of Unemployment Duration

The basic search model of unemployment duration has been developed by Mortensen (1970) and McCall (1970). In recent years, the approach of Kiefer and Neumann (1979a, 1979b, 1981) has been used by several researchers in empirical studies. It is based on the analysis of a rational individual's decision to accept or to reject job offers assumed to be available at random with a known probability distribution. In the standard search model, jobs are described by the wage proffered. The wages are modeled as random variables with a known probability distribution. The model posits that an optimal decision rule of an unemployed individual i at time t consists in fixing a reservation wage $V(i, t)$. A wage offer w is accepted when it exceeds this reservation wage level (cf. Hall, Lippmann, and McCall 1976).

In general, the reservation wage is defined by the net benefits expected from further job searching. A rational individual will accept a job offer if the expected benefits of the job exceed those of further searching. The conditional probability of accepting a job equals the probability of a wage offer exceeding the reservation wage. The exit rate from unemployment is then defined as the product of the rate at which offers become available and the conditional probability that the job will be accepted. The exit rate $[h (i, t)]$ from unemployment is defined as a function of the reservation wage $[V (i, t)]$, of the probability distribution of job offers faced by individual i at time t $[F (w \mid i, t)]$, and of the rate at which job offers become available $[g (i, t)]$:

$$h(i, t) = g(i, t) \{1 - F[V(i, t) \mid i, t]\} \qquad (12.1)$$

The basic search model usually assumes stationarity as well as an infinite time horizon, which implies that the reservation wage remains constant over time. However, this specification is rather restrictive. Even if one assumes homogeneity of environment over short periods, reservation wages will not be constant. A finite time horizon for job search will result in varying reservation wages. Apart from that, the assumption of a stationary process of job offers appears to be questionable. If work contracts are regarded as the result of search activities by both employers and employees (see, e.g., Galler 1985), the rate at which these job offers become available to an individual may depend on the duration of unemployment. Rational employers searching for a worker to fill a given vacancy will de-

fine some minimum requirements with regard to qualifications and abili-
ties. If the duration of unemployment is used as a screening device, the
chances of an unemployed individual being offered a job will probably
decline with an increasing duration of unemployment even if the total
number of jobs available remains constant.

Even for the simplified approach based on the assumption of stationarity, in general no direct solution for the reservation wage can be obtained.
Kiefer and Neumann (1981), in a discrete time approach, represent the
reservation wage as a function of the wage offer distribution, the net transfer received, and the discount rate along with the duration of unemployment. They then apply a linear approximation to obtain an operable representation of the reservation wage relation that can be estimated from
empirical data by probit or logit procedures.

A similar approach can be used for a nonstationary continuous-time formulation of the model. For the estimation of a continuous-time model the
integrated hazard rate must be derived. Therefore it is preferable to start
from a general representation of the logarithm of the hazard rate and then
to apply a linear expansion. This will lead to the class of proportional hazard models. In general, the exit rate from unemployment will depend on
the rate of offers becoming available, the conditional wage offer distribution, the reservation wage, and the current transfer income $z(i, t)$. If no
stationarity is assumed, expectations with regard to future job offers and
transfers will also determine the reservation wage. With the impact of
expectations collapsed into a variable $Q(i, t)$, a general representation of
the hazard rate is:

$$\ln h(i, t) = h^*[\, g(i, t),\, F(w \mid i, t),\, z(i, t),\, Q(i, t)] \qquad (12.2)$$

Since expectations are formed on the basis of information available, the
terms entering the hazard rate (equation 12.2) may be modeled as functions of the vector of observed characteristics $x(i, t)$ of the individual, of a
vector of labor market indicators $y(t)$, and of the duration of unemployment t, as well as unobserved variables $e(i, t)$. A linear expansion with
respect to the observed variables $x(i, t)$ and $y(t)$ and some function $k(t)$
representing duration dependence of unemployment results in the following relation, with an error term $R(i, t)$ describing the approximation
error and the impact of the unobserved variables $e(i, t)$:

$$\ln h(i, t) = h_0 + \alpha' x(i, t) + \beta' y(t) + \pi k(t) + R(i, t) \qquad (12.3)$$

Parameter estimates based on such a linear approximation provide a basis
for inferences about the structure of the true relation. However without

additional assumptions regarding the error $R(i, t)$, the model cannot be estimated.

Specifications of Unobserved Heterogeneity

By definition, the error term of the simplified model (equation 12.3) represents deviations of the model from the true relation. It may be interpreted as a specification error caused by the omission of variables relevant for explanation but not included into the model or by the approximation to the true functional form. Such specification errors imply biased estimation results and may even lead to wrong conclusions with regard to the true hazard rate of the individual.

The most simple formulation of the duration model neglects the heterogeneity term $R(i, t)$. In this case either omitted covariates, or a departure from proportionality, or an inadequate model of duration dependence, may lead to a severe bias in the estimates of the form of duration dependence and the influence of covariates. For example, when the "true" model is a mixture of Weibull models $[k(t) = \ln t]$ with different scale parameters h_0, but a simple Weibull model is used for estimation, the estimated form parameter π as well as the estimated parameters of the covariates α and β will be biased downward (Lancaster 1985).

One obtains a less restrictive specification if the form of the baseline hazard is not explicitly modeled and inference is drawn from Cox's partial likelihood. However, the Cox model does not provide estimates for the form of duration dependence $k(t)$. For this purpose, alternative approaches, like that of Breslow, have to be used (cf. Kalbfleisch and Prentice 1980). In the presence of unobserved heterogeneity, the estimates from a partial likelihood approach are biased downward. The magnitude of the bias is determined by the influence of the omitted variables on the duration in a state (Struthers and Kalbfleisch 1986). The direction of the bias resulting from nonproportionality depends on the form of the true underlying model. Nevertheless the relative importance of the covariates remains unchanged, at least to a first-order approximation (Solomon 1984).

One way to treat the error term more explicitly is to model it by a time-invariant constant that is specific to the individual observation. The individual hazard rates are proportional up to an unknown heterogeneity factor $h_0(i)$ given the values of the explanatory variables. The usual approach to unobserved heterogeneity is adopted, when these terms are supposed to be realizations of a random variable. The marginal distribution of such models will, in general, no longer belong to the class of proportional hazard models. Thus a constant heterogeneity term may catch both individual heterogeneity and a departure from the supposed form of time dependence.

If a parametric form of the probability distribution of the heterogeneity term is assumed, such a model can be estimated directly by maximum-likelihood methods. Moreover, the combination of a parametric hazard model and a parametric heterogeneity specification yields a flexible class of duration distributions and allows for the representations of various aspects of heterogeneity. If sufficient prior information on the properties of heterogeneity is available, the methods of Hougaard (1984, 1986) can be used to select an appropriate distribution for the heterogeneity term (e.g., log-normal, gamma, or inverse Gaussian distributions). However, economic theory provides only limited information with regard to the distribution of unobserved heterogeneity. Also the nonlinear structure of the true relation may result in a nonstandard distribution of the error terms of the approximate model. As a consequence, parametric estimators based on standard distributional assumptions may give biased estimates as demonstrated by Heckman and Singer (1984). This makes a nonparametric approach to unobserved heterogeneity attractive.

Semi-parametric models with a parametric specification of the base-line hazard and a nonparametric specification of the heterogeneity term pose problems of identifiability and require nonstandard maximum-likelihood estimation techniques. If the set of distribution functions used to represent individual heterogeneity is not restricted to a parametric class, maximum-likelihood estimators may not even be consistent (Neyman and Scott 1948). Heckman and Singer (1984) proved the identifiability of such models and the consistency of a semi-parametric maximum-likelihood estimator under some additional assumptions on the distribution of heterogeneity and the admissible parameters. Simulation results suggest good properties in the estimation of structural parameters, while estimates of the distribution of heterogeneity, even in large samples, hardly recover the underlying true distribution (Heckman and Singer 1984).

However, in Heckman and Singer's nonparametric approach to unobserved heterogeneity some basic problems remain. In their empirical work Trussell and Richards (1985) report the strong dependence of the semi-parametric estimators on the choice of a parametric base-line hazard. One way to circumvent this difficulty is to adopt a nonparametric specification both of duration dependence and of the heterogeneity term. In the case of a heterogeneity term with finite expectation and in the presence of at least one regressor, Elbers and Ridder (1982) demonstrated the identifiability of such a model.

An inspection of their proof, which uses the deviations of the empirical duration distributions from proportionality, suggests that a large amount of exact data would be needed to recover the form of the hazard, the influence of the covariates, and the functional form of the heterogeneity term. An implementation of their proof strategy would require numerical differentiation and integration. These procedures are very sensitive to small perturbations in the values of the estimated survival function. Furthermore, one needs to know the complete survival function for all values of the covariates. Given the limitations of the data, it seems impossible to estimate both duration dependence and heterogeneity nonparametrically.

A compromise between a fully nonparametric and a parametric specification of duration dependence may be to adopt a partially parametric dummy variable approach as an approximation to a nonparametric formulation of duration dependence (see, e.g., Trussell and Richards 1985). This approach models duration dependence by dummy variables that represent predetermined time intervals with constant rates. This is not a fully nonparametric approach since the intervals have to be fixed a priori. However, it allows a flexible specification of duration dependence so that misspecifications can, to a large extent, be avoided. This is especially true if many dummy variables are used.

Since a dummy variable specification implies some restrictions for the form of duration dependence, it can, in principle, be combined with a nonparametric specification of unobserved heterogeneity. Thus it provides a flexible specification for both duration dependence and for unobserved heterogeneity. One would expect unobserved heterogeneity to be empirically of less importance for a partially parametric model than for other, more specific formulations of duration dependence, because dummy variables may approximate the empirical distribution of unemployment durations as closely as required. Especially if a comparatively large number of dummy variables is employed, the identification of unobserved heterogeneity, while theoretically possible, would demand a large amount of exact data.

The Data Base and Models Used for Estimation

As an example for the consequences of different specifications of duration dependence and unobserved heterogeneity, we have estimated different versions of a hazard rate model for unemployment durations. Our data base is the information of the first two waves of the German Socio-Economic Panel Study. This panel study was started in 1984 by the Sonderforschungsbereich 3, in order to collect longitudinal data on the population living in private households in West Germany (cf. Hanefeld 1984). Experience with these data is still limited. Up until now only a few analyses have been conducted. Therefore the analyses reported here are exploratory in character.

For each person in the sample, each wave of the Socio-Economic Panel

Study records employment status in the previous year by retrospective interviewing. Combining the data from the first two waves for each individual covers a period of twenty-four months, starting from January 1983. Within this period, the start and the end of individual spells of work, unemployment, schooling, or nonparticipation in the labor force can be dated by month. As explanatory variables we use available information on individual characteristics as well as on the family and the household. However, because of the protection of individual privacy, no regional information is supplied that allows the use of regional labor market indicators as explanatory variables.

The analysis was restricted to unemployed men, since women in the labor market are bound by different conditions in respect to household production and labor market participation. To avoid problems of left censoring, only those individuals who had become unemployed during the period under consideration were included in the sample. In the data base, the beginning and the end of an unemployment spell was defined by comparing the individual's status in two consecutive months. Because this status is recorded only by month, the start and the end of each spell was dated to the middle of the respective month except for those unemployed for only one month. For these cases a duration of a quarter of a month was assumed. Observations were marked as right censored after the month of November if they remained in the same status in December but no information was available on the status during January of the following year. For the same reason, spells starting in December but not followed in January were excluded from the sample since it was not possible to decide whether the spell had been completed during December or whether the observation was censored on the right.

For the present analysis three proportional hazard model specifications have been used that differ only in the specification of duration dependence of the exit rate from unemployment. First, an exponential model with no duration dependence has been considered. In the second model, duration dependence of the Weibull type has been assumed. The third specification uses dummy variables μ that indicate durations of one to three months and more than three months, respectively:

$$\text{Model (1): } \ln[h(i, t)] = \alpha' \, x(i, t) \tag{12.4}$$

$$\text{Model (2): } \ln[h(i, t)] = \alpha' \, x(i, t) + (\Phi - 1)\ln(t) + \ln(\Phi) \tag{12.5}$$

$$\text{Model (3): } \ln[h(i, t) = \alpha' \, x(i, t) + \mu(t) \tag{12.6}$$

Only a few explanatory variables have been included in each model. First, a dummy variable is used to indicate non-German nationality. Age is represented by a set of dummy variables for different age brackets. For education, dummy variables are introduced for individuals without formal professional training and for those with university degrees. In the present specification, unemployment transfers are only represented by a dummy variable that takes the value of one for those months in which unemployment compensation was received. No variables related to family size or to the marginal utility of income have been included. The same is true for labor market indicators, since no regional information was supplied and indicators on the national level showed too little variation to be used as explanatory variables.

Additionally, a dummy variable was introduced for the month of December 1983 to represent the effect of recall errors. Since the information on two consecutive years was collected in respective waves of the panel study, some inconsistencies naturally occur. A significant proportion of respondents who reported being unemployed in December 1983 did not report being unemployed for January 1984. This is, to some extent, probably caused by recall errors. The dummy variable is intended to catch this effect. For the same reason, observations starting in January 1984 have been excluded from the sample since at least some portion of them were left censored due to underreporting in the first wave.

To assess the sensitivity of the estimates with regard to unobserved heterogeneity, all three models have been estimated both under the assumption of no unobserved heterogeneity and under a nonparametric specification of unobserved heterogeneity based on the Heckman-Singer approach. For unobserved heterogeneity, estimation started with a sufficiently large number of support points $[\theta(i)]$ of the mixing distribution. Then the number of points was reduced if either the probability mass of a point approached zero or two points of support converged during the iteration process.

Estimation Results

The model specifications without unobserved heterogeneity were estimated using standard maximum-likelihood procedures. For numerical maximization of the log-likelihood function, we used the quadratic-hill-climbing procedure developed by Goldfeld and Quandt (1972). For nonparametric estimation of the mixing distribution for unobserved heterogeneity, the EM-algorithm was applied (cf. Redner and Walker 1984). This approach required extensive computations.

For the models without unobserved heterogeneity, the parameter estimates are reported together with the *t*-ratios. However, for the semiparametric models no computationally feasible bound for the variance of the estimators is available. Note that the reported t-ratios have no strict justification when computed under the wrong model.

The parameter estimates for the specification without unobserved heterogeneity (see Table 12.1) are similar to the findings of other studies. The exit rate from unemployment is lower for foreigners than for German nationals. Young people leave unemployment faster than the reference group in the middle age bracket, while older people show a significantly lower exit rate. Men without professional qualifications leave unemployment at a slower rate than the reference group with formal professional training, while the group with university degrees shows substantially higher exit rates. From a theoretical point of view, one would expect more qualified people to search longer for a job. The exit rate is substantially lower for people receiving unemployment benefits. Finally, the dummy variable for December 1983 shows a significant positive effect of recall errors on the exit rate.

The parameter estimates for the covariates prove to be robust with regard to the specification of duration dependence assumed. Except for the constant, there are only slight differences in the estimates between the three model specifications. This result is in accordance with the findings of Trussell and Richards (1985).

Both the Weibull specification (equation 12.5) and the dummy variable representation (equation 12.6) show significant negative duration dependence of the exit rate if no unobserved heterogeneity is introduced. This is consistent with the results of other empirical studies (see, e.g., Egle 1979). However, at least in the context of conventional economic search theory, one would rather expect the exit rate to rise with prolonged unemployment since unemployment benefits decrease as well as expected income and individual wealth. But eventually other relationships might be derived if screening by potential employers dependent on unemployment duration is considered.

If unobserved heterogeneity is introduced, quite different effects occur. For the dummy variable specification of duration dependence (equation 12.6) almost no unobserved heterogeneity is found. In the estimation process, the mixing distribution degenerates to one point equal to the constant term of the corresponding model without unobserved heterogeneity. The parameter estimates are practically identical to those for the simple model. The remaining differences result from the slow convergence properties of the EM-algorithm.

Apparently, the step function assumed for duration dependence fits the data sufficiently well so that no variation remains that could be attributed to unobserved heterogeneity. However, the partially parametric specification of duration dependence is not very well suited for a combination of

Table 12.1. Parameter Estimates for Hazard Rate Models of Unemployment Duration for
Unemployed Men under 65 Years in West Germany ($N = 441$)

Model	No Unobserved Heterogeneity			With Unobserved Heterogeneity		
	(1)	(2)	(3)	(1)	(2)	(3)
Log-likelihood	−71.9	−65.7	−44.9	−62.3	−51.9	−44.9
Foreigner	−.1317	−.1163	−.1036	−.1086	−.1440	−.1035
	(.93)	(.82)	(.73)	—	—	—
Age under 25	.6819	.6463	.6105	.8401	1.3314	.6108
	(3.77)	(3.57)	(3.37)	—	—	—
25–34	.3614	.3553	.3324	.4613	.2343	.3326
	(1.84)	(1.81)	(1.69)	—	—	—
45–54	−.1280	−.0766	−.0839	−.0590	−.2995	−.0837
	(.52)	(.31)	(.34)	—	—	—
55–64	−.9806	−.8850	−.8307	−1.1312	−2.2432	−.8309
	(2.62)	(2.37)	(2.22)	—	—	—
Education						
No professional training	−.3697	−.3760	−.3844	−.5183	−1.7249	−.3846
	(2.46)	(2.50)	(2.56)	—	—	—
University	.6804	.5779	.4970	.5942	−.1571	.4969
	(2.84)	(2.41)	(2.07)	—	—	—
Unemployment benefits	−.1989	−.2071	−.2102	−.1992	.2432	−.2103
	(1.51)	(1.57)	(1.56)	—	—	—
December 1983	.9442	.9096	.8868	.9244	.7532	.8868
	(5.15)	(4.94)	(4.82)	—	—	—
Constant (mean)	.4051	.3247	1.0607	.4616	1.7649	1.0604
	(2.40)	(1.91)	(5.77)	—	—	—
Weibull parameter (Φ)	—	.8483	—	—	1.9167	—
	—	(3.39)	—	—	—	—
Duration						
μ_1: 1–3 months	—	—	−.8942	—	—	−.8939
	—	—	(5.76)	—	—	—
μ_2: 4+ months	—	—	−.9584	—	—	−.9576
	—	—	(6.66)	—	—	—
Mixing distribution						
Point θ_1	—	—	—	−.8862	−2.8868	−.0245
p_1	—	—	—	.2272	.2989	.5499
Point θ_2	—	—	—	−.1794	−.2583	.0299
p_2	—	—	—	.5713	.4151	.4501
Point θ_3	—	—	—	1.5077	3.3919	—
p_3	—	—	—	.2015	.2860	—

Source: Socio-Economic Panel Study, first and second wave.
Note: *t*-values are in parentheses.

positive duration dependence with a mixing distribution. A mixture of constant hazard rates will give negative duration dependence within each interval. Thus a mixture of increasing step functions results in a rather irregular form for the marginal hazard rate. This may also be the reason the estimates show negative duration dependence.

In contrast to the dummy variable approach, a substantial variation of the heterogeneity term was estimated for the specifications in equation 12.4 without any duration dependence. This is plausible since introducing unobserved heterogeneity allows a better fit to the observed distribution of durations than is achieved by a simple exponential model with a constant rate. In comparison to an exponential model, the density function of a mixture of exponentials is steeper for short durations and flatter for longer ones. The largest changes in the parameter estimates occur for the age-specific dummy variables. The coefficients estimated for the younger age brackets rise while those for the older people are reduced. A similar increase in the impact of education can be observed.

Compared to the other two models, the changes in the parameter estimates are largest for the Weibull specification (equation 12.5). The most important changes occur in the parameters of education and of unemployment benefits and also in the Weibull form parameter. While significant negative duration dependence ($\Phi < 1$) was estimated for the specification without unobserved heterogeneity, controlling for unobserved heterogeneity resulted in strong positive duration dependence ($\Phi > 1$). This resembles the results of Heckman and Singer (1984) based on the Kiefer-Neumann data. Since positive duration dependence may appear more plausible from a theoretical point of view, these estimates may be seen to favor a nonparametric specification of unobserved heterogeneity.

The same is true for the negative coefficient of high qualification as compared to the positive value derived from the specification without unobserved heterogeneity. Lower exit rates for highly qualified individuals are in accordance with economic theory. By contrast, the positive estimate for the impact of unemployment benefits does not agree with prior theoretical beliefs. Here the negative value of the other models appears to be more plausible. However, as the t-ratios for the model without unobserved heterogeneity suggest, this result may not be significant. In general, the estimates appear to support the argument by Heckman and Singer (1984) that a nonparametric approach to unobserved heterogeneity will result in less biased parameter estimates. However, such conclusions should be drawn with care. The rather large values of the coefficients, the sign-change of two coefficients, and the value of the Weibull parameter give rise to the question of whether the estimates represent true causal pendencies or reflect some peculiarities of the model or of the data.

A Weibull model with positive duration dependence implies a probability density with a unique mode at a nonzero location, while negative duration dependence implies a mode at zero. The position of the mode depends on the Weibull form parameter Φ given the values of the explanatory variables. If, for instance, the process of data collection causes the observed durations to concentrate around some specific values, a mixture of Weibull models with positive duration dependence may fit the empirical frequency distribution better than a model with negative duration dependence. The modes of the estimated conditional densities can be forced to coincide with the modes of the empirical frequency distribution by the choice of appropriate heterogeneity terms. Thus estimated positive duration dependence may reflect deficiencies in the data rather than a true causal relationship.

To get an impression of the distribution of durations implied by the estimates, the probability densities have been computed from the model conditional on the estimates for the heterogeneity parameter using the sample values of the explanatory variables (see Figure 12.1). These conditional probability densities have been aggregated to the marginal density for the sample and have been compared to a nonparametric estimate of the duration density.

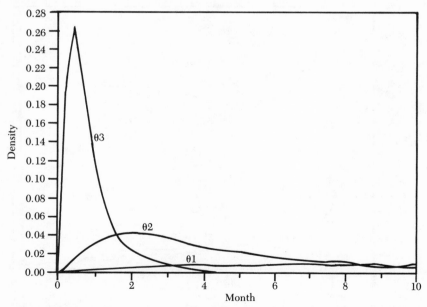

Figure 12.1. Estimated Densities Conditional on the Estimated Support Points in a Weibull Model with 3 Support Points

The plot (Figure 12.1) of the conditional Weibull densities, given the heterogeneity term, shows a partitioning of the sample in three groups with distinct distributions of unemployment durations. The largest value for the heterogeneity parameter (θ_3) gives a strongly skewed conditional density function with a mode at less than one month. In contrast, the mode of durations is about ten months for the smallest estimate (θ_1). The marginal density function is again unimodal with a mode at a comparatively short duration of unemployment.

The nonparametric estimate of the marginal density function (Figure 12.2) reveals the empirical density's rather peculiar shape. Exits are frequent for very short durations. After a sharp decline the frequencies then show a rather flat profile. The mixed Weibull density function shows a good fit for very short durations and for durations over four months. In the interval between, the model apparently overestimates the empirical frequencies.

The shape of the empirical density function for very short durations reflects, to some degree, the procedure used for determining unemployment durations. By definition, there are no spells ending before a duration of a quarter of one month. After that point, completed durations are measured in multiples of full months while censoring is assumed in the

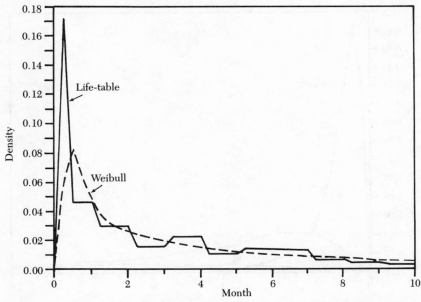

Figure 12.2. Marginal Density of Sample Observations: Life-Table Estimates and Estimates Based on a Weibull Model with 3 Support Points

middle of the month. Thus, the data actually represent a discrete frequency distribution.

If a mixture model based on the Weibull specification is fitted to such a distribution, a strong positive duration dependence is obtained, for it implies a strongly skewed unimodal distribution. If, in contrast, one assumes negative duration dependence, the largest probability would be attributed to the first short-duration interval. This is not supported by the data, however, since the empirical frequencies are zero for the first quarter of a month.

This explanation is confirmed by the observation that even larger values of the Weibull parameter are obtained if more support points are introduced for the mixing distribution of the heterogeneity term. The conditional density corresponding to the largest value of the heterogeneity term becomes even more skewed and concentrated at very short durations. At the same time, in a model with five points of support, the hump that occurs in the empirical frequency distribution at about four months of duration is reflected by an additional partition of the sample.

This implies that the estimate of positive duration dependence may represent an artifact due to inaccuracies of the data rather than a true causal relationship. If the observed distribution of durations is truncated from below, it is difficult to discriminate empirically between a Weibull model with negative duration dependence (mode at zero) and a mixture of models with positive duration dependence. The data may not contain enough information to identify the true form of duration dependence.

Conclusions

Even if unobserved heterogeneity is considered explicitly in models of unemployment duration it still is rather difficult to discriminate empirically between true duration dependence and the effects of unobserved heterogeneity. Economic theory provides little guidance with regard to the functional form of duration dependence or the specification of unobserved heterogeneity. Nevertheless, given the data available, some restrictions both on the form of duration dependence and on the distribution of unobserved heterogeneity are required to achieve identifiability of the models. If unobserved heterogeneity is neglected, a nonparametric specification of duration dependence becomes feasible. Such models do not allow causal analyses with regard to duration dependence. However, they do provide an instrument for exploratory data analyses.

If a functional form is assumed for duration dependence, a nonparametric approach to unobserved heterogeneity may appear appropriate since little prior information is available on the distribution of unobserved heterogeneity. Moreover, parameter estimates are sensitive with regard to parametric specifications of the mixing distribution. On the other hand, semi-parametric estimates seem to be sensitive to deficiencies in the data. Since no restrictions are introduced for the mixing distribution, errors in the data may affect the estimates to a large degree. Thus there is an obvious trade-off between the quality of the data and the prior information required for estimation.

Unobserved Heterogeneity in Hazard Rate Models: A Test and an Illustration from a Study of Career Mobility

Introduction

In recent years, the increasing availability of event history data in bio-medical, economics and social science research has led to the widespread application of continuous-time hazard rate models. When using such methods, researchers often assume that they have measured and included the relevant causal influences in the model. But most scientists will agree that in any particular empirical analysis, this is hardly ever the case. Usually some important factors could not be measured or were ignored, creating a spurious change over time in estimated transition rates.

There is a growing literature addressing the issue of omitted variable bias and the problems of how to test and parametrically represent unobserved heterogeneity in continuous-time hazard rate models (see, for example, Tuma 1985; Heckman and Singer 1984; Tuma and Hannan 1984; Chamberlain 1985; Trussell and Richards 1985; Waldman 1985; Galler and Poetter 1987; Arminger 1987). Unfortunately at this point, computer pro-

This paper results from work undertaken as part of the West German life-history project, which is based in the Max Planck Institute for Human Development and Education, and supported by grants of the Deutsche Forschungsgemeinschaft. For helpful comments on an earlier draft, we wish to thank Michael T. Hannan, Ellen Skinner, Nancy B. Tuma, and Ulrich Poetter.

grams designed to alleviate these problems are very specialized and not available to everyone.

The purpose of this paper is, therefore, to propose a test for neglected heterogeneity in continuous-time hazard rate models that can be done easily using generally available statistical program packages, like GLIM (Roger and Peacock 1983), SAS (1985), or BMDP (Petersen 1986a, 1986b). Our test for neglected heterogeneity combines the results of Lancaster (1985), Kiefer (1984), and Burdett et al. (1985). The derivation of the test statistic follows Lancaster (1985). Utilizing White's information matrix test Lancaster (1985) proposed a general test for neglected heterogeneity in duration models. It is assumed that the models are misspecified by the neglect of a random multiplicative heterogeneity in the hazard rate. Lancaster's approach of constructing diagnostics can be applied to any duration model, but he does not consider censored data. We shall generalize his approach to allow for right-censored observations, but we use another variance estimator of the test statistic. This variance estimator was proposed by Burdett et al. (1985). They derived an estimator which is conditionally on the estimated parameter values, whereas Lancaster estimates the unconditional variance which is needed for the construction of the information matrix test.

In the next section we first show how unmeasured heterogeneity creates spurious time dependence in observed transition rates. Then we derive a test procedure which detects this kind of misspecification. In the last section we give an example of the application of this test, analyzing career trajectories of German men from three birth cohorts.

Testing for Neglected Heterogeneity

Models for event history data are usually specified in terms of the hazard rate. Let T denote the random duration and let $\mathbf{x}$ be the vector of measured covariates. Then the hazard rate is given by

$$\lambda\,(t \mid \mathbf{x}) = \lim_{\Delta t \to 0} \frac{1}{\Delta t}\,\Pr(t \leq T < t + \Delta t \mid T \geq t, \mathbf{x}). \qquad (13.1)$$

Survivor function and density function are

$$S(t \mid \mathbf{x}) = \exp\left(-\int_{o}^{t} \lambda\,(s \mid \mathbf{x})\,ds\right), \qquad (13.2)$$

$$f(t \mid \mathbf{x}) = \lambda\,(t \mid \mathbf{x})\,S(t \mid \mathbf{x}). \qquad (13.3)$$

In (13.1) it is assumed that the variation in the hazard rate depends only on variation in the measured covariates, that is, we have assumed that all relevant causal variables have been included in the model. But in many applications there will be variation in the hazard rates that is not adequately measured by the variables in **x**. If such unmeasured heterogeneity is important, then neglecting it will give biased estimates. Let us consider an example. Suppose that a population is divided into two subpopulations x_1 and x_2, and that in each subpopulation the hazard is constant, but the two hazard rates are not equal, for example,

$$\lambda(t \mid x_1) = 0.1, \lambda(t \mid x_2) = 0.4. \tag{13.4}$$

Furthermore, let p_i be the probability that an individual belongs to subpopulation i, $i = 1, 2$. The hazard rate in the population is then

$$\lambda(t) = \frac{\sum_i f(t \mid x_i) \, p_i}{\sum_i S(t \mid x_i) \, p_i} \tag{13.5}$$

For the above values of $\lambda(t|x_i)$ and for $p_1 = p_2 = 0.5$ the hazard rates are given in Figure 13.1.

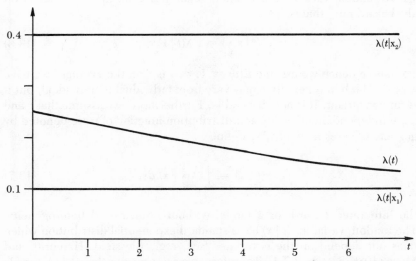

Figure 13.1. The Hazard Rate Path of the Subpopulations and the Total Population ($\lambda(t \mid x_1) = 0.1$ and $\lambda(t \mid x_2) = 0.4$)

Individuals with high rates will experience an event early and persons with high durations will systematically be the individuals with low rates. Therefore the rate in the total population will decline as time elapses. For further examples see Vaupel and Yashin (1985) or Blossfeld, Hamerle, and Mayer (1986). The above mentioned result is general. People will differ along various neglected variables and observed dynamics at the population level will differ from the underlying dynamics at the individual level. In general, failure to control for unobserved variables leads to a bias toward negative duration dependence, that is, it can lead to an estimated hazard that declines more steeply, or rises more slowly than the true hazard. If the unmeasured heterogeneity is correlated with x, then we also expect that neglecting unobserved heterogeneity will result in biased estimates of the regression coefficients. Most of the hazard rate models used in social sciences to analyze event history data do not account for unobserved heterogeneity, and nearly all available computer programs only estimate models without unobserved heterogeneity. But estimating such a model we cannot be sure if the underlying model is correct or if we have misspecified the model neglecting important unobserved variables. Therefore, we need a test procedure which detects this kind of misspecification, and if possible, we should be able to calculate the test statistic with available computer programs. In addition, it should not use a special form for the distribution of the heterogeneity.

To include unobserved heterogeneity explicitly in the model, a nonnegative random variable v is defined which has a multiplicative effect on the hazard rate, that is,

$$\lambda(t \mid \mathbf{x}, v) = v \, \lambda(t \mid \mathbf{x}). \tag{13.6}$$

For convenience we assume $E(v) = 1$, that is, "on the average" we have $\lambda(t \mid \mathbf{x})$. The heterogeneity v may vary from individual to individual, but it is time invariant. It is not observable. Furthermore, we assume that v and $\mathbf{x}$ are independent. Density and distribution function of v are denoted by $g(v)$ and $G(v)$ respectively. We define

$$r(t \mid \mathbf{x}) = \int_{o}^{t} \lambda(s \mid \mathbf{x}) \, ds, \tag{13.7}$$

the integrated hazard for a model without unmeasured heterogeneity. The random variable $r(t \mid \mathbf{x})$ has a standard exponential distribution which does not depend on the covariates (see, e.g., Blossfeld, Hamerle, and Mayer 1986, section 3.7.1). Therefore, we can consider the $r(t_i \mid \mathbf{x}_i)$, $i = 1$, . . . , n, as residuals, if we replace unknown parameters by maximum likelihood estimates. Residuals as defined above are "generalized residuals" in the sense of Cox and Snell (1968) (see also Crowley and Hu 1977). We shall see that the test statistic will only depend on these residuals which are calculated from models that ignore unobserved heterogeneity. Therefore, common computer packages can be used. For example, the residuals of the exponential, the Weibull, and the log-logistic model are given by

$$r(t \mid \mathbf{x}) = t \, \exp(\mathbf{x}'\hat{\boldsymbol{\alpha}}) \text{ (exponential model)} \tag{13.8}$$

$$r(t \mid \mathbf{x}) = t^{\alpha} \, \exp(\mathbf{x}'\hat{\boldsymbol{\alpha}}) \text{ (Weibull model)} \tag{13.9}$$

$$r(t \mid \mathbf{x}) = \log(1 + t^{\alpha} \, (\mathbf{x} \, \hat{\boldsymbol{\beta}})) \text{ (log-logistic model)}. \tag{13.10}$$

Now we again introduce the heterogeneity v and we obtain for the survivor function of T, given $\mathbf{x}$ and v

$$S\,(t \mid \mathbf{x},v) = \exp(-v \, r(t \mid \mathbf{x})), \tag{13.11}$$

and on integrating this equation with regard to the distribution of v, we find that

$$\begin{aligned} S(t \mid \mathbf{x}) &= \int \exp(-v \, r(t \mid \mathbf{x})) \, g(v) \, dv \\ &= E_v \, (\exp(-v \, r(t \mid \mathbf{x}))). \end{aligned} \tag{13.12}$$

The density function $f(t \mid \mathbf{x},v)$ is given by

$$\begin{aligned} f(t \mid \mathbf{x},v) &= v \, r'(t \mid \mathbf{x}) \, \exp(-v \, r(t \mid \mathbf{x})) \\ &= v \, \lambda(t \mid \mathbf{x}) \, \exp(-v \, r(t \mid \mathbf{x})). \end{aligned} \tag{13.13}$$

Now we develop the test statistic to examine neglected heterogeneity. The distribution of v is not known, and hence we need a test statistic which does not require knowledge about the form of the distribution of v. Let $\mathrm{Var}(v) = \sigma^2$. The null hypothesis is that there is no neglected heterogeneity. This can be expressed as $\sigma^2 = 0$. With the alternative hypothesis of small σ^2 we approximate the density $f(t \mid \mathbf{x},v)$ and the survivor function $S(t \mid \mathbf{x},v)$ with a Taylor expansion around $v_0 = 1$. Differentiating $S(t \mid \mathbf{x},v)$ with respect to v we obtain

$$\frac{dS(t \mid \mathbf{x},v)}{dv} = -r(t \mid \mathbf{x}) \, \exp(-v \, r(t \mid \mathbf{x}))$$

$$\frac{d^2S(t \mid \mathbf{x},v)}{dv^2} = r^2(t \mid \mathbf{x}) \, \exp(-v \, r(t \mid \mathbf{x})), \tag{13.14}$$

and for the Taylor expansions we have

$$S(t|\mathbf{x},v) = \exp(-r(t \mid \mathbf{x})) - r(t \mid \mathbf{x}) \exp(-r(t \mid \mathbf{x})) (v - 1)$$
$$+ 1/2 \; r^2(t \mid \mathbf{x}) \exp(-r(t \mid \mathbf{x})) (v - 1)^2 + R. \qquad (13.15)$$

Integrating $S(t|\mathbf{x},v)$ with respect to the distribution of v and neglecting terms of higher order than two, we can write

$$S(t|\mathbf{x}) \approx \exp(-r(t \mid \mathbf{x})) + \sigma^2/2 \; r^2(t \mid \mathbf{x}) \exp(-r(t \mid \mathbf{x}))$$
$$= S(t \mid \mathbf{x},1) (1 + \sigma^2/2 \; r^2(t \mid \mathbf{x})). \qquad (13.16)$$

For the density $f(t|\mathbf{x})$ we obtain

$$f(t|\mathbf{x}) = - \frac{dS(t \mid \mathbf{x})}{dt} \approx r'(t \mid \mathbf{x})\exp(-r(t \mid \mathbf{x})) - \sigma^2/2 \; [2r(t \mid \mathbf{x})r'(t \mid \mathbf{x})$$
$$\exp(-r(t \mid \mathbf{x})) + r^2(t \mid \mathbf{x}) \exp(-r(t \mid \mathbf{x})) (-r'(t \mid \mathbf{x}))]$$
$$= f(t \mid \mathbf{x},1) - \sigma^2 \; r(t \mid \mathbf{x}) f(t \mid \mathbf{x}) + \sigma^2/2 \; r^2(t \mid \mathbf{x}) f(t \mid \mathbf{x},1)$$
$$= f(t \mid \mathbf{x},1) [1 + \sigma^2/2 \; r^2(t \mid \mathbf{x}) - \sigma^2 \; r(t \mid \mathbf{x})] \qquad (13.17)$$

Now we assume that the functional form of $f(t \mid \mathbf{x})$ and $S(t \mid \mathbf{x})$ is known up to a finite dimensional parameter vector $\boldsymbol{\theta}$. $\boldsymbol{\theta}$ contains the regression coefficients β as well as further parameters determining time dependence. We write $f(t \mid \mathbf{x}; \boldsymbol{\theta})$ and $S(t \mid \mathbf{x}; \boldsymbol{\theta})$. We introduce a censoring indicator δ_i where $\delta_i = 0$ if the duration of individual i is right censored and $\delta_i = 1$ otherwise. The log-likelihood contribution is given by

$$\log L = \delta \log f(t \mid \mathbf{x}; \boldsymbol{\theta}) + (1 - \delta) \log S(t \mid \mathbf{x}; \boldsymbol{\theta}), \qquad (13.18)$$

where we dropped the subscript i to simplify notation. Using (13.6) and (13.7) as an approximation of the true survivor function and the true density function for small σ we have

$$\log L = \delta[\log f(t \mid \mathbf{x}, 1; \boldsymbol{\theta}) + \log (1 + \sigma^2(1/2 \; r^2(t \mid \mathbf{x}; \boldsymbol{\theta}) - r(t \mid \mathbf{x}; \boldsymbol{\theta}))]$$
$$+ (1 - \delta) [\log S(t \mid \mathbf{x}, 1; \boldsymbol{\theta}) (1 + \sigma^2/2 \; r^2(t \mid \mathbf{x}; \boldsymbol{\theta})].$$
$$13.19$$

The proposed test for neglected heterogeneity is a score test for the hypothesis $\sigma^2 = 0$. Let $\hat{\boldsymbol{\theta}}$ denote the maximum likelihood estimates under the null hypothesis, that is, when σ^2 is known to be zero. To derive the test statistic we have to calculate the score function at the point $(\hat{\boldsymbol{\theta}}, 0)$. We obtain

$$\frac{\partial \log L}{\partial \theta_j}\bigg|_{(\theta,\sigma^2)} = (\hat{\theta},0) = 0 \text{ for all } j,$$

$$\frac{\partial \log L}{\partial \sigma^2} = \delta \frac{1/2\ r^2(t \mid \mathbf{x};\ \theta) - r(t \mid \mathbf{x};\ \theta)}{1 + \sigma^2(1/2\ r^2(t \mid \mathbf{x};\ \theta) - r(t \mid \mathbf{x};\ \theta))}$$
$$+ (1 - \delta) \frac{r^2(t \mid \mathbf{x};\theta)/2}{1 + \sigma^2/2 r^2(t \mid \mathbf{x};\theta)} \qquad (13.20)$$

Evaluating $\dfrac{\partial \log L}{\partial \sigma^2}$ at $(\hat{\theta},0)$ and collecting terms we see that

$$\frac{\partial \log L}{\partial \sigma^2}\bigg|_{(\theta,\sigma^2)} = (\hat{\theta},0) = 1/2\ r^2(t \mid \mathbf{x};\hat{\theta}) - \delta r(t \mid \mathbf{x};\hat{\theta}). \quad (13.21)$$

Using the total likelihood function the score test for the null hypothesis $\sigma^2 = 0$ is based on the quantity

$$S = \frac{1}{2n} \sum_{i=1}^{n} (r^2(t_i \mid \mathbf{x}_i;\hat{\theta}) - 2\delta_i r(t_i \mid \mathbf{x}_i;\hat{\theta})). \qquad (13.22)$$

The $r(t_i|\mathbf{x}_i;\hat{\theta})$ in (13.22) are the maximum likelihood estimates of the integrated hazards for the model without heterogeneity. Therefore, common computer programs for duration models (e.g. SAS, GLIM, BMDP, RATE) can be used for the computation of S.

The variance of S can be estimated by

$$\text{Var}\ (S) = \frac{1}{4n^2} \sum_{i=1}^{n} (s_i - \bar{s})^2 \qquad (13.23)$$

where $s_i = r^2(t_i|\mathbf{x}_i;\hat{\theta}) - 2\delta_i r(t_i|\mathbf{x}_i;\hat{\theta})$ and $\bar{s}$ is the sample mean of s_i. This conditional estimate of the variance of the test statistic was proposed by Burdett et al. (1985), whereas Lancaster (1985) uses an unconditional variance estimator which is more difficult to obtain in the case of censored durations.

The test statistic

$$\frac{S}{\sqrt{\text{Var}\ (S)}} \qquad (13.24)$$

is asymptotically standard normal, conditionally on the estimated value of $\hat{\theta}$. We use a one-tailed test because the alternative hypothesis is $\sigma^2 > 0$.

$$(13.17)$$

The proposed test statistic applies quite general provided that the generalized residuals can be calculated. It is a score test for neglected heterogeneity when the variance of the heterogeneity is small.

An Illustration of the Test for Unobserved Heterogeneity

As an example of the test for unobserved heterogeneity, we analyze the career trajectories of German men from three birth cohorts. In social mobility research, job-shift rates are hypothesized to decline as a function of time in a job because of job-specific investments in human capital (Mincer 1974). Therefore, a standard continuous-time model for individual career processes would be any model that allows for a monotonic decrease in the rate of leaving a job (Tuma and Hannan 1984; Blossfeld and Hamerle 1987). In the present case, we use a Weibull model to estimate the job-shift rates of German males in the Federal Republic of Germany.

The data are taken from the West German Life History Study (Mayer and Brückner 1989). This data base includes information from 2,171 German respondents from the cohorts of 1929–31, 1939–41, and 1949–51, and is representative of the native-born German population of the Federal Republic of Germany (Mayer and Brückner 1989, Blossfeld 1987). The data were collected retrospectively by asking the respondents to reconstruct, with exact dates, their life histories. Thus, the data provide the almost complete information about career trajectories, because they tell us the timing of all job moves in sequence. In particular the data-base contains information about the month in which each job held by the respondents started and ended.

In this example, the dependent variable is the number of months a man spent in a job before he moved or censoring occurred. The hazard function depends on education (measured in years; see Blossfeld and Hamerle 1987), on prestige of the job (Wegener 1985), on the number of previous jobs, on the employee's general labor force experience at the time a job was entered (measured in months), and on two dummy variables, indicating the membership of the birth cohort (reference group: cohort 1929–31). In the Weibull model the duration t in a job is used as a proxy for job-specific training.

We assume that there are also unobserved variables, which can be summarized in variable v (omitting subscripts for individual observations), which multiplicatively influences the job-shift rate of each person. Because hazard rates must be positive, also v must be positive. Since v is unobserved, it is reasonable to assume that v has a mean of unity (Tuma and Hannan 1984). That is, on average the job-shift rate equals the deterministic function of the included covariates in the Weibull model. The hazard considered is

$$\lambda\,(t|x,v) = v\,\alpha\,t^{\alpha-1}\,\exp(x'\beta)\,, \tag{13.25}$$

Survivor function and probability density are

$$S(t|x,v) = \exp(-v\,\exp(x'\beta)t^{\alpha})\,, \tag{13.26}$$

$$f(t|x,v) = \lambda\,(t|x,v)\,S(t|x,v). \tag{13.27}$$

Assume further that v has an exponential distribution, then multiplying $f(t|x,v)$ by the probability density of the heterogeneity $h(v) = \exp(-v)$ and integrating over all possible values of v gives the density of the observed job-shift rate that is not dependent on the disturbance

$$
\begin{aligned}
f(t|x) &= \alpha t^{\alpha-1}\,\exp(x'\beta)\int_0^{\infty} v\,\exp(-v\,(1\,+\,\exp(x'\beta)t^{\alpha})dv \\
&= \frac{\alpha t^{\alpha-1}\,\exp(x'\beta)}{(1\,+\,\exp(x'\beta)t^{\alpha})^2}\,.
\end{aligned} \tag{13.28}
$$

Notice that the observed job-shift rate has a log-logistic distribution even though each individual's job-shift rate is assumed to be Weibull distributed. Therefore, if there is standard exponentially distributed unobserved heterogeneity in the job-shift model, our proposed test for unobserved heterogeneity should give a significant result for the Weibull model and a nonsignificant result for the log-logistic model.

The parameter estimates for these two models are obtained by means of the algorithm described by Roger and Peacock (1983), using GLIM. The estimates are reported in Table 13.1.

Model 1 in Table 13.1 assumes that the job-shift rate is Weibull distributed. The estimates show that education and the number of previous jobs had a significant and positive effect on the rate of leaving jobs. With increasing education and increasing number of jobs, people are more mobile. Also significant and positive are the effects of the cohort dummies. Each younger cohort shows more mobility than each older one. Significant and negative is the effect of general labor force experience and prestige. That is, the longer the experience and the higher the prestige of the job, the less people move. The duration dependence is also negative, indicating that the longer a person has been in a job the less likely it is that the person will change, presumably because of job-specific investments in human capital. This finding is in accordance with human capital theory (Mincer 1974).

Using our proposed score test, we examine the null hypothesis that there is no neglected heterogeneity in our job-shift model. Estimates of

Table 13.1. Maximum-Likelihood Estimates of the Effects on the Rate of Leaving Jobs[a]

	Model 1 "Weibull Model"	Model 2 "Log-Logistic Model"
Constant	−3.4240	−4.3330
	(0.1433)	(0.1992)
Duration	0.8266	1.2340
	(0.0129)	(0.0195)
Education	0.0715	0.0104
	(0.0145)	(0.0209)
Prestige	−0.0049	−0.0072
	(0.0014)	(0.0019)
Number of previously held jobs	0.1592	0.2661
	(0.0122)	(0.0199)
General labor force experience	−0.0086	−0.0126
	(0.0005)	(0.0006)
Cohort 1939–41	0.1218	0.1244
	(0.0485)	(0.0726)
Cohort 1949–51	0.3325	0.3244
	(0.0530)	(0.0803)
−2log L	5632	3294
Test statistic for unobserved heterogeneity	5.10	2.60

[a]Standard errors in parentheses.

the cumulative hazards of the given Weibull model are easily obtained with SPSS (Blossfeld, Hamerle, Mayer 1986). The asymptotically $N(0;1)$ distributed test statistic is highly significant ($z = 5.11$), indicating that there is unobserved heterogeneity in our job-shift model which may lead to spurious findings.

Model 2 assumes, therefore, that the job-shift rate has a Weibull distribution for any job-person unit, but has a log-logistic distribution within the population, due to an unobserved standard exponentially distributed random term for each person. As Table 13.1 shows, all estimates for the observed covariates have the same sign as in the Weibull model and show the same pattern of statistical significances. The duration dependence is positive, indicating that the rate in the population has a nonmonotonic shape even when each individual's rate is assumed to be declining. This may be seen as an example of the general finding described above, namely, that unobserved heterogeneity creates spurious time dependence in observed transition rates.

However, when the score test for the log-logistic model is again calculated, the test statistic still shows a significant result, although it is much lower than in the Weibull model ($z = 2.60$). In other words, there is still unobserved heterogeneity in our job-shift model. Only a part of the originally neglected heterogeneity could be controlled for by a standard exponential distribution.

This leads us to the question of how to specify the disturbance's distribution in continuous-time hazard rate models. Unfortunately, in most cases there is no theory or prior research that can provide a convincing rationale for specifying any particular distribution of the disturbance (Tuma and Hannan 1984). Moreover, Heckman and Singer (1984) as well as Galler and Poetter (1987), who estimated several models with different assumptions about the distribution of the disturbance, conclude with warnings not to make causal decisions about distributions of the disturbance. We simply need more research on this topic. Nevertheless, given a specific transition rate model to be used in empirical research, our proposed test can at least show whether there is unobserved heterogeneity and whether the estimations are affected by omitted influences. The test statistic, therefore, provides a useful instrument for model evaluation.

Conclusion

In this chapter we have shown how unmeasured heterogeneity can create spurious time dependence in observed transition rates. Because it is often the case in empirical research that important factors cannot not be measured or are ignored, it is very likely that models are misspecified. Unfortunately, to date unobserved heterogeneity could only be estimated using very specialized computer programs, not available to everyone. Our purpose was, therefore, to propose a test for neglected heterogeneity in continuous-time hazard rate models that can be done easily using generally available program packages.

The proposed test for unobserved heterogeneity combines the results of Lancaster (1985), Kiefer (1984), and Burdett et al. (1985). It is a score test appropriate for cases in which the variance of the heterogeneity is small and it can be applied quite generally, provided that the generalized residuals can be calculated.

The test was demonstrated using data on the career trajectories of German males from the German Life History Study. Using a Weibull model, the test for unobserved heterogeneity showed a highly significant result, indicating that there is unobserved heterogeneity. Assuming that this unobserved heterogeneity would have a standard exponential distribution, leading to a log-logistic distribution within the population, we used the test for unobserved heterogeneity again to examine the log-logistic distribution. The test statistic again showed a significant result, although a much lower one than for the Weibull model. Thus, only a part of the originally neglected heterogeneity could be controlled for by a standard exponential distributed random variable.

Although further research is required to investigate how to represent parametrically unobserved heterogeneity in continuous-time hazard rate models, our proposed test for unobserved heterogeneity nevertheless provides a useful first step in evaluating models.

14 *Gerhard Arminger*

Testing against Misspecification in Parametric Rate Models

Misspecification of Models

A crucial issue in the interpretation of results from fitting statistical models to empirical data is the underlying but rarely voiced assumption that the class of models fitted to the data contains the true model of the random mechanism generating the data. If this is not the case, the parameters estimated from a wrong model can easily be heavily biased and lead to wrong conclusions about the nature of relationships and causal mechanism. The main problem in rate models—as in any other regression model such as generalized linear models or covariance structure models—is to use the correct functional form of the rate, especially the dependence on time and on relevant covariates, including functions of explanatory variables and interactions. Since the interpretation of results from model-fitting depends completely on the assumption that a correct model has been estimated, it is desirable to conduct general tests against misspecification without knowing the form of alternative hypotheses. Although such tests have been developed in econometrics (cf. the seminal work of Hausman 1978; White 1980a, 1980b, 1981, 1982; White and Domowitz 1984) for linear and nonlinear regression models as well as for general maximum-likelihood estimation procedures, these tests have rarely been applied, even in the econometric literature. One of the main obstacles to their more frequent use may be the test's reliance on asymptotic theory, whose requisite large sample sizes may be hard to obtain in econometric data sets. However, large samples are quite common in fields such as sociology, psychology, demography, and epidemiology. Here the tests should certainly be applied to prevent researchers from drawing wrong conclusions from their estimates. Since this chapter focuses on parametric rate models, which are usually estimated by maximum-likelihood methods, the tests that White (1982) derived from ML estimation under misspecification will be applied. Weights for Hausman-type tests (Hausman 1978) against inconsistency of parameters will be chosen by considering deviance increments in rate models, which were developed in a companion paper (Arminger 1986).

ML Estimation of Misspecified Models

Before applying the matrix information test of White (1982) and Hausman-type tests to rate models, White's key results (1982) are briefly reviewed. For the results to hold true, the regularity assumptions of White have to be fulfilled and differentiation under the integral sign must be allowed. Let $U_1 \sim 1 \times M, i = 1, \ldots, n$ be independently identically distributed random vectors with true density $g(\mathbf{u})$. The assumed model for the random vector $\mathbf{U}$ is a parameterized family $f(\mathbf{u}, \boldsymbol{\theta})$ of densities dominated by the same measure v as $g(\mathbf{u})$ which we assume to be the Lebesgue measure $\lambda(\mathbf{u})$. $\boldsymbol{\theta}$ is a $p \times 1$ vector. If the model is correctly specified, the family $f(\mathbf{u}, \boldsymbol{\theta})$ contains as an element $g(\mathbf{u}) = f(\mathbf{u}, \boldsymbol{\theta}_0)$.

A quasi-maximum-likelihood (QML) estimator $\hat{\boldsymbol{\theta}}_n$ maximizes the quasi-loglikelihood for a given n

$$L_n(\boldsymbol{\theta}) = \frac{1}{n} \sum_{i=1}^{n} \ln f(\mathbf{u}_i, \boldsymbol{\theta}) \tag{14.1}$$

If $g(\mathbf{u}) = f(\mathbf{u}, \boldsymbol{\theta}_0)$, $L_n(\boldsymbol{\theta})$ is the loglikelihood of the sample. Under suitable regularity assumptions $L_n(\boldsymbol{\theta})$ almost surely converges against the expected value of $\ln f(\mathbf{u}, \boldsymbol{\theta})$, which is $\int \ln f(\mathbf{u}, \boldsymbol{\theta}) g(\mathbf{u}) \, d\lambda (\mathbf{u})$. If $E_g[\ln f(\mathbf{u}, \boldsymbol{\theta})]$ has a unique maximum at $\boldsymbol{\theta}_*$, the QMLE $\hat{\boldsymbol{\theta}}_n$ almost surely converges to $\boldsymbol{\theta}_*$. The last condition is identical to the condition that the Kullback-Leibler information criterion (KLIC), which measures the discrepancy between two densities

$$I(g; f, \boldsymbol{\theta}) = \int \ln \frac{g(\mathbf{u})}{f(\mathbf{u}, \boldsymbol{\theta})} g(\mathbf{u}) \, d\lambda(\mathbf{u}), \tag{14.2}$$

has a unique minimum at $\boldsymbol{\theta}_*$. $\boldsymbol{\theta}_*$ is the value of $\boldsymbol{\theta}$ that minimizes the discrepancy between $g(\mathbf{u})$ and $f(\mathbf{u}, \boldsymbol{\theta})$. Hence, $\hat{\boldsymbol{\theta}}_n$ may also be called the minimum ignorance estimator. The KLIC $I(g; f, \boldsymbol{\theta}) \geq 0$ and is equal to 0 only for $g(\mathbf{u}) = f(\mathbf{u}, \boldsymbol{\theta})$ almost everywhere. Hence, if $g(\mathbf{u}) = f(\mathbf{u}, \boldsymbol{\theta}_0)$, the vector $\boldsymbol{\theta}_*$ that minimizes $I(g; f, \boldsymbol{\theta})$ must be equal to $\boldsymbol{\theta}_0$, and $\boldsymbol{\theta}_n$ converges to $\boldsymbol{\theta}_0$. In this case, $L_n(\boldsymbol{\theta})$ converges towards $E_{\boldsymbol{\theta}_0}[\ln f(\mathbf{u}, \boldsymbol{\theta})]$ and $\hat{\boldsymbol{\theta}}_n$ is the ML estimator converging towards $\boldsymbol{\theta}_0$ if $E_{\boldsymbol{\theta}_0}[\ln f(\mathbf{u}, \boldsymbol{\theta})]$ has a unique maximum at $\boldsymbol{\theta}_0$. The last condition is the classical condition of identifiability in ML estimation.

Even if $g(\mathbf{u}) \neq f(\mathbf{u}, \boldsymbol{\theta}_0)$, $g(\mathbf{u})$ may be parameterized in such a way that $\boldsymbol{\theta}_0$ and $\boldsymbol{\theta}_*$ may be identical in some components. As a simple example consider a normal linear regression model with stochastic regressor matrices $\mathbf{X}_1 \sim n \times p_1$ and $\mathbf{X}_2 \sim n \times p_2$ and dependent vector $\mathbf{y} \sim n \times 1$:

$$\mathbf{y} = \mathbf{X}_1 \boldsymbol{\beta}_1 + \mathbf{X}_2 \boldsymbol{\beta}_2 + \boldsymbol{\epsilon}, \ \boldsymbol{\epsilon} \sim N(\mathbf{O}, \sigma^2 \mathbf{I}) \tag{14.3}$$

The QML estimator $\boldsymbol{\beta}_1$, based only on the misspecified model $\mathbf{y} = \mathbf{X}_1 \boldsymbol{\beta}_1 + \tilde{\boldsymbol{\epsilon}}$, will converge almost surely to

$$\boldsymbol{\beta}_{1*} = \boldsymbol{\beta}_1 + \mathbf{M} \boldsymbol{\beta}_2 \tag{14.4}$$

where $\mathbf{M}$ is the stochastic limit of $(\frac{1}{n} \mathbf{X}_1^T \mathbf{X}_1)^{-1} (\frac{1}{n} \mathbf{X}_1^T \mathbf{X}_2)$. Then $\boldsymbol{\beta}_{1*} = \boldsymbol{\beta}_1$ only if either $\boldsymbol{\beta}_2 = \mathbf{0}$ (no misspecification!) or if the stochastic limit of $\frac{1}{n} \mathbf{X}_1^T \mathbf{X}_2 = \mathbf{0}$, that is, if $\mathbf{X}_1$ and $\mathbf{X}_2$ are orthogonal. Although $\boldsymbol{\beta}_1$ will be correctly estimated in the second case, the model will still be misspecified, yielding inconsistent estimates not for $\boldsymbol{\beta}_1$ but for σ^2 through the heteroskedasticity introduced by $\mathbf{X}_2 \boldsymbol{\beta}_2$. This example shows why one is interested in tests against general misspecification as well as tests against inconsistency of certain parameters of special relevance.

Assuming almost sure convergence of $\hat{\boldsymbol{\theta}}_n$ towards $\boldsymbol{\theta}_*$ and suitable regularity conditions to ensure asymptotic normality, the asymptotic covariance matrix is derived by a Taylor expansion about $\boldsymbol{\theta}_*$:

$$\frac{\partial L_n(\hat{\boldsymbol{\theta}})}{\partial \boldsymbol{\theta}} = \frac{\partial L_n(\boldsymbol{\theta}_*)}{\partial \boldsymbol{\theta}} + \frac{\partial^2 L_n(\bar{\boldsymbol{\theta}})}{\partial \boldsymbol{\theta} \, \partial \boldsymbol{\theta}^T} (\hat{\boldsymbol{\theta}} - \boldsymbol{\theta}_*), \text{ where}$$

$\hat{\boldsymbol{\theta}}$ is the QML estimator, and

$\hat{\boldsymbol{\theta}} \in l(\hat{\boldsymbol{\theta}}, \boldsymbol{\theta}_*)$ with $l(\hat{\boldsymbol{\theta}}, \boldsymbol{\theta}_*)$ denoting the line

segment between $\hat{\boldsymbol{\theta}}$ and $\boldsymbol{\theta}_*$. $\tag{14.5}$

Since $\partial L_n(\hat{\boldsymbol{\theta}}/\partial \boldsymbol{\theta}) = \mathbf{0}$, multiplication by $\sqrt{n}$ yields:

$$\sqrt{n}\,(\hat{\boldsymbol{\theta}} - \boldsymbol{\theta}_*) = -\left(\frac{\partial^2 L_n(\tilde{\boldsymbol{\theta}})}{\partial\boldsymbol{\theta}\,\partial\boldsymbol{\theta}^T}\right)^{-1} \times \sqrt{n}\left(\frac{\partial L_n(\boldsymbol{\theta}_*)}{\partial\boldsymbol{\theta}}\right) \tag{14.6}$$

$\boldsymbol{\theta}_*$ minimizes the KLIC $I[g; f(\mathbf{u}, \boldsymbol{\theta})]$ or, equivalently, maximizes E_g (ln $f(\mathbf{u}, \boldsymbol{\theta})$). Hence, one finds for the expected value and the covariance matrix of the score function:

$$E_g(\sqrt{n}\,\frac{\partial L_n(\boldsymbol{\theta}_*)}{\partial\boldsymbol{\theta}}) = \frac{1}{\sqrt{n}} \sum_{1=1}^{n} \int \frac{\partial \ln f(\mathbf{u}, \boldsymbol{\theta}_*)}{\partial\boldsymbol{\theta}}\, g(\mathbf{u})\, d\lambda\,(\mathbf{u})$$

$$= \frac{1}{\sqrt{n}} \sum_{i=1}^{n} \frac{\partial}{\partial\boldsymbol{\theta}}\, E_g\,[\ln f(\mathbf{u}, \boldsymbol{\theta}_*)] = \mathbf{0} \tag{14.7}$$

$$V(\sqrt{n}\,\frac{\partial L_n(\boldsymbol{\theta}_*)}{\partial\boldsymbol{\theta}}) = \frac{1}{n} \sum_{i=1}^{n} \int \frac{\partial \ln f(\mathbf{u}, \boldsymbol{\theta}_*)}{\partial\boldsymbol{\theta}} \frac{\partial \ln f(\mathbf{u}, \boldsymbol{\theta}_*)}{\partial\boldsymbol{\theta}^T}\, g(\mathbf{u})\, d\lambda\,(\mathbf{u})$$

$$= \int \frac{\partial \ln f(\mathbf{u}, \boldsymbol{\theta}_*)}{\partial\boldsymbol{\theta}} \frac{\partial \ln f(\mathbf{u}, \boldsymbol{\theta}_*)}{\partial\boldsymbol{\theta}^T}\, g(\mathbf{u})\, d\lambda\,(\mathbf{u}) \equiv \mathbf{B}(\boldsymbol{\theta}_*) \tag{14.8}$$

Since $\hat{\boldsymbol{\theta}}_n$ converges to $\boldsymbol{\theta}_*$, the observed information matrix in $\tilde{\boldsymbol{\theta}} \in l(\boldsymbol{\theta}, \boldsymbol{\theta}_*)$ converges to the expected information matrix:

$$\frac{\partial^2(L_n(\tilde{\boldsymbol{\theta}}))}{\partial\boldsymbol{\theta}\,\partial\boldsymbol{\theta}^T} = \frac{1}{n} \sum_{i=1}^{n} \frac{\partial^2 \ln f(\mathbf{u}, \tilde{\boldsymbol{\theta}})}{\partial\boldsymbol{\theta}\,\partial\boldsymbol{\theta}^T} \xrightarrow{a.s.} \int \frac{\partial^2 \ln f(\mathbf{u}, \boldsymbol{\theta}^*)}{\partial\boldsymbol{\theta}\,\partial\boldsymbol{\theta}^T}\, g(\mathbf{u})\, d\lambda(\mathbf{u}) \equiv \mathbf{A}(\boldsymbol{\theta}_*)$$
$$\tag{14.9}$$

The main result of this section is the finding that the relation $\mathbf{A}(\boldsymbol{\theta}_*) = -\mathbf{B}(\boldsymbol{\theta}_*)$ holds true if $g(\mathbf{u}) = f(\mathbf{u}, \boldsymbol{\theta}_0)$, for example if the model is correctly specified. This result is obtained immediately by differentiating $\partial ln\, f(\mathbf{u}, \boldsymbol{\theta})/\partial\boldsymbol{\theta}$ with respect to $\boldsymbol{\theta}$ and computing the expected value.

$$E_g\left[\frac{\partial^2 \ln f(\mathbf{u}, \boldsymbol{\theta})}{\partial\boldsymbol{\theta}\,\partial\boldsymbol{\theta}^2}\right] = \int\int\left[\frac{\partial^2 f(\mathbf{u}, \boldsymbol{\theta})}{\partial\boldsymbol{\theta}\,\partial\boldsymbol{\theta}^T} f(\mathbf{u}, \boldsymbol{\theta}) - \frac{\partial f(\mathbf{u}, \boldsymbol{\theta})}{\partial\boldsymbol{\theta}} \frac{\partial f(\mathbf{u}, \boldsymbol{\theta})}{\partial\boldsymbol{\theta}^T}\right]$$
$$f(\mathbf{u}, \boldsymbol{\theta})^{-2}\, g(\mathbf{u})\, d\lambda(\mathbf{u}) \tag{14.10}$$

The integral

$$\int \frac{\partial^2 f(\mathbf{u}, \boldsymbol{\theta})}{\partial\boldsymbol{\theta}\,\partial\boldsymbol{\theta}^T} f(\mathbf{u}, \boldsymbol{\theta})^{-1}\, g(\mathbf{u})\, d\lambda(\mathbf{u}) \tag{14.11}$$

will be 0 if $g(\mathbf{u}) = f(\mathbf{u}, \boldsymbol{\theta}_0)$, with $\boldsymbol{\theta} = \boldsymbol{\theta}_0$.

Hence, in general the vector $\sqrt{n}\,(\hat{\boldsymbol{\theta}}_n - \boldsymbol{\theta}_*)$ will be asymptotically normally distributed with asymptotic covariance matrix $\Sigma(\theta_*) = A(\theta_*)^{-1}B(\theta_*)A(\theta_*)^{-1}$, which is simplified by $A(\theta_*) = -B(\theta_*)$, if the model is correctly specified. In practice $A(\theta_*)$, $B(\theta_*)$ will be consistently estimated by

$$B_n(\hat{\theta}) = \frac{1}{n}\sum_{i=1}^{n}\left(\frac{\partial \ln f(u_i, \hat{\theta})}{\partial \theta}\right)\left(\frac{\partial \ln f(u_i, \hat{\theta})}{\partial \theta^T}\right) \qquad (14.12)$$

$$A_n(\hat{\theta}) = \frac{1}{n}\sum_{i=1}^{n}\frac{\partial^2 \ln f(u_i, \hat{\theta})}{\partial \theta\, \partial \theta^T} \qquad (14.13)$$

The result that $A(\theta_*) = -B(\theta_*)$ only if no misspecification is present is the basis of White's (1982) information matrix test against general misspecification. For the construction of a test against parameter inconsistency the following results about QML estimation with weights are useful.

Assume now that $U_i = (Y, X)_i$ with true density $\tilde{g}(y_i, x_i) = g(y_i|x_i)\, p(x_i)$ and supposed density $\tilde{f}(y_i, x_i) = f(y_i|x_i, \theta)\, p(x_i)$, both of which are dominated by the Lebesgue measure. $p(x_i)$ is a nonspecified, nondegenerate density. Assume further a positive normed weight function dependent on X only with $\int w(x)p(x)d\lambda(x) = 1$.

Now consider the kernel of the unweighted and the weighted quasi-loglikelihood functions, which are maximized with respect to θ.

$$k_n(\theta) = \frac{1}{n}\sum_{i=1}^{n}\ln f(y_i|x_i, \theta) \xrightarrow{a.s.} \int\int \ln f(y|x, \theta)\, g(y|x)\, d\lambda(y)\, p(x)\, d\lambda(x) \qquad (14.14)$$

$$\tilde{k}_n(\theta) = \frac{1}{n}\sum_{i=1}^{n} w(x_i)\ln f(y_i|x_i, \theta)$$
$$\xrightarrow{a.s.} \int\int \ln f(y|x, \theta)\, g(y|x)\, d\lambda(y)\, p(x)\, w(x)\, d\lambda(x) \qquad (14.15)$$

If the true structure $g(y|x)$ equals $f(y|x, \theta_0)$, then both limits are maximized at θ_0 for any weight function $w(x)$.

However, if the true structure $g(y|x)$ is not a member of the family $f(y|x, \theta)$ the limits will be maximized at different points θ_* and θ_{**} unless the functions $p(x)$ and $p(x)w(x)$ are both members of the subspace of functions that is orthogonal to the function

$$h(\mathbf{x}, \boldsymbol{\theta}_*) = \int \frac{\partial \ln f(\mathbf{y}|\mathbf{x}, \boldsymbol{\theta})}{\partial \boldsymbol{\theta}} g(\mathbf{y}|\mathbf{x}) \, d\lambda(\mathbf{y}) \tag{14.16}$$

with regard to the inner product

$$< h(\mathbf{x}, \boldsymbol{\theta}_*), p(\mathbf{x}) > \, = \int h(\mathbf{x}, \boldsymbol{\theta}_*) \, p(\mathbf{x}) \, d\lambda(\mathbf{x}). \tag{14.17}$$

The difference between the unweighted estimator $\hat{\boldsymbol{\theta}}_n$ for $\boldsymbol{\theta}_*$ and the weighted estimator $\tilde{\boldsymbol{\theta}}_n$ for $\boldsymbol{\theta}_{**}$ forms the basis of a Hausman-type test (Hausman 1978, White 1982).

Testing against Misspecification

White's Information Matrix Test

If the model is not misspecified—that is, $g(\mathbf{u}) = f(\mathbf{u}, \boldsymbol{\theta}_0)$—the matrix $\mathbf{A}(\boldsymbol{\theta}_0) = -\mathbf{B}(\boldsymbol{\theta}_0)$, or alternatively $\mathbf{A}(\boldsymbol{\theta}_0) + \mathbf{B}(\boldsymbol{\theta}_0) = \mathbf{0}$. To construct a test of the Wald type, the following notation is used. The symbol *lowtri* stands for the operation of stacking the lower triangular of a symmetric matrix in a column vector. If $\mathbf{A} = (a_i)$ $i, j, = 1, \ldots, p$, then *lowtri* $\mathbf{A} = (a_{11}, a_{21}, a_{22}, a_{31}, \ldots, a_{pp-1}, a_{pp})^T$ will have $q = p(p + 1)/2$ elements.

$$\mathbf{d}(\mathbf{u}_i, \hat{\boldsymbol{\theta}}_n) \sim q \times 1 =$$
$$lowtri \left[\left(\frac{\partial \ln f(\mathbf{u}_i, \hat{\boldsymbol{\theta}}_n)}{\partial \boldsymbol{\theta}} \right) \left(\frac{\partial \ln f(\mathbf{u}_i, \hat{\boldsymbol{\theta}}_n)}{\partial \boldsymbol{\theta}^T} \right) + \frac{\partial^2 \ln f(\mathbf{u}_i, \hat{\boldsymbol{\theta}}_n)}{\partial \boldsymbol{\vartheta} \, \partial \boldsymbol{\theta}^T} \right] \tag{14.18}$$

$$\mathbf{D}_n(\hat{\boldsymbol{\theta}}_n) = \frac{1}{n} \sum_{i=1}^{n} \mathbf{d}(\mathbf{u}_i, \hat{\boldsymbol{\theta}}_n) \tag{14.19}$$

$$\mathbf{D}(\boldsymbol{\theta}_*) = \int \mathbf{d}(\mathbf{u}, \boldsymbol{\theta}_*) \, g(\mathbf{u}) \, d\lambda(\mathbf{u}) \tag{14.20}$$

A Taylor expansion about $\boldsymbol{\theta}_*$ yields

$$\sqrt{n} \, \mathbf{D}_n(\hat{\boldsymbol{\theta}}_n) = \sqrt{n} \, \mathbf{D}_n(\boldsymbol{\theta}_*) + \nabla \mathbf{D}_n(\tilde{\boldsymbol{\theta}}) \sqrt{n} \, (\hat{\boldsymbol{\theta}}_n - \boldsymbol{\theta}_*), \tag{14.21}$$

with

$$\nabla \mathbf{D}_n(\tilde{\boldsymbol{\theta}}) = \frac{1}{n} \sum_{i=1}^{n} \frac{\partial}{\partial \boldsymbol{\theta}} [\mathbf{d}(\mathbf{u}_i, \tilde{\boldsymbol{\theta}})] \sim q \times q, \tag{14.22}$$

with $\tilde{\boldsymbol{\theta}}$ an element of the line segment $l(\hat{\boldsymbol{\theta}}_n, \boldsymbol{\theta}_*)$. Using the expansion of equation 14.6 and equation 14.13 one finds

$$\sqrt{n}\ \mathbf{D}_n(\hat{\boldsymbol{\theta}}_n) = -[\mathbf{A}_n\ (\tilde{\tilde{\boldsymbol{\theta}}})]^{-1}\ \frac{1}{\sqrt{n}}\ \sum_{i=1}^{n}\ \frac{\partial\ \ln\ f(\mathbf{u}_i,\ \boldsymbol{\theta}_*)}{\partial\boldsymbol{\theta}} \qquad (14.23)$$

with $\tilde{\tilde{\boldsymbol{\theta}}}$ an element of the line segment $l(\hat{\boldsymbol{\theta}}_n,\ \boldsymbol{\theta}_*)$. Combining equations 14.21, 14.22, and 14.23 gives the result

$$\sqrt{n}\ \mathbf{D}_n(\hat{\boldsymbol{\theta}}_n) = \frac{1}{\sqrt{n}}\ \sum_{i=1}^{n}\ \left[\mathbf{d}(\mathbf{u}_i,\ \boldsymbol{\theta}_*) - \nabla\mathbf{D}_n\ (\tilde{\boldsymbol{\theta}})\mathbf{A}_n\ (\tilde{\tilde{\boldsymbol{\theta}}})^{-1}\ \frac{\partial\ \ln\ f(\mathbf{u}_i,\ \boldsymbol{\theta}^*)}{\partial\boldsymbol{\theta}}\right] \qquad (14.24)$$

With $\mathbf{D}_n(\hat{\boldsymbol{\theta}}_n)$ and $\mathbf{A}_n(\tilde{\tilde{\boldsymbol{\theta}}})$ almost surely converging against $\mathbf{D}(\boldsymbol{\theta}_*)$ and $\mathbf{A}(\boldsymbol{\theta}_*)$, the asymptotic second moment matrix of $\sqrt{n}\ \mathbf{D}_n(\hat{\boldsymbol{\theta}}_n)$ is given by $\mathbf{M}(\boldsymbol{\theta}_*)$:

$$\mathbf{M}(\boldsymbol{\theta}_*) = E_g\{[\mathbf{d}(\mathbf{u},\ \boldsymbol{\theta}_*) - \nabla\mathbf{D}(\boldsymbol{\theta}_*)\ \mathbf{A}(\boldsymbol{\theta}_*)^{-1}\ \frac{\partial\ \ln\ f(\mathbf{u},\ \boldsymbol{\theta}_*)}{\partial\boldsymbol{\theta}}]$$

$$\times\ [\mathbf{d}(\mathbf{u},\ \boldsymbol{\theta}_*) - \nabla\mathbf{D}(\boldsymbol{\theta}_*)\ \mathbf{A}(\boldsymbol{\theta}_*)^{-1}\ \frac{\partial\ \ln\ f(\mathbf{u},\boldsymbol{\theta}_*)}{\partial\boldsymbol{\theta}}]^T\} \qquad (14.25)$$

$\mathbf{M}(\boldsymbol{\theta}_*)$ is consistently estimated by

$$\mathbf{M}_n(\hat{\boldsymbol{\theta}}_n) = \frac{1}{n}\ \sum_{i=1}^{n}\ \{[\mathbf{d}(\mathbf{u}_i,\ \hat{\boldsymbol{\theta}}_n) - \nabla\mathbf{D}_n(\hat{\boldsymbol{\theta}}_n)\ \mathbf{A}_n(\hat{\boldsymbol{\theta}})^{-1}\ \frac{\partial\ \ln\ f(\mathbf{u}_i,\ \hat{\boldsymbol{\theta}}_n)}{\partial\boldsymbol{\theta}}]$$

$$\times\ [\mathbf{d}(\mathbf{u}_i,\ \hat{\boldsymbol{\theta}}_n) - \nabla\mathbf{D}_n(\hat{\boldsymbol{\theta}}_n)\ \mathbf{A}_n(\hat{\boldsymbol{\theta}}_n)^{-1}\ \frac{\partial\ \ln\ f(\mathbf{u}_i,\ \hat{\boldsymbol{\theta}}_n)}{\partial\boldsymbol{\theta}}]^T\} \qquad (14.26)$$

If the model is not misspecified, the expected value of $\sqrt{n}\ \mathbf{D}_n(\hat{\boldsymbol{\theta}}_n) = \sqrt{n}\ \mathbf{D}(\boldsymbol{\theta}_0) = \mathbf{0}$ and the matrix $\mathbf{M}(\boldsymbol{\theta}_0)$ will be the asymptotic covariance matrix of $\sqrt{n}\ \mathbf{D}_n(\hat{\boldsymbol{\theta}}_n)$. The central result of White (1982) is the asymptotic normal distribution of $\sqrt{n}\ \mathbf{D}_n(\hat{\boldsymbol{\theta}}_n)$ and hence the central chi square distribution of the Wald statistic:

$$W_n = n\mathbf{D}_n(\hat{\boldsymbol{\theta}}_n)^T[\mathbf{M}_n(\hat{\boldsymbol{\theta}}_n)]^{-1}\ \mathbf{D}_n(\hat{\boldsymbol{\theta}}_n), \qquad (14.27)$$

with q degrees of freedom if the model is correctly specified. A necessary condition for the Wald statistic to exist is the nonsingularity of $\mathbf{M}_n(\hat{\boldsymbol{\theta}}_n)$, which can in practice always be ensured by deleting linear dependent rows and columns in $\mathbf{M}_n(\hat{\boldsymbol{\theta}}_n)$ and the corresponding rows in $\mathbf{D}_n(\boldsymbol{\theta}_n)$ and by reducing the degrees in freedom accordingly.

The Wald statistic is very cumbersome to compute because of the third derivatives of the quasi-loglikelihood function in the asymptotic covariance matrix $\mathbf{M}(\boldsymbol{\theta}_*)$. However, Lancaster (1984) has shown a way to estimate $\mathbf{M}(\boldsymbol{\theta}_*)$ without computing third derivatives if the model is correctly specified. Let $\hat{\mathbf{Z}}_1$ denote the $n \times q$ matrix with $\hat{\mathbf{z}}_{i1} = \mathbf{d}(\mathbf{u}_i, \hat{\boldsymbol{\theta}}_n)^T$, $i = 1, \ldots, n$, and let $\hat{\mathbf{Z}}_2$ denote the $n \times p$ matrix of first derivatives with $\hat{\mathbf{z}}_{i2} = \partial \ln f(\mathbf{u}_i, \hat{\boldsymbol{\theta}}_n)/\partial \boldsymbol{\theta}^T$, $i = 1, \ldots, n$. Lancaster's main result is that $\mathbf{M}(\boldsymbol{\theta}_*)$ may be estimated by

$$\mathbf{V}_n(\hat{\boldsymbol{\theta}}_n) = n^{-1}[\hat{\mathbf{Z}}_1^T\hat{\mathbf{Z}}_1 - \hat{\mathbf{Z}}_1\hat{\mathbf{Z}}_2(\hat{\mathbf{Z}}_2^T\hat{\mathbf{Z}}_2)^{-1}\hat{\mathbf{Z}}_2^T\hat{\mathbf{Z}}_1] \tag{14.28}$$

Since $\mathbf{D}_n(\hat{\boldsymbol{\theta}}_n) = n^{-1}\mathbf{1}^T\hat{\mathbf{Z}}_1$ with $\mathbf{1} \sim n \times 1$ a vector of ones, the statistic of equation 14.27 may be written as

$$W_n = n^{-1} \mathbf{1}^T\hat{\mathbf{Z}}_1[\mathbf{V}_n(\hat{\boldsymbol{\theta}}_n)]^{-1}\hat{\mathbf{Z}}_1^T\mathbf{1} \tag{14.29}$$

$$= \mathbf{1}^T\hat{\mathbf{Z}}_1[\hat{\mathbf{Z}}_1^T\mathbf{Z}_1 - \hat{\mathbf{Z}}_1\hat{\mathbf{Z}}_2(\hat{\mathbf{Z}}_2^T\hat{\mathbf{Z}}_2)^{-1}\hat{\mathbf{Z}}_2^T\hat{\mathbf{Z}}_1]^{-1}\hat{\mathbf{Z}}_1^T\mathbf{1} \tag{14.30}$$

which is easily computed by regressing $\hat{\mathbf{Z}}_1$ against $\hat{\mathbf{Z}}_2$ and inverting the SSE matrix $n\mathbf{V}_n(\hat{\boldsymbol{\theta}}_n)$. As pointed out above, White's information matrix test is a test against general misspecification. If the hypothesis of no misspecification is rejected, at least the usual ML covariance estimators $-\mathbf{A}_n(\hat{\boldsymbol{\theta}}_n)^{-1}$ or $\mathbf{B}(\hat{\boldsymbol{\theta}}_n)^{-1}$ will not be consistent estimators of the covariance matrix of parameters $\hat{\boldsymbol{\theta}}_n$. Inconsistency of the QMLE for parameters of interest may also be implied. However, as shown before in the context of a simple regression model, model misspecification in some of the parameters of the model does not necessarily result in inconsistent estimation of the parameters of interest. To detect inconsistency of parameter estimates, tests of the Hausman type (Hausman 1978, White 1982) are used.

Hausman Tests with Weight Functions

As shown earlier in this chapter, the unweighted and the weighted QML estimators $\hat{\boldsymbol{\theta}}_n$ and $\tilde{\boldsymbol{\theta}}_n$ are both consistent estimators of $\boldsymbol{\theta}_0$, if the model is correctly specified. However, if the model is misspecified, the QML and the weighted QML estimator will generally diverge. Let $\hat{\boldsymbol{\theta}}_n$ and $\tilde{\boldsymbol{\theta}}_n$ be the QML estimates maximizing the quasi-loglikelihood functions of equations 14.14 and 14.15. Assuming that the weight function $w(\mathbf{x})$ is nonorthogonal in the sense of equation 14.16, the probability limits $\boldsymbol{\theta}_*$ of $\hat{\boldsymbol{\theta}}_n$ and $\boldsymbol{\theta}_{**}$ of $\tilde{\boldsymbol{\theta}}_n$ will not be equal, unless $g(\mathbf{y}|\mathbf{x})$ is an element of the family $f(\mathbf{y}|\mathbf{x}, \boldsymbol{\theta})$. Hence one should consider the difference $(\tilde{\boldsymbol{\theta}}_n - \hat{\boldsymbol{\theta}}_n)$, which almost surely converges to $\theta_{**} - \theta_*$, which is 0 only if both $\bar{\theta}_n$ and $\hat{\theta}_n$ are consistent estimators of 0.

The asymptotic distribution of $(\bar{\theta}_n - \hat{\theta}_n)$ is derived by looking at the joint distribution of $(\hat{\theta}_n - \theta_*)$ and $(\bar{\theta}_n - \theta_{**})$. A Taylor expansion about θ_* and θ_{**}, in analogy to equations 14.5 and 14.6, yields with $p_i(\theta) = \partial \ln f(y_i|x_i, \theta)/\partial\theta \sim p \times 1$ and $Q_i(\theta) = \partial^2 \ln f(y_i|x_i, \theta)/\partial\theta \, \partial\theta^T \sim p \times p$:

$$\begin{bmatrix} \sqrt{n}\,(\hat{\theta}_n - \theta_*) \\[2ex] \sqrt{n}\,(\bar{\theta}_n - \theta_{**}) \end{bmatrix} = \begin{bmatrix} -[\frac{1}{n} \sum_i Q_i(\tilde{\theta})]^{-1} \frac{1}{\sqrt{n}} \sum_i p_i(\theta_*) \\[2ex] -[\frac{1}{n} \sum_i Q_i(\tilde{\tilde{\theta}})w(x_i)]^{-1} \frac{1}{\sqrt{n}} p_i(\theta_{**})w(x_i) \end{bmatrix} \quad (14.31)$$

with $\theta \in l(\hat{\theta}_n, \theta_*)$ and $\tilde{\tilde{\theta}} \in l(\bar{\theta}_n, \theta_{**})$. If we assume that the following means converge almost surely to their limits, given by:

$$A_n(\tilde{\theta}) = \frac{1}{n} \sum_i Q_i(\tilde{\theta}) \xrightarrow{a.s.} E_g[Q_i(\theta_*)] = A(\theta_*) \qquad 14.32$$

$$B_n(\theta_*) = \frac{1}{n} \sum_i p_i(\theta_*)p_i(\theta_*)^T \xrightarrow{a.s.} E_g[p_i(\theta_*)p_i(\theta_*)^T] = B(\theta_*) \qquad (14.33)$$

$$G_n(\tilde{\theta}) = \frac{1}{n} \sum_i Q_i(\tilde{\tilde{\theta}})w(x_i) \xrightarrow{a.s.} E_g[Q_i(\theta_{**})w(x)] = G(\theta_{**}) \qquad (14.34)$$

$$H_n(\theta) = \frac{1}{n} \sum_i p_i(\theta_{**})p_i(\theta_{**})^T w(x_i)^2 \xrightarrow{a.s.} E_g[p_i(\theta_{**})p_i(\theta_{**})^T w(x_i)^2] = H(\theta_{**})$$

$$(14.35)$$

$$R_n(\tilde{\theta}, \tilde{\tilde{\theta}}) = \frac{1}{n} \sum_i p_i(\tilde{\theta})p_i(\tilde{\tilde{\theta}})^T w(x_i) \xrightarrow{a.s.} E_g[p_i(\theta_*)p_i(\theta_{**})^T w(x_i)] = R(\theta_*, \theta_{**}),$$

$$(14.36)$$

then the asymptotic covariance matrix of the vector $\sqrt{n}[(\hat{\theta}_n - \theta_*)^T,$ $(\bar{\theta}_n - \theta_*)^T]^T$ is given by

$$K(\theta_*, \theta_{**}) = \begin{bmatrix} A(\theta_*)^{-1} B(\theta_*)A(\theta_*)^{-1}, & A(\theta_*)^{-1} R(\theta_*, \theta_{**})G(\theta_{**})^{-1} \\ G(\theta_*)^{-1} R(\theta_*, \theta_{**})^T A(\theta_*)^{-1}, & G(\theta_{**})^{-1} H(\theta_{**})^{-1} G(\theta_{**})^{-1} \end{bmatrix}$$

$$(14.37)$$

Hence, the difference $\sqrt{n}(\bar{\theta}_n - \hat{\theta}_n)$ will asymptotically follow a normal distribution with expected value $\sqrt{n}(\theta_{**} - \theta_*)$ and covariance matrix $V(\theta_{**}, \theta_*)$.

$$V(\boldsymbol{\theta}_{**}, \boldsymbol{\theta}_*) = G(\boldsymbol{\theta}_{**})^{-1} H(\boldsymbol{\theta}_{**})G(\boldsymbol{\theta}_{**})^{-1} + A(\boldsymbol{\theta}_*)^{-1} B(\boldsymbol{\theta}_*)A(\boldsymbol{\theta}_*)^{-1}$$
$$- G(\boldsymbol{\theta}_{**})^{-1} R(\boldsymbol{\theta}_*, \boldsymbol{\theta}_{**})^T A(\boldsymbol{\theta}_*)^{-1} - A(\boldsymbol{\theta}_*)^{-1} R(\boldsymbol{\theta}_*, \boldsymbol{\theta}_{**})G(\boldsymbol{\theta}_{**})^{-1} \quad (14.38)$$

$V(\boldsymbol{\theta}_{**}, \boldsymbol{\theta}_*)$ is estimated consistently by substituting $A_n(\hat{\boldsymbol{\theta}}_n)$, $B_n(\hat{\boldsymbol{\theta}}_n)$, $G_n(\tilde{\boldsymbol{\theta}}_n)$, $H_n(\tilde{\boldsymbol{\theta}}_n)$ and $R(\hat{\boldsymbol{\theta}}_n, \tilde{\boldsymbol{\theta}}_n)$ into their expected values. As shown by White (1982), the Hausman statistic

$$h_n = n(\tilde{\boldsymbol{\theta}}_n - \hat{\boldsymbol{\theta}}_n)^T V(\tilde{\boldsymbol{\theta}}_n, \hat{\boldsymbol{\theta}}_n)^{-1} (\tilde{\boldsymbol{\theta}}_n - \hat{\boldsymbol{\theta}}_n) \quad (14.39)$$

will follow a central chi square distribution with p degrees of freedom, if the model is not misspecified in the sense, that $\tilde{\boldsymbol{\theta}}_n$ and $\hat{\boldsymbol{\theta}}_n$ estimate consistently $\boldsymbol{\theta}_0$. Since the covariance matrix is cumbersome to compute from equations 14.33 to 14.36, it may be useful to estimate V in equation 14.38 by applying Lemma 2.1 of Hausman (1978). If the model is correctly specified (that is, if $g(y|x) = f(y|x, \boldsymbol{\theta}_0)$, then $\sqrt{n}(\hat{\boldsymbol{\theta}}_n - \boldsymbol{\theta}_0) \overset{\Delta}{\sim} N(O, B(\boldsymbol{\theta}_0)^{-1})$, and $\sqrt{n}(\tilde{\boldsymbol{\theta}}_n - \boldsymbol{\theta}_0) \overset{\Delta}{\sim} N(O, H(\boldsymbol{\theta}_0)^{-1})$. If the model is not misspecified, $\hat{\boldsymbol{\theta}}_n$ will be the ML estimator attaining the asymptotic Rao-Cramér bound for the covariance matrix of $\sqrt{n}(\tilde{\boldsymbol{\theta}}_n - \boldsymbol{\theta}_0)$. The covariance matrix $H(\boldsymbol{\theta}_0)$ will be greater than $B(\boldsymbol{\theta}_0)$ and $H(\boldsymbol{\theta}_0) - B(\boldsymbol{\theta}_0)$ will be positive semi-definite. On the other hand, it may be shown that the difference $\sqrt{n} \, \hat{q}_n = \sqrt{n}(\tilde{\boldsymbol{\theta}}_n - \hat{\boldsymbol{\theta}}_n)$ is uncorrelated with $\sqrt{n}(\hat{\boldsymbol{\theta}}_n - \boldsymbol{\theta}_0)$. Hence for the covariance matrix of $\sqrt{n} \, \hat{q}_n$, which is denoted by $V(\sqrt{n} \, \hat{q}_n)$, we find that

$$\sqrt{n}(\tilde{\boldsymbol{\theta}}_n - \boldsymbol{\theta}_0) = \sqrt{n}(\hat{\boldsymbol{\theta}}_n - \boldsymbol{\theta}_0) + \sqrt{n} \, \hat{q}_n \quad (14.40)$$

$$H(\boldsymbol{\theta}_0)^{-1} = B(\boldsymbol{\theta}_0)^{-1} + V(\sqrt{n} \, \hat{q}_n) \quad (14.41)$$

Hence, a simple test statistic is given by

$$h_n = n(\tilde{\boldsymbol{\theta}}_n - \hat{\boldsymbol{\theta}}_n)^T [H_n(\tilde{\boldsymbol{\theta}}_n)^{-1} - B(\hat{\boldsymbol{\theta}})^{-1}] (\tilde{\boldsymbol{\theta}}_n - \hat{\boldsymbol{\theta}}_n) \quad (14.42)$$

While the matrix in equation 14.38 is always estimated by a positive definite matrix, the positive definiteness of the estimated covariance matrix in equation 14.42 depends crucially on the correct specification of the model. Hence, if the model is misspecified, empirical researchers will often find the estimated covariance matrix will not be positive definite.

The power of a Hausman test depends primarily on the weight function $w(x)$. As Hausman (1978) and White (1982) point out, the weights should be chosen in such a way that the difference $(\boldsymbol{\theta}_{**} - \boldsymbol{\theta}_*)$ is large if misspecification is present. One intuitively expects such a behavior if the weights are chosen inversely to the fit of the model. Data points that are fitted well should be given low weights and points that are fitted badly should have high weights. The choice of such weights is discussed in the next section within the context of parametric rate models.

Application to Parametric Rate Models

Let T_i, $i = 1, \ldots, n$ be continuous independent random variables describing length of time until an event occurs. The density of the event times is characterized by the transition $r_i(t_i)$, which is parameterized in $\boldsymbol{\beta} \sim p \times 1$ with explanatory variables x_i (cf. Kalbfleisch and Prentice 1980, Tuma and Hannan 1984). Here only the most simple case of a single event is considered, which may readily be generalized to repeated events. The starting value of T_i is set to 0.

$$r_i(t_i) \quad = g(t_i, \boldsymbol{\beta}) \geq 0 \text{ (parametric rate model)} \qquad (14.43)$$

$$S_i(t_i) \quad = \exp(-\int_0^t r_i(\tau) \, d\tau) \text{ (survivor function)} \qquad (14.44)$$

$$f(t_i|r_i(t_i)) = r_i(t_i)S_i(t_i) \text{ (density function)} \qquad (14.45)$$

Maximum likelihood estimators of $\boldsymbol{\beta}$ are computed by maximizing the loglikelihood function with respect to $\boldsymbol{\beta}$ by taking into account the effect of right censoring. The individual loglikelihood $L_i(\boldsymbol{\beta}|t_i)$ is given by:

$$L_i(\boldsymbol{\beta}|t_i) = c_i \ln r_i(t_i) - \int_0^{t_i} r_i(\tau)d\tau, \qquad (14.46)$$

with

$$c_i = \begin{cases} 1 \text{ if } t_i \text{ is the time of an event} \\ 0 \text{ if } T_i \text{ is censored at } t_i \end{cases}$$

To apply the tests discussed in the previous section, one has to compute the first and second derivatives of $L_i(\boldsymbol{\beta}|t_i)$ with respect to $\boldsymbol{\beta}$ for the unweighted as well as the weighted loglikelihood functions. The weights may be chosen by considering that the deviance increments d_i discussed in the companion paper (Arminger 1986) are good indicators of the fit of the model for the individual data points. The formula for the deviance increments is given by:

$$d_i = 2[c_i(\ln t_i^{-1} - 1)] - c_i \ln \hat{r}_i(t_i) + \int_0^{t_i} \hat{r}_i(\tau) \, d\tau, \qquad (14.47)$$

with $\hat{r}_i(t_i)$ as the ML estimate of $r_i(t_i)$ from the unweighted loglikelihood function.

Since the weights should be functions of the explanatory variables x_i and not of the dependent variable, the deviance increments d_i may either be thought of as prior weights or may be considered as functions of x_i. Using an argument analogous to White (1980a, 1980b), the deviance increments are regressed on a vector of ones, the first derivatives and on their cross-products, and the fitted values $\hat{d}_i$ are used as prior weights. Since the weights must be positive, I chose a generalized linear model for $\hat{d}_i$ with a Gamma distribution as error distribution and the natural logarithm as link function.

As an illustration, I consider a sample of 250 national labor unions in the United States taken from a larger body of data discussed in detail by Freeman et al. (1983) and analyzed previously by Hannan and Tuma (1985). The substantive question is the dependence of the rate of death of a union through disbanding on the size of founding (S measured on a logarithmic scale) and on the duration time. Since new organizations are thought to face a higher risk of disbanding than older organizations, a Weibull model with shape parameter $\alpha > 0$ and regression coefficients β_1, β_2 is fitted

$$r(t) = \alpha t^{\alpha-1} \exp(\beta_1 + \beta_2 S) \qquad (14.48)$$

The event time is measured in years. The first and second derivatives for such a model are as follows:

$$r(t) = \alpha t^{\alpha-1} \exp(\mathbf{x}\boldsymbol{\beta}), \qquad (14.49)$$

is a Weibull rate with $\alpha \geq 0$ shape parameter, $\mathbf{x} \sim 1 \times p$ row vector of explanatory variables, and $\boldsymbol{\beta} \sim p \times 1$ column vector of regression coefficients. Let c_i be the dummy variable indicating right censoring. The individual loglikelihood is then given by:

$$l(\alpha, \boldsymbol{\beta}|t, c) = c \ln \alpha + (\alpha-1)c \ln t + c \, \mathbf{x}\boldsymbol{\beta} - t^a \exp(\mathbf{x}\boldsymbol{\beta}) \qquad (14.50)$$

$$\frac{\partial L}{\partial \alpha} = \alpha^{-1}c + c \ln t - t^a \exp(\mathbf{x}\boldsymbol{\beta}) \ln t \sim 1 \times 1 \qquad (14.51)$$

$$\frac{\partial L}{\partial \boldsymbol{\beta}} = [c - t^a \exp(\mathbf{x}\boldsymbol{\beta})]\mathbf{x}^T \sim p \times 1 \qquad (14.52)$$

$$\frac{\partial^2 L}{\partial \alpha^2} = -\alpha^{-2} c - t^a \exp(\mathbf{x}\boldsymbol{\beta})\,(\ln t)^2 \sim 1 \times 1 \qquad (14.53)$$

$$\frac{\partial^2 L}{\partial \alpha \,\partial \boldsymbol{\beta}^T} = -t^a \exp(\mathbf{x}\boldsymbol{\beta})\mathbf{x}\ln t \sim 1 \times p \qquad (14.54)$$

$$\frac{\partial^2 L}{\partial \boldsymbol{\beta} \,\partial \boldsymbol{\beta}^T} = -t^a \exp(\mathbf{x}\boldsymbol{\beta})\mathbf{x}^T\mathbf{x} \sim p \times p \qquad (14.55)$$

Using equation 14.30 a Wald statistic $W_n = 165.1$ is computed for White's information matrix test. With three degrees of freedom this test statistic indicates a strong discrepancy between the estimates of the information matrix computed from the first and second derivatives. Assuming now that the model is misspecified, the covariance matrix $\Sigma(\boldsymbol{\theta}_*)$ derived

Table 14.1. Parameter Estimates and Estimated Asymptotic Covariance Matrix from the Unweighted Loglikelihood Function

	Estimated Parameters		
	α	β_1	β_2
	0.5742	−1.01746	−0.34031
	Estimated Covariance Matrix of Parameters		
	α	β_1	β_2
α	0.00592		
β_1	−0.02467	0.39115	
β_2	0.00028	−0.04533	0.00720

Table 14.2. Parameter Estimates and Estimated Asymptotic Covariance Matrix from the Weighted Loglikelihood Function with Weights d_i

	Estimated Parameters		
	α	β_1	β_2
	0.5555	−2.21803	0.04815
	Estimated Covariance Matrix of Parameters		
	α	β_1	β_2
α	0.00744		
β_1	−0.02487	0.11245	
β_2	−0.00049	−0.00017	0.00018

from equations 14.8 and 14.9 must be used as a covariance matrix for the estimated parameters (see Table 14.1).

If the deviance increments d_i obtained from the unweighted QML estimation are used as prior weights, one finds the results shown in Table 14.2. Inspection of the difference between the weighted and the unweighted estimators shows only a small difference in α, but large differences in β_1 and β_2. Computing the Wald statistic for the Hausman test from equation 14.39 yields a value of 117.3, which is again highly significant with three degrees of freedom. The information matrix test as well as the Hausman test point out clearly that the model is very probably misspecified. This result is to be expected by using only one explanatory variable.

References
Indexes

References

Aalen, O. O. 1978. "Nonparametric inference for a family of counting processes." *Annals of Statistics* 6 (4): 701–726.

Abraham, K. G., and J. L. Medoff. 1985. "Length of service and promotions in union and nonunion work groups." *Industrial and Labor Relations Review* 38 (3): 410–420.

Albrecht, G. 1972. *Soziologie der geographischen Mobilität*. Stuttgart: Enke.

Allison, P. D. 1982. "Discrete-time methods for the analysis of event histories." In *Sociological methodology 1982*, ed. S. Leinhardt, San Francisco: Jossey-Bass.

Allison, P. D. 1984. *Event history analysis: Regression for longitudinal event data*. Beverly Hills: Sage.

Allison, P. D. 1985. "Survival analysis of backward recurrence times." *Journal of the American Statistical Association* 80: 315–322.

Amemiya, T. 1985. *Advanced econometrics*. Cambridge, Mass.: Harvard University Press.

Andreß, H.-J. 1985. *Multivariate Analyse von Verlaufsdaten*. Mannheim: Zentrum für Umfragen, Methoden, und Analysen (ZUMA).

Arminger, G. 1984. "Analysis of event histories with generalized linear models." In *Stochastic modelling of social processes*, ed. A. Diekmann and P. Mitter, 245–282. Orlando, Fla.: Academic Press.

Arminger, G. 1986. "Deviance, deviance residuals, and a coefficient of determination for parametric rate models." Paper presented at the conference Applications of Event History Analysis in Life Course Research, Max-Planck-Institut für Bildungsforschung, June 5–7, Berlin.

Arminger, G. 1987. "Testing against misspecification in parametric rate models." In *Applications of Event History Analysis in Life Course Research*, ed. K. U. Mayer and N. B. Tuma, 679–699. Berlin: Max-Planck-Institut für Bildungsforschung.

Arvidsson, A., et al. 1980. *Kvinnor och barn: Intervjuer med kvinnor om familj och arbete*. Stockholm: National Central Bureau of Statistics, Information i prognosfrågor, 1982: 4.

Atkinson, A. B., J. Gomulka, and J. Micklewright. 1984. "Unemployment benefit, duration and incentives in Britain." *Journal of Public Economics* 23: 3–26.

Averitt, R. 1968. *The dual economy*. New York: McGraw-Hill.

Azariadis, C. 1975. "Implicit contracts and underemployment equilibria." *Journal of Political Economy* 83: 1183–1202.

Bailey, K. R. 1983. "The asymptotic joint distribution of regression and survival estimates in the Cox regression model." *Annals of Statistics* 11 (1): 39–48.

Bailey, K. R. 1984. "Asymptotic equivalence between the Cox estimator and the general ML estimators of regression and survival parameters in the Cox model." *Annals of Statistics* 12 (2): 730–736.

Bailey, D., and A. Parikh. 1985. "An analysis of duration of unemployment: 1967–1979." *Empirical Economics* 10: 131–142.

Baltes, P. B., F. Dittmann-Kohli, and R. Dixon. 1986. "Multidisciplinary propositions on the development of intelligence during adulthood and old age." In *Human development and the life course: Multidisciplinary perspectives*, ed. A. B. Sørensen, F. E. Weinert, and L. R. Sherrod. Hillsdale, N.J., and London: Erlbaum.

Baron, J., and W. Bielby. 1980. "Bringing the firms back in: Stratification and the economic segmentation of work." *American Sociological Review* 45: 737–765.

Baron, J., and W. Bielby. 1984. "The organization of work in a segmented economy." *American Sociological Review* 49: 454–473.

Bartel, A. P. 1982. "Wages, nonwage job characteristics, and labor mobility." *Industrial and Labor Relations Review* 35 (4): 578–589.

Bartel, A. P., and G. J. Borjas. 1977. "Middle-age job mobility: Its determinants and consequences." In *Men in pre-retirement years*, ed. S. U. Wolfbein, 39–97. Philadelphia: Temple University Press.

Baydar, N., N. B. Tuma, and L. L. Wu. 1987. "The impact of left-censoring of migration histories on inferences: A Monte Carlo simulation study." MS, Princeton University.

Becker, G. S. 1975. *Human capital: A theoretical and empirical analysis, with special reference to education*, 2d ed. Chicago: University of Chicago Press.

Bell, D. 1973. *The coming of post-industrial society*. New York: Basic Books.

Berg, I. 1970. *Education and jobs: The great training robbery*. New York: Praeger.

Bernard, P., and J. Renaud. 1976. "Contre-mobilité et effets différés." *Sociologie et sociétés*, 8.

Bertaux, D. 1974. "Mobilité sociale biographique: Une critique de l'approche transversale." *Revue française de sociologie* 15: 329–362.

Bertaux, D., and M. Kohli. 1984. "The life story approach: A continental view." *Annual Review of Sociology* 10: 215–262.

Bielby, W. T., and J. N. Baron. 1983. "Organizations, technology, and worker attachment to the firm." *Research in Social Stratification and Mobility*, ed. R. Robinson, vol. 3, 77–113. Greenwich, Conn.: JAI Press.

Bills, D. B. N.d. "Educational credentials and hiring decisions: What employers look for in entry level employees." Department of Sociology, University of Iowa.

Birg, H. 1985. "Interregionale demo-ökonomische Modelle für die Bundesrepublik Deutschland: Eine Zwischenbilanz." Institut für Bevölkerungsforschung und Sozialpolitik, IBS-Materialien no. 18: 23. Universität Bielefeld.

Birg, H., J. Huinink, H. Koch, and H. Vorholt. 1984. *Kohortenanalytische Darstellung der Geburtenentwicklung in der Bundesrepublik Deutschland*, IBS Materialien no. 10. Bielefeld.

Blau, F. D., and L. M. Kahn. 1981. "Race and sex differences in quits by young workers." *Industrial and Labor Relations Review* 34: 536–577.

Blau, P. 1977. *Inequality and heterogeneity: A primitive theory of social structure.* New York: Free Press.

Blau, P., and O. Duncan. 1967. *The American occupational structure.* New York: Wiley.

Blossfeld, H.-P. 1985a. "Berufseintritt und Berufsverlauf—Eine Kohortenanalyse über die Bedeutung des ersten Berufs in der Erwerbsbiographie." *Mitteilungen aus der Arbeitsmarkt- und Berufsforschung* 2: 177–197.

Blossfeld, H.-P. 1985b. *Bildungsexpansion und Berufschancen.* Frankfurt: Campus.

Blossfeld, H.-P. 1986. "Career opportunities in the Federal Republic of Germany: A dynamic approach to the study of life-course, cohort, and period effects." *European Sociological Review* 2 (3): 208–225.

Blossfeld, H.-P. 1987. "Zur Repräsentativität der Sfb 3-Lebensverlaufsstudie: Ein Vergleich mit Daten aus der amtlichen Statistik." *Allgemeines Statistisches Archiv* 71: 126–144.

Blossfeld, H.-P. 1987. "Labor market entry and the sexual segregation of careers in the Federal Republic of Germany." *American Journal of Sociology* 93 (1): 89–118.

Blossfeld, H.-P., A. Hamerle, and K. U. Mayer. 1986. *Ereignisanalyse. Statistische Theorie und Anwendung in den Wirtschafts- und Sozialwissenschaften.* Frankfurt am Main: Campus Verlag.

Blossfeld, H.-P., A. Hamerle, and K. U. Mayer. 1989. *Event history analysis.* Hillsdale, N.J.: Erlbaum.

Blossfeld, H.-P., and A. Hamerle. 1987. "Interpreting career mobility as a multi-episode process." Sonderforschungsbereich 3, Working Paper no. 236. Frankfurt am Main.

Bluedorn, A. C. 1982. "The theories of turnover: Causes, effects, and meaning." In *Research on the sociology of organizations*, ed. S. B. Bacharach. Greenwich, Conn.: JAI Press.

Bogue, D., and M. J. Hagood. 1953. *Differential migration in the corn and cotton belts: Subregional migration in the United States, 1939–40*, vol. 2. Oxford, Ohio: Nymphenburger.

Borus, M. E., ed. 1984. *Youth and the labor market: Analyses of the national longitudinal survey.* Kalamazoo, Mich.: W. E. Upjohn Institute for Employment Research.

Bourdieu, P., and J. C. Passeron. 1971. *Die Illusion der Chancengleichheit: Untersuchungen zur Soziologie des Bildungswesens am Beispiel Frankreichs.* Stuttgart: Klett Verlag.

Braverman, H. 1974. *Labor and monopoly capital.* New York: Monthly Review Press.

Breiger, R. 1981. "The social class structure of occupational mobility." *American Journal of Sociology* 87: 578–611.

Brown, A., and K. Kiernan. 1981. "Cohabitation in Great Britain: Evidence from the General Household Survey." *Population Trends* 25 (1): 4–10.

Brown, C. 1982. "Dead-end jobs and youth unemployment." In *The youth labor market problem: Its nature, causes, and consequences,* ed. R. P. Freeman and D. A. Wise. Chicago: University of Chicago Press.

Büchtemann, C. F., and U. Brasche 1985. "Recurrent unemployment: Longitudinal evidence for the Federal Republic of Germany." SAMF-Arbeitspapier nr. 1985–3, Berlin.

Büchtemann, C. F., and Infratest Sozialforschung. 1983. *Die Bewältigung von Arbeitslosigkeit im zeitlichen Verlauf.* Bonn: Bundesminister für Arbeit und Sozialordnung.

Bundesminister für Raumordnung, Bauwesen und Städtebau, ed. 1978. "Raumordnungsbericht der Bundesregierung 1978." Bonn: Deutscher Bundestag (Drucksache 8/2378).

Bundsminister für Raumordnung, Bauwesen und Städtebau, ed. 1982. "Raumordnungsbericht der Bundesregierung 1982." Bonn: Deutscher Bundestag (Drucksache 10/210).

Bundesminister für Raumordnung, Bauwesen und Städtebau, ed. 1986. "Raumordnungsbericht der Bundesregierung 1986." Bonn: Deutscher Bundestag (Drucksache 10/6027).

Burawoy, M. 1979. *Manufacturing consent.* Chicago: University of Chicago Press.

Burdett, K., N. Kiefer, and S. Shama. 1985. "Layoff and duration dependence in a model of turn over." *Journal of Econometric* 28:51–69.

Buttler, G. 1984. "Arbeitsmarktanalyse, Aufgaben und Möglichkeiten." In *Arbeitsmarktanalyse,* ed. G. Buttler, 7–16. Göttingen: Vandenhoeck und Ruprecht.

Carroll, G. 1987. *Publish and perish: The organizational ecology of newspaper industries.* Greenwich, Conn.: JAI Press.

Carroll, G. R., and K. U. Mayer. 1986. "Job-shift patterns in the Federal Republic of Germany: The effects of social class, industrial sector, and organizational size." *American Sociological Review* 51 (3): 323–341.

Chamberlain, G. 1985. "Heterogeneity, omitted variable bias, and duration dependence." In *Longitudinal analysis of labor market data,* ed. J. J. Heckman and B. Singer, 3–38. Cambridge: Cambridge University Press.

Clark, K., and L. H. Summers. 1979. "Labor dynamics and unemployment: A reconsideration." *Brookings Papers on Economic Activity* 1: 13–60.

Coale, A. J., and D. R. McNeil. 1972. "The distribution by age of the frequency of first marriage in a female cohort." *Journal of the American Statistical Association* 67 (340): 743–749.

Coleman, J. S. 1981. *Longitudinal data analysis.* New York: Basic Books.

Coleman, J. S. 1984. "The transition from school to work." In *Research in Social Stratification and Mobility,* ed. R. Robinson, vol. 3. Greenwich, Conn.: JAI Press.

Coleman, J. S., E. Katz, and H. Menzel. 1957. "The diffusion of an innovation among physicians." *Sociometry* 20: 253–270.

Courgeau, D. 1984. "Relations entre cycle de vie et migrations." *Population* 39: 483–514.

Courgeau, D. 1985. "Interrelation between spatial mobility, family, and career life-cycle: A French survey." *European Sociological Review* 1: 139–163.

Cox, D. R. 1972. "Regression models and life tables." *Journal of the Royal Statistical Society* B 34: 187–202.

Cox, D. R. 1975: "Partial likelihood." *Biometrika* 62: 269–276.

Cox, D. R., and D. Oakes. 1984. *Analysis of Survival Data.* London: Chapman and Hall.

Cox, D. R., and E. J. Snell. 1968. "A general definition of residuals." *Journal of the Royal Statistical Society* B 30: 248–275.

Crowley, J., and M. Hu. 1977. "Covariance analysis of heart transplant survival data." *Journal of the American Statistical Association* 72: 27–36.

Davis, K. 1984. "Wives and work: The sex role revolution and its consequences." *Population and Development Review* 10 (3): 397–417.

Derenbach, R. 1984. "Berufliche Eingliederung der nachwachsenden Generation: Forschungen zur Raumentwicklung," vol. 13. Bonn: Bundesforschungsanstalt für Landeskunde und Raumordnung.

Dessler, G. 1984. *Personnel management,* 3d ed. Reston, Va.: Reston Publishing.

Diekmann, A. 1980: *Dynamische Modelle sozialer Prozesse.* Stuttgart: Teubner.

Diekmann, A. 1987a. "Determinanten des Heiratsalters und Scheidungsrisikos. Eine Analyse soziodemographischer Umfragedaten mit Modellen und statistischen Schätzmethoden der Verlaufsdatenanalyse." Habilitationsschrift, Institut für Soziologie, Universität München.

Diekmann, A. 1987b. "Effects of education, occupational characteristics, and cohort on the 'family cycle.'" In *Applications of Event History Analysis in Life Course Research,* ed. K. U. Mayer and N. B. Tuma, 404–431. Berlin: Max-Planck-Institut für Bildungsforschung.

Diekmann, A., and P. Mitter. 1983. "The 'sickle hypothesis': A time dependent Poisson model with applications to deviant behavior and occupational mobility." *Journal of Mathematical Sociology* 9: 85–101.

Diekmann, A., and P. Mitter. 1984a. "A comparison of the 'sickle function' with alternative stochastic models of divorce rates." In *Stochastic modelling of social processes,* ed. A. Diekmann and P. Mitter 123–153. Orlando, Fla.: Academic Press.

Diekmann, A., and P. Mitter. 1984b. *Methoden zur Analyse von Zeitverläufen.* Stuttgart: Teubner.

Dinkel, R. 1983. "Analyse und Prognose der Fruchtbarkeit am Beispiel der Bundesrepublik Deutschland." *Zeitschrift für Bevölkerungswissenschaft* 9 (1): 47–72.

DiPrete, T. A. 1981. "Unemployment over the life cycle: Racial differences and the effect of changing economic conditions." *American Journal of Sociology* 87: 286–307.

DiPrete, T. A., and W. T. Soule. 1986. "The organization of career lines: Equal employment opportunity and status advancement in a federal bureaucracy." *American Sociological Review* 51 (3): 295–309.

Doeringer, P. B., and M. J. Piore. 1971. *Internal labor markets and manpower analysis.* Lexington, Mass.: D. C. Heath.

Edwards, R. 1979. *Contested terrain.* New York: Basic Books.

Efron, B. 1977. "The efficiency of Cox's likelihood function for censored data." *Journal of the American Statistical Association* 72: 557–565.

Egle, F. 1979. "Strukturalisierung der Arbeitslosigkeit und Segmentation des Arbeitsmarktes." In *Beiträge zur Arbeitsmarkt- und Berufsforschung,* ed. C. Brinkmann et al., vol. 33. Nürnberg.

Egle, F. 1984. "Arbeitsmarktindikatoren." In *Arbeitsmarktanalyse,* ed. G. Buttler, 53–67. Göttingen: Vandenhoeck und Ruprecht.

Ehrenberg, R. G., and R. S. Smith. 1988. *Modern labor economics: Theory and public policy.* Glenview, Ill.: Scott, Foresman.

Elandt-Johnson, R. C., and N. L. Johnson. 1980. *Survival models and data analysis.* New York: John Wiley and Sons.

Elbers, C., and G. Ridder. 1982. "True and spurious duration dependence: The identifiability of the proportional hazard model." *Review of Economic Studies* 49: 403–410.

Elder, G. H. 1974. *Children of the great depression: Social change in life experience.* Chicago: University of Chicago Press.

Elder, G. H. 1985. "Perspectives on the life course." In *Life course dynamics: Trajectories and transitions, 1968–1980,* ed. G. H. Elder. Ithaca: Cornell University Press.

Elder, G. H. 1986. "Military times and turning points in men's lives." *Developmental Psychology* 22 (2): 233–245.

Elder, G. H., and S. L. Bailey. 1986. "The timing of military service in men's lives." In *Social stress and family development,* ed. J. Aldous and D. Klein. New York: Guilford Press.

Erikson, E. 1968. *Identity, youth and crisis.* New York: Norton.

Erikson, R., and J. Goldthorpe. 1985. "Are American rates of social mobility exceptionally high? New evidence on an old issue." *European Sociological Review* 1 (1): 1–22.

Erikson, E., and J. Goldthorpe. 1987. "Worklife and intergenerational class mobility: A Comparative analysis." Paper presented to the Research Committee on Social Stratification and Mobility of the International Sociological Association, Nürnberg, April 22–25.

Espenshade, T. J. 1983. "Marriage, divorce, and remarriage from retrospective data: A multiregional approach." *Environment and Planning* A 15: 1633–1652.

Featherman, D. L. 1986. "Biography, society, and history: Individual development as a population process." In *Human development and the life course: Multidisciplinary perspectives,* ed. A. B. Sørensen, F. E. Weinert, and L. R. Sherrod. Hillsdale, N.J., and London: Erlbaum.

Featherman, D. L., and R. M. Hauser. 1978. *Opportunity and change.* New York: Academic Press.

Featherman, D. L., and T. Petersen. 1986. "Markers of aging: Modeling the clocks that time us." *Research on Aging* 8 (3): 339–365.

Featherman, D. L., and K. Selbee. 1989. "Class formation and class mobility: A new approach with counts from life history data." In *Social change and the life course.* Vol. 1: *Social structures and human lives,* ed. M. W. Riley. Newburyport: Sage.

Featherman, D. L., L. K. Selbee, and K. U. Mayer. 1989. "Social class and the structuring of the life course in Norway and West Germany." In *Age structuring in comparative perspective*, ed. D. Kertzer, and K. W. Schaie. Hillsdale, N.J.: Erlbaum.

Featherman, D. L., and A. B. Sørensen. 1983. "Societal transformation in Norway and change in the life-course transition into adulthood." *Acta Sociologica* 26: 105–126.

Feldstein, M. A. 1975. "The importance of temporary layoffs: An empirical analysis." *Brookings Papers on Economic Activity* 3: 725–744.

Felmlee, D. H. 1982. "Women's job mobility processes." *American Sociological Review* 47 (1): 142–151.

Felmlee, D. H., and D. Eder. 1983. "Contextual effects in the classroom: The impact of ability grouping on student attention." *Sociology of Education* 7: 77–87.

Finnäs, F. 1983. "Fertility trends of Swedish women, 1960–1977: A study of birth intervals in selected cohorts of women born between 1927 and 1952." In *Fertility of Swedish Women Born 1927–1960*, ed. L. Johansson and F. Finnäs. Stockholm: Statistics Sweden, Urval no. 14.

Finnäs, F. and J. M. Hoem. 1980. "Starting age and subsequent birth intervals in cohabitational unions in current Danish cohorts, 1975." *Demography* 17: 275–295.

Flinn, C. J. 1986. "Wages and mobility of young workers." *Journal of Political Economy* 94 (3), pt. 2: S88–S110.

Foner, A., and D. Kertzer. 1978. "Transitions over the life course: Lessons from age-set societies." *American Journal of Sociology* 83 (5): 1081–1104.

Frank, R. H. 1985. *Choosing the right pond. Human behavior and the quest for status*. New York: Oxford University Press.

Freeman, J., G. R. Carroll, and M. Hannan. 1983. "The liability of newness: Age dependence in organizational death rates." *American Sociological Review* 48: 692–710.

Freeman, R. B., and J. L. Medoff. 1984. *What do unions do?* New York: Basic Books.

Freeman, R. B., and D. A. Wise, eds. 1982. *The youth labor market problem: Its nature, causes, and consequences*. Chicago: University of Chicago Press.

Freiburghaus, D. 1978. *Dynamik der Arbeitslosigkeit*. Meisenheim am Glan: Hain.

Friedlaender, D., and R. J. Roshier. 1966. "A study of internal migration in England and Wales. Part 2." *Population Studies* 20: 45–59.

Friedrich, W., and G. Ronning 1985. "Technischer Fortschritt: Auswirkungen auf Wirtschaft und Arbeitsmarkt." ifo-Schnelldienst, 22/85: 13–25.

Galler, H. P. 1985. "Labor supply, labor demand and occupational mobility." In *Yearbook 1983/84 of the Institute for Advanced Study*, ed. P. Wapnewski, 123–134. Berlin.

Galler, H., and U. Poetter. 1987. "Unobserved heterogeneity in models of unemployment duration." In *Applications of Event History Analysis in Life Course Research*, ed. K. U. Mayer and N. B. Tuma, 628–650. Berlin: Max-Planck-Institut für Bildungsforschung.

Galtung, J. 1967. *Theory and methods of social research.* London: Allen and Unwin.

Geipel, R. 1965. *Sozialräumliche Strukturen des Bildungswesens.* Frankfurt: Diesterweg.

Giddens, A. 1973. *The class structure of the advanced societies.* London: Hutchinson.

Gilks, W. R., and J. N. Hobcraft. 1981. "Modelling age-specific nuptiality in England and Wales." London: Word Fertility Survey.

Girod, R. 1971. *Mobilité sociale: faits établis et problèmes ouverts.* Geneva: Droz.

Goldfeld, S., and R. Quandt. 1972. *Nonlinear methods in econometrics.* Amsterdam: North-Holland.

Goldthorpe, J. 1980. *Social mobility and class structure in modern Britain.* Oxford: Clarendon Press.

Goldthorpe, J., and C. Payne. 1986. "Trends in intergenerational class mobility in England and Wales, 1971–1983." *Sociology* 20: 1–20.

Granovetter, M. 1986. "Labor mobility, internal markets, and job matching: A comparison of the sociological and economic approaches." In *Research in Social Stratification and Mobility,* ed. R. Robinson, vol. 5, 3–39. Greenwich, Conn.: JAI Press.

Grubel, H. G., and A. Scott. 1967. "Determinants of migration: The highly skilled." *International Migration* 5: 127–139.

Hachen, D. S. 1983. "Class, labor markets, and career mobility." Ph.D. diss., Madison, Wis., University of Wisconsin.

Hachen, D. S. 1988. "The competing risks model." *Sociological Methods and Research* 17: 21–54.

Halaby, C. N. 1982. "Job-shift differences between men and women in the workplace." *Social Science Research* 11 (1): 1–29.

Halaby, C. N. 1986. "Worker attachment and workplace authority." *American Sociological Review* 51 (5), 634–649.

Hall, J., S. A. Lippmann, and J. McCall. 1976. "Expected utility maximizing job search." In *Studies in the Economics of Search,* ed. S. A. Lippmann and J. McCall, 133–155. Amsterdam: North-Holland.

Hall, R. E. 1970. "Why is unemployment so high at full employment?" *Brookings Papers on Economic Activity* 3: 369–402.

Haller, M., and R. Hodge. 1981. "Class and status as dimensions of career mobility: Some insights from the Austrian case." *Zeitschrift für Soziologie* 10: 133–150.

Hamblin, R., B. Jacobsen, and J. L. L. Miller. 1973. *A mathematical theory of social change.* New York: John Wiley and Sons.

Hamerle, A. 1985. "Regressionsmodelle für gruppierte Verweildauern und Lebenszeiten." *Zeitschrift für Operations Research* B 29: 243–260.

Hamermesh, D. 1977. *Jobless pay and the economy.* Baltimore: Johns Hopkins University Press.

Hanefeld, U. 1984. "Das Sozio-Ökonomische Panel—Eine Längsschnittstudie für die Bundesrepublik Deutschland." *Vierteljahreshefte zur Wirtschaftsforschung* 4 (1984): 391–406.

Hannan, M., and N. B. Tuma. 1979. "Methods for temporal analysis." *Annual Review of Sociology* 5: 303–328.

Harrell, F. 1980. "The PHGLM procedure." In SAS Supplemental Library User's Guide, 1980 ed. Cary, N.C.: SAS Institute.

Hartmann, H. I. 1987. "Internal labor markets and gender: A case study of promotion." In *Gender in the Workplace,* ed. C. Brown, and J. A. Pechman, 59–105. Washington: Brookings Institution.

Hauser, P. M. 1979. "Introduction and overview." In *World population and development: Challenges and prospects,* ed. P. M. Hauser. Syracuse: Syracuse University Press.

Hausman, J. 1978. "Specification tests in econometrics," *Econometrica* 46: 1251–1271.

Hausman, J., and D. Wise. 1978. "A conditional probit model for qualitative choice: Discrete decisions recognizing interdependence and heterogeneous preferences." *Econometrica* 46: 403–427.

Heberle, R. 1936. "Die Bedeutung der Wanderungen im sozialen Leben der Völker." In *Reine und angewandte Soziologie: Eine Festgabe für Ferdinand Tönnies.* Leipzig: Buske.

Heckman, J. J., and G. Borjas. 1980. "Does unemployment cause future unemployment? Definitions, questions and answers from a continuous time model of heterogeneity and state dependence." *Economica* 47: 247–283.

Heckman, J. J., and B. Singer. 1982. "The identification problem in econometric models for duration data." In *Advances in Econometrics,* ed. W. Hildenbrand, 39–77. New York: Cambridge University Press.

Heckman, J. J., and B. Singer. 1984. "A method for minimizing the impact of distributional assumptions in econometric models for duration data." *Econometrica* 52 (2): 63–132, 271–320.

Heckman, J. J., and B. Singer. 1986. "Econometric analysis of longitudinal data." In *Handbook of Econometrics,* ed. Z. Griliches and M. D. Intriligator, vol. 3, 1689–1763. Amsterdam.

Helberger, C. 1982. "Arbeitslosigkeit als Gegenstand mikroökonomischer Theorien zur Funktionsweise der Arbeitsmärkte." *DIW-Vierteljahreshefte zur Wirtschaftsforschung* 4/82: 398–412.

Hernes, G. 1972. "The process of entry into first marriage." *American Sociological Review* 37 (2): 173–182.

Hernes, G. 1976. "Structural change in social processes." *American Journal of Sociology* 82: 513–547.

Hjort, N. L. 1984. "Weak convergence of cumulative intensity processes when parameters are estimated, with applications to goodness of fit tests in models with censoring." Research Report no. 764. Oslo: Norwegian Computing Center.

Hobcraft, J. N., and G. Rodriguez. 1980. "Methodological issues in life table analysis of life histories." Paper prepared for the IUSSP-WFS-CPS Seminar on the Analysis of Maternity Histories, London, 1980.

Hoem, J. M. 1983. "Distortions caused by nonobservation of periods of cohabitation before the latest." *Demography* 20 (4): 491–506.

Hoem, J. M. 1985. "Weighting, misclassification, and other issues in the analysis of survey samples of life histories." In *Longitudinal analysis of labor market data*, ed. J. J. Heckman and B. Singer. Cambridge: Cambridge University Press.

Hoem, J. M., D. Madsen, J. L. Nielsen, E.-M. Ohlsen, H. O. Hansen, and B. Rennermalm. 1980. "Experiments in modelling recent Danish fertility curves." *Demography* 18 (2): 231–244.

Hoem, J. M., and B. Rennermalm. 1985. "Modern family initiation in Sweden: Experience of women born between 1936 and 1960." *European Journal of Population* 1 (1): 81–112.

Hoem, J. M., and R. Selmer. 1984. "The negligible influence of premarital cohabitation on marital fertility in current Danish cohorts, 1975." *Demography* 21 (2): 193–206.

Hoepflinger, F. 1987. *Wandel der Familienbildung in Westeuropa*. Frankfurt: Campus.

Hofbauer, H., and E. Nagel. 1973. "Regionale Mobilität bei männlichen Erwerbspersonen in der Bundesrepublik Deutschland." *Mitteilungen aus der Arbeitsmarkt- und Berufsforschung* 6: 255–272.

Hoffmeyer-Zlotnik, J., H. P. Kirschner, M. Weidenback, and E. Brueckner. 1984. "Methodenreport 'Lebensverläufe.'" Mannheim: ZUMA-Technischer Bericht No. T84108.

Hogan, D. P. 1982. *Transitions and social change: The early lives of American men*. New York: Academic Press.

Horstmann, K. 1976. "Zur Soziologie der Wanderungen." *Handbuch der empirischen Sozialforschung*. Vol. 5, *Soziale Schichtung und Mobilität*, ed. R. König. Stuttgart: dtv.

Hougaard, P. 1984. "Life table methods for heterogeneous populations: Distributions describing the heterogeneity." *Biomerika* 71: 75–83.

Hougaard, P. 1986. "Survival models for heterogeneous populations derived from stable distributions," *Biometrika* 73: 387–396.

Huinink, J. 1987a. "Kohortenanalyse der Geburtenentwicklung in der Bundesrepublik Deutschland." In *Lebenslauf und Familienentwicklung*. A. Herlth, and K. P. Strohmeier, eds., Leverkusen: Leske und Buderich.

Huinink, J. 1987b. "Soziale Herkunft, Bildung und das Alter bei der Geburt des ersten Kindes," *Zeitschrift für Soziologie* 16 (5): 367–384.

Hujer, F., and H. Schneider 1986. "Ökonometrische Ansätze zur Analyse von Paneldaten: Schätzung und Vergleich von Übergangsratenmodellen." Sonderforschungsbereich 3, Working Paper no. 190. Frankfurt.

Hyrenius, H. 1941. *Studier rörande den utomäktenskapliga fruktsamhetens variationer*. Skrift no. 28 utgiven av Fahlbeckska stiftelsen. Lund: Gleerup.

Jacoby, S. M. 1985. *Employing Bureaucracy: Managers, Unions and the Transformation of Work in American Industry*. New York: Columbia University Press.

Kalbfleisch, J. D., and R. L. Prentice. 1980. *The statistical analysis of failure time data*. New York: John Wiley & Sons.

Kalleberg, A. L., and A. B. Sørensen. 1979. "The sociology of labor markets." *Annual Review of Sociology* 5: 351–379.

Kandel, D. B., and K. Yamaguchi. 1987. "Job mobility and drug use." *American Journal of Sociology* 92 (4): 836–878.

Kaplan, E. L., and P. Meier. 1958. "Nonparametric estimation from incomplete observations." *Journal of the American Statistical Association* 53 (282): 457–481.

Keeley, M. C. 1979. "An analysis of the age pattern of first marriage." In *International Economic Review* 20:527–544.

Kern, H., and M. Schumann. 1970. *Industriearbeit und Arbeiterbewusstsein.* Frankfurt am Main: Europäische Verlagsanstalt.

Kiefer, N. 1984. "A simple test for heterogeneity in exponential models of duration," *Journal of Labour Economics* 2: 539–549.

Kiefer, N., and G. Neumann. 1979a. "Estimation of wage offer distributions and reservation wages." In *Studies in the Economics of Search*, ed. S. A. Lippmann and J. McCall. Amsterdam: North Holland.

Kiefer, N., and G. Neumann. 1979b. "An empirical job search model with a test of the constant reservation-wage hypothesis." *Journal of Political Economy* 87: 89–107.

Kiefer, N., and G. Neumann. 1981. "Structural and reduced form approaches to analyzing unemployment durations." In *Studies in Labor Markets*, ed. S. Rosen, 171–185. Chicago: University of Chicago Press.

Kiel, W. 1985. "Datenhandbuch zur Lebenslagen-Studie." Sonderforschungsbereich 3. Frankfurt.

Kiernan, K. 1979. "Characteristics of young people who move interregionally: A longitudinal study." In *Regional demographic development*, ed. J. Hobcraft and P. Rees. London: Croom Helm.

Konda, S. L., and S. Stewman. 1980. "An opportunity demand model and markovian labor supply models: Comparative tests in organizations." *American Sociological Review* 45 (2): 276–301.

König, W., and W. Müller. 1986. "Educational system and labour markets as determinants of worklife mobility in France and West Germany: A comparison of men's career mobility, 1965–1970." *European Sociological Review* 2 (2): 73–96.

Kosta, J., I. Krings, and B. Lutz. 1970. *Probleme der Klassifikation von Erwerbstätigen und Tätigkeiten.* München: Institut für sozialwissenschaftliche Forschung.

Kraus, V. 1976. "Social grading of occupations in Israel'. Ph.D. diss., Hebrew University, Jerusalem.

Lancaster, T. 1984. "The covariance matrix of the information matrix test." *Econometrica* 52: 1051–1053.

Lancaster, T. 1985. "Generalized residuals and heterogeneous duration models with applications to the Weibull model." *Journal of Econometrics* 28: 155–169.

Lansing, J. B., and E. Mueller. 1967. "The geographic mobility of labor," MS, University of Michigan, Ann Arbor.

Lawless, J. F. 1982. *Statistical models and methods for lifetime data.* New York: John Wiley & Sons.

Lempert-Helm, I. 1985. "Zugangs- und Verbleibsrisiken der Arbeitslosigkeit im

Zeitvergleich." In *Mobilitätsprozesse auf dem Arbeitsmarkt*, ed. R. Hujer and H. Knepel, 193–222. Frankfurt: Campus.

Linton, R. 1939. "A neglected aspect of social organization." *American Journal of Sociology* 45: 870–886.

Lippmann, S. A., and J. J. McCall. 1976a. "The economics of job search: A survey." *Economic Inquiry* 14: 155–189, 347–368.

Lippmann, S. A., and J. J. McCall. 1976b. "Job search in a dynamic economy." *Journal of Economic Theory* 12: 365–390.

Long, L. H. 1973. "Migration differentials by education and occupation: Trends and variations." *Demography* 19: 243–258.

Lyberg, I. 1984. "Att fråga om barn: Teknisk beskrivning av undersökningen 'Kvinnor i Sverige.'" Bakgrundsmaterial från Prognosinstitutet, 1984 (4). Stockholm: Statistics Sweden.

Mahajan, V., and R. A. Peterson. 1985. *Models for innovation diffusion*. Beverly Hills, Calif.: Sage.

Mammey, K. 1979. "Räumliche Aspekte in der sozialen Mobilität in der Bundesrepublik Deutschland." In *Soziale Strukturen und individuelle Mobilität*, ed. H. Tegtmayer, Wiesbaden: Boldt.

March, J. C., and J. G. March. 1981. "Performance sampling and Weibull distributions." *Administrative Science Quarterly*, 26: 90–92.

Mare, R. D. 1981. "Change and stability in educational stratification." *American Sociological Review* 46: 72–88.

Mare, R. D., C. Winship, and W. N. Kubitschek. 1984. "The transition from youth to adulthood: Understanding the age pattern of employment." *American Journal of Sociology* 90: 326–358.

Marel, K. 1980. *Inter- und intraregionale Mobilität*. Wiesbaden: Boldt.

Marini, M. M. 1985. "Determinants of the timing of adult role entry." *Social Science Research* 14: 309–350.

Marx, K. 1867. "Das Kapital. Kritik der politischen Ökonomie." In K. Marx and F. Engels, *Werke*, vol. 23. Berlin: Dietz, 1970.

Matović, M. R. 1985. *"The Stockholm marriage": Family formation and choice of partner in Stockholm, 1850–1890*. (In Swedish, with a long summary in English). Stockholm: Liber Förlag.

Matras, J. 1984. "On schooling and employment in the transition of Israeli males to adulthood." MS, Max-Planck-Institut für Bildungsforschung, Berlin.

Matras, J., G. Noam, and I. Bar-Haim. 1984. "Young Israelis on the threshold: A study of the 1954 cohort of Israeli men." Brookdale Institute Discussion Paper D0284, Jerusalem.

Mayer, K. U. 1977. "Ungleiche Chancen und Klassenbildung." *Soziale Welt* 28: 466–493.

Mayer, K. U. 1979a. "Berufliche Tätigkeiten, berufliche Stellung und beruflicher Status—empirische Vergleiche zum Klassifikationsproblem." In *Sozialstrukturanalyse mit Umfragedaten*, ed. F. U. Pappi. Königstein: Athenäum.

Mayer, K. U. 1979b. "Strukturwandel im Beschäftigungssystem und berufliche Mobilität zwischen Generationen." *Zeitschrift für Bevölkerungswissenschaft* 3: 267–298.

Mayer, K. U. 1979c. "Lebensverläufe und Wohlfahrtsentwicklung." Antrag auf

Einrichtung und Finanzierung des Sonderforschungsbereichs 3, *"Mikroanalytische Grundlagen der Gesellschaftspolotik."* Frankfurt am Main: 181–217.

Mayer, K. U. 1986. "Structural constraints on the life course." *Human Development* 29 (3): 163–170.

Mayer, K. U., and E. Brückner. 1989. *Lebensverläufe und Wohlfahrtsentwicklung. Konzeption, Design und Methodik der Erhebung von Lebensverläufen der Geburtsjahrgänge 1929–1931, 1939–1941, 1949–1951,* Materialien aus der Bildungsforschung Nr. 35, Berlin: Max-Planck-Institut für Bildungsforschung.

Mayer, K. U., and G. R. Carroll. 1987. "Jobs and classes: Structural constraints on career mobility." *European Sociological Review* 3 (1): 14–38.

Mayer, K. U., D. L. Featherman, K. Selbee, and T. Colbjornssen. 1989. "Class mobility during the working life: A comparison of Germany and Norway." In *Cross-national research in sociology.* ed. M. Kohn. Newbury Park: Sage.

Mayer, K. U., and J. Huinink. 1989. "Age, period, and cohort in the study of life course: A comparison of classical A–P–C–analysis with event history analysis or farewell to Lexis." In *Proceedings of the workshop on Methodological Issues in Longitudinal Research I: Data and General Designs,* ed. D. Magnusson. Cambridge: Cambridge University press.

Mayer, K. U., and W. Müller. 1986. "The state and the structure of the life course." In *Human development and the life course: Multidisciplinary perspectives,* ed. A. B. Sørensen, F. E. Weinert, and L. R. Sherrod. Hillsdale, N.J., and London: Erlbaum.

Mayer, K. U., and M. Wagner. 1986. "Der Auszug von Kindern aus dem elterlichen Haushalt—ein Erklärungsmodell für die Geburtsjahrgänge 1929–31, 1939–41, und 1949–51." In *Demographische Probleme der Haushaltsökonomie,* ed. K. F. Zimmermann. Bochum: Brockmeyer.

Mayer, K. U., and N. B. Tuma, eds. 1987. *Applications of event history analysis in life course research.* Materialien aus der Bildungsforschung nr. 30. Berlin: Max-Planck-Institut für Bildungsforschung.

McCall, J. (1970): "Economics of information and job search." *Quarterly Journal of Economics* 84: 113–126.

McGinnis, R. 1968. "A stochastic model for social mobility." *American Sociological Review* 33: 712–722.

McKenna, C. J. 1985. *Uncertainty and the labour market: Recent developments in job search theory.* Brighton: Harvester Press.

Medoff, J. L., and K. G. Abraham. 1980. "Experience, performance, and earnings." *Quarterly Journal of Economics* 95 (4): 703–736.

Meitzen, M. E. 1986. "Differences in male and female job-quitting behavior." *Journal of Labor Economics* 4 (2): 151–167.

Meyer, R. H., and Wise, D. A. 1982. "High school preparation and early labor force experience." In *The youth labor market problem: Its nature, causes, and consequences,* ed. R. B. Freeman, and D. A. Wise. Chicago: University of Chicago Press.

Michael, R. T., and N. B. Tuma. 1985. "Entry into marriage and parenthood by young men and women: The influence of family background." *Demography* 22 (4): 515–544.

Mincer, J. 1974. *Schooling, experience, and earnings.* New York: Columbia University Press.

Mitter, P. 1987. "Compound arrival times." In *Applications of event history analysis in life course research,* ed. K. U. Mayer and N. B. Tuma. Berlin: Max-Planck-Institut für Bildungsforschung.

Moffitt, R. 1985. "Unemployment insurance and the distribution of unemployment spells." *Journal of Econometrics* 28: 85–101.

Morgan, J. J., and G. J. Duncan. 1983. *Five thousand American families,* vol. 10. Ann Arbor: University of Michigan.

Morrison, P. A. 1972. *Population movements and the shape of urban growth: Implications for public policy.* Santa Monica, Calif.: Rand Corporation.

Mortensen, D. 1970. "Job search, the duration of unemployment and the Phillips curve." *American Economic Review* 60: 847–862.

Müller, W. 1983. "Wege und Grenzen der Tertiarisierung: Wandel der Berufsstruktur in der Bundesrepublik Deutschland 1950–1980." In *Krise der Arbeitsgesellschaft? Verhandlungen des 21. Deutschen Soziologentages in Bamberg,* ed. J. Matthes. Frankfurt: Campus.

Müller, W. 1986. "Women's labor force participation over the life course: A model case of social change." In *Life-span development and behavior,* ed. P. B. Baltes, D. L. Featherman, and M. Lerner, vol. 7. Hillsdale, N.J., and London: Erlbaum.

Musgrove, F. 1963. *The migratory elite.* London: Heinemann.

Namboodiri, K., and C. M. Suchindran. 1987. *Life table techniques and their applications.* Orlando, Fla.: Academic Press.

Nelson, W. 1972. "Theory and applications of hazard plotting for censored failure data." *Technometrics* 14 (4): 945–966.

Nelson, W. 1982. *Applied life data analysis.* New York: John Wiley and Sons.

Neugarten, B. L., J. W. Moore, and J. C. Lowe. 1965. "Age norms, age constraints, and adult socialization." *American Journal of Sociology* 70: 710–717.

Neyman, J., and E. L. Scott. 1948. "Consistent estimates based on partially consistent observations." *Econometrica* 16: 1–32.

Niedzwetzki, K. 1979. "Raumordnungsbericht." Vol. 12, "Die Wanderungen: Räumliche Mobilität und Regionalpolitik." Schwäbisch-Gmünd: Regionalverband Baden-Württemberg.

Noyelle, T. J. 1987. *Beyond industrial dualism. Markets and job segmentation in the new economy.* Boulder, Colo.: Westview Press.

Olzak, S. 1986. "A competition model of ethnic collective action in American cities, 1877–1889." In *Competitive ethnic relations,* ed. S. Olzak and J. Nagel. Orlando, Fla.: Academic Press.

Olzak, S. 1987. "Causes of ethnic protest and conflict in urban America, 1877–1889." *Social Science Research* 16: 185–210.

Oppenheimer, V. K. 1974. "The life-cycle squeeze: The interaction of men's occupational and family life cycles." *Demography* 11: 227–245.

Ornstein, M. 1976. *Entry into the American labor force.* New York: Academic Press.

Osterman, P. 1980: *Getting started: The youth labor market.* Cambridge, Mass.: MIT Press.

Osterman, P. 1984. "Introduction: The nature and importance of internal labor markets." In *Internal labor markets*, ed. P. Osterman, 1–22. Cambridge, Mass.: MIT Press.

Page, H. J., B. Ferry, J. H. Shah, and R. Lesthaeghe. 1980. "The most recent births: Analytical potential and some underlying problems." Paper prepared for the IUSSP-WFS-CPS Seminar on the Analysis of Maternity Histories, London.

Papastefanou, G. 1987. "Gender differences in family formation: Modelling the life course specificity of social differentiation." In *Applications of Event History Analysis in Life Course Research*, ed. K. U. Mayer and N. B. Tuma, 327–403. Berlin: Max-Planck-Institut für Bildungsforschung.

Parkin, F. 1971. *Class inequality and political order.* London: McGibben and Kee.

Parkin, F. 1974. "Strategies of social closure in class formation." In *The social analysis of class structure*, ed. F. Parkin. London: Tavistock.

Peisert, H. 1967. *Soziale Lage und Bildungschancen in Deutschland.* München: Piper.

Petersen, T. 1986a. "Estimating fully parametric hazard rate models with time-dependent covariates. Use of maximum likelihood." *Sociological Methods and Research* 14 (3): 219–246.

Petersen, T. 1986b. "Fitting parametric survival models with time-dependent covariates." *Journal of the Royal Statistical Society* C 35 (3): 281–288.

Petersen, T. 1988. "Specification and estimation of continuous state space hazard rate models." *Sociological Methodology.* San Francisco: Jossey-Bass.

Prentice, R. L., J. D. Kalbfleisch, A. V. Peterson, Jr., N. Flournoy, V. T. Farewell, and N. E. Breslow. 1978. "The analysis of failure times in the presence of competing risks." *Biometrics* 34: 541–554.

Prescott, R. B. 1922. "Law and growth in forecasting demand." *Journal of the American Statistical Association* 18: 471–479.

Quetelet, A. 1914. *Soziale Physik. Abhandlung über die Entwicklung der Fähigkeit des Menschen,* vol. 1, trans. (from the French ed. of 1869) Valentine Dorn. Jena: Gustav Fischer.

Quigley, J. M., and D. H. Weinberg. 1977. "Intra-urban residential mobility: A review and synthesis." *International Regional Science Review* 2: 41–66.

Qvist, J., and B. Rennermalm. 1985. *Att bilda familj: Samboende, äktenskap och barnafödande bland kvinnor födda 1936–60.* Urval no. 17. Stockholm: Statistics Sweden.

Raven, J. C. 1958. *Standard progressive matrices.* London: Lewis.

Redner, R., and H. Walker. 1984. "Mixture densities, maximum likelihood and the EM-algorithm." *SIAM Review* 26: 195–239.

Riley, M. W., M. E. Johnson, and A. Foner. 1972. *Aging and Society: A Sociology of Age Stratification,* vol. 3. New York: Russell Sage.

Rindfuss, R. R., L. L. Bumpass, and J. A. Palmore. 1985. "Analyzing selected fertility histories: Does the restriction bias the results?" MS.

Rindfuss, R. R., P. S. Morgan, and L. G. Swicegood. 1984. "The transition to motherhood: The intersection of structural and temporal dimensions." *American Sociological Review* 49 (3): 359–372.

Rodriguez, G., and J. Trussell. 1980. "Maximum likelihood estimation of the parameters of Coale's model nuptiality schedule from survey data." Technical Bulletin no. 7. London: World Fertility Survey.

Roger, J. H., and S. D. Peacock. 1983. "Fitting the scale as a GLIM parameter for Weibull, extreme value, logistic and log-logistic regression models with censored data." GLIM-Newsletter 6: 30–37.

Rosenbaum, J. E. 1984. *Career mobility in a corporate hierarchy.* New York: Academic Press.

Salant, S. W. 1977. "Search theory and duration data: A theory of sorts." *Quarterly Journal of Economics* 91: 39–57.

Sandefur, G. D. 1981. "Organizational boundaries and upward job shifts." *Social Science Research* 10 (1): 67–82.

Sandefur, G. D., and W. J. Scott. 1981. "A dynamic analysis of migration: An assessment of the effects of age, family, and career variables." *Demography* 18: 355–368.

SAS User's Guide: Statistics, Version 5 Edition, 1985. Cary, N.C., 507–557.

Schervish, P. 1983. *The structural determinants of unemployment.* New York: Academic Press.

Schreiber, K. H. 1975. *Wanderungsursachen und idealtypische Verhaltensmuster mobiler Bevölkerungsgruppen.* Frankfurt: Kramer.

Selmer, R. 1984. "Cohabitation without marriage—marriage and births [in Norwegian cohorts]." (In Norwegian with a summary in English.) Artikler no. 146. Oslo: Central Bureau of Statistics of Norway.

Sengenberger, W. 1975. *Arbeitsmarktstruktur—Ansätze zu einem Modell des segmentierten Arbeitsmarkts.* Frankfurt and München: Aspekte Verlag.

Shavit-Streifler, Y. J. 1983. "Tracking in Israeli education: Its consequences for ethnic inequality in educational attainment." Ph.D. diss., University of Wisconsin–Madison.

Shavit, Y. 1984. "Tracking and ethnicity in Israeli secondary education." *American Sociological Review* 49: 210–220.

Shavit, Y., and D. L. Featherman. 1988. "Schooling, tracking, and teenage intelligence." *Sociology of Education* 61: 42–51.

Shaw, R. P. 1975. *Migration theory and fact.* Philadelphia: Regional Science Research Institute.

Shyrock, H. S., and C. B. Nam. 1986. "Educational selectivity of interregional migration." *Social Forces* 3: 299–310.

Skvoretz, J. 1984. "Career mobility as a Poisson process: An application to the career dynamics of men and women in the U.S. Office of the Comptroller of the Currency from the Civil War to World War II." *Social Science Research* 13 (2): 198–220.

Smooha, S. 1978. *Israeli: Pluralism and conflict.* Berkeley: University of California Press.

Snipp, M. 1985. "Occupational mobility and social class: Insights from men's career mobility." *American Sociological Review* 50: 475–493.

Solomon, P. J. 1984. "Effect of misspecification of regression models in the analysis of survival data." *Biometrika* 71: 291–298.

Sørensen, A. B. 1977a. "The structure of inequality and the process of attainment." *American Sociological Review* 42: 965–978.

Sørensen, A. B. 1977b. "Estimating rates from retrospective questions." In *Sociological Methodology*, ed. D. Heise. San Francisco: Jossey-Bass.

Sørensen, A. B. 1979. "A model and a metric for the process of intergenerational status attainment." *American Journal of Sociology* 85: 361–384.

Sørensen, A. B. 1983. "Processes of allocation to open and closed positions in social structure." *Zeitschrift für Soziologie* 12 (3): 203–224.

Sørensen, A. B. 1984. "Interpreting time dependency in career processes." In *Stochastic modeling of social processes*, ed. A. Diekmann, and P. Mitter. New York: Academic Press.

Sørensen, A. B. 1987. "Employment relations and employment processes." In *Unemployment: Theory, policy and structure*, ed. P. J. Pedersen, and R. Lund. New York: de Gruyter.

Sørensen, A. B., and S. Fuerst. 1978. "Black-white differences in the occurence of job shifts." *Sociology and Social Research* 62 (4): 537–557.

Sørensen, A. B., and N. B. Tuma. 1981. "Labor market structures and job mobility." In *Research in Social Stratification and Mobility*, ed. R. Robinson, vol. 1, 67–94. Greenwich, Conn.: JAI Press.

Sørensen, A., J. Allmendinger, and A. B. Sørensen. 1986. "Intergenerational mobility as a life course process." Paper presented at the meeting of the American Sociological Association, New York.

Sørensen, A., and A. B. Sørensen. 1986. "An event history analysis of the process of entry into first marriage." *Current Perspectives on Aging and the Life Cycle* 2: 53–71.

Spenner, K. I., L. B. Otto, and V. R. A. Call. 1982. *Career lines and careers.* Lexington, Mass.: Lexington Books.

Spilerman, S. 1977. "Careers, labor market structure and socioeconomic achievement." *American Journal of Sociology* 83: 551–593.

Spilerman, S. 1986. "Organizational rules and features of work careers." In *Research in Social Stratification and Mobility*, ed. R. Robinson, vol. 5, 41–102. Greenwich, Conn.: JAI Press.

Spilerman, S., and T. Petersen. 1988. "Organizational structure and the determinants of promotions." MS, Columbia University and Harvard University.

Staatliche Zentralverwaltung für Statistik. 1986. *Statistisches Jahrbuch der Deutschen Demokratischen Republik.* Berlin: Staatsverlag der DDR.

Statistisches Bundesamt. Various years, 1983–1986. *Gebiet und Bevölkerung.* Stuttgart: Kohlhammer.

Statistisches Bundesamt. Various years, 1962–1982. *Statistisches Jahrbuch der Bundesrepublik Deutschland.* Stuttgart: Kohlhammer.

Stewman, S., and S. L. Konda. 1983. "Careers and organizational labor markets: Demographic models of organizational behavior." *American Journal of Sociology* 88 (4): 637–685.

Stinchcombe, A. L. 1974. *Creating efficient industrial administrations.* New York: Academic Press.

Stinchcombe, A. L. 1979. "Social mobility in industrial labor markets." *Acta Sociologica* 22: 217–245.

Stinchcombe, A. L. 1983. *Economic sociology.* Orlando, Fla.: Academic Press.

Strohmeier, K. P. 1985. *Familienentwicklung in Nordrhein-Westfalen.* Schriftenreihe des Ministerpräsidenten des Landes Nordrhein-Westfalen, no. 47. Düsseldorf.

Struthers, C. A., and J. D. Kalbfleisch. 1986. "Misspecified proportional hazard models." *Biometrika* 73: 363–369.

Suval, E. M., and C. H. Hamilton. 1964. "Some new evidence on educational selectivity in migration to and from the South." *Social Forces* 43: 536–547.

Tilly, C. 1985. *Big structures, large processes, huge comparisons.* New York: Russell Sage.

Thurow, L. C. 1975. *Generating inequality: Mechanisms of distribution in the U.S. economy.* New York: Basic Books.

Trost, J. 1978. "A renewed social institution: Non-marital cohabitation." *Acta Sociologica* 21 (4): 303–315.

Trussell, J., and D. E. Bloom. 1983. "Estimating the co-variates of age at marriage and first birth." *Population Studies* 37 (3): 403–416.

Trussell, J., and T. Richards. 1985. "Correcting for unmeasured heterogeneity in hazard models using the Heckman-Singer procedure." In *Sociological Methodology,* ed. N. B. Tuma. San Francisco: Jossey-Bass.

Tuma, N. B. 1976. "Rewards, resources, and the rate of mobility: A nonstationary multivariate stochastic model." *American Sociological Review* 41 (2): 338–360.

Tuma, N. B. 1979. *Invoking RATE.* 2d ed. Menlo Park, Calif.: SRI International.

Tuma, N. B. 1985. "Effects of labor market structure on job-shift patterns." In *Longitudinal analysis of labor market data,* ed. J. J. Heckman and B. Singer, 327–363. Cambridge: Cambridge University Press.

Tuma, N. B., and M. T. Hannan. 1984. *Social dynamics: Models and methods.* Orlando, Fla.: Academic Press.

Tuma, N. B., and R. T. Michael 1986. "A comparison of statistical models for life course analysis with an application to first marriage." *Current Perspectives on Aging and the Life Cycle* 2: 107–146.

Tuma, N. B., and P. K. Robins. 1980. "A dynamic model of employment behavior: An application to the Seattle and Denver income maintenance experiments." *Econometrica* 48: 1031–1052.

U.S. Bureau of the Census. 1983. *June 1980 U.S. current population survey: Selected variables—females.* (Machine readable data file, 71,407 logical records.) First DAAPPP 1983 edition. Palo Alto, Calif.: Data Archive on Adolescent Pregnancy and Pregnancy Prevention, American Institutes for Research.

Vaupel, J. W., and A. I. Yashin. 1985. "The deviant dynamics of death in heterogeneous populations." In *Sociological Methodology,* ed. N. B. Tuma, 179–211. San Francisco: Jossey-Bass.

Viscusi, W. K. 1980. "Sex differences in worker quitting." *Review of Economics and Statistics* 62 (3): 388–398.

Waite, L. J., and S. E. Berryman. 1986. "Jobs stability among young women: A comparison of traditional and nontraditional occupations." *American Journal of Sociology* 92 (3): 568–595.

Waldman, D. M. 1985. "Computation in duration models with heterogeneity." *Journal of Econometrics* 28: 127–134.

Weber, M. 1964. *Wirtschaft und Gesellschaft.* Köln and Berlin: Kiepenheuer & Witsch.

Weber, M. 1968. *Economy and society.* New York: Bedminster Press.

Wegener, B. 1985. "Gibt es Sozialprestige?" *Zeitschrift für Soziologie* 14: 209–235.

Weiss, A. 1984. "Determinants of quit behavior." *Journal of Labor Economics* 2 (3): 371–387.

White, H. C. 1970. *Chains of opportunity.* Cambridge, Mass.: Harvard University Press.

White, H. 1980a. "Nonlinear regression on cross section data." *Econometrica* 48: 721–746.

White, H. 1980b. "A heteroskedasticity—Consistent covariance matrix estimator and a direct test for heteroskedaticity." *Econometrica* 48: 817–838.

White, H. 1981. "Consequences and detection of misspecified nonlinear regression models." *Journal of the American Statistical Association* 76: 419–433.

White, H. 1982. "Maximum likelihood estimation of misspecified models." *Econometrica* 50: 1–25.

White, H., and I. Domowitz. 1984. "Nonlinear regression with dependent observations." *Econometrica* 52: 143–161.

White, R. W., and R. P. Althauser. 1984. "Internal labor markets, promotions, and workers' skill: An indirect test of skill ILMs." *Social Science Research* 13 (4): 373–392.

Wiedenbeck, M. 1982. "Zum Problem repräsentativer Querschnitte von kleinen Teilgruppen der Bevölkerung am Beispiel des Projekts 'Lebensverläufe und Wohlfahrtsentwicklung.'" *ZUMA-Nachrichten* 10: 21–34.

Williamson, O. E. 1975. *Markets and hierarchies. Analysis and antitrust implications.* New York: Free Press.

Wise, D. A. 1975. "Personal attributes, job performance, and probability of promotion." *Econometrica* 43 (5–6): 913–931.

Wright, E. O. 1979. *Class structure and income determination.* New York: Academic Press.

Wu, L. L. 1986. "Age dependence in rates of first marriage: An exploratory analysis of women in the United States, 1880–1970." Ph.D. diss., Department of Sociology, Stanford University.

Zentralarchiv für Empirische Sozialforschung der Universität zu Köln und Zentrum für Umfragen, Methoden und Analysen (ZUMA), eds. 1987. *Allgemeine Bevölkerungsumfrage der Sozialwissenschaften.* Kumulierter Datensatz 1980–1984, Codebook ZA-Nr. 1335.

Index of Proper Names

Index

Advancement rules, 70

Age, 4, 7, 8, 55; and seniority, as factors in departure decisions, 16, 71, 74–75, 77, 80–86, 88, 90, 94–95; at marriage, 18, 170, 171–183, 190–199; differences, and job stability among Israeli men, 63–64, 66, 67; and educational selectivity in migration, 131, 135–142, 144; and unemployment duration, 234; and job shifts, 249

AIDS (Acquired Immune Deficiency Syndrome), 15

ALLBUS project, 178n5

Auslesewirkungen (selection), 130

Authority, 29, 62

Berlin, West, 117, 134, 145. *See also* Germany, West

Bias, 20, 102, 229, 253; problem of, in sampling theory, 18; selection, 57; restriction, in the analysis of births and marriages, 203–225; toward negative duration dependence, 244

Birth control, 165

Birth rates. *See* Fertility patterns

BMPD program. *See* Computer programs, BMPD program

British General Household Survey. *See* Data sets, British General Household Survey

Capitalism, 31, 34; in West Germany, 35, 39

Career(s): beginnings, of Israeli men, job shifts in, 15–16, 53–68; orderly and chaotic, Spilerman on, 54–55, 65; incentives, 69–95; ladders, 70, 74, 94, 104. *See also* Career mobility

Career mobility, 241–52; downward, 65,

66, 68; structural constraints on, 23–52; of men, intergenerational, 24

—upward, 24, 44; and job shifts, among Israeli men, 55, 56, 65, 67, 68; and downward and lateral job shifts, distinction between, 65; and education, 67

Childbearing, 55, 62, 117, 123. *See also* Family; Fertility patterns

Child care, 95, 123, 124, 125. *See also* Family; Fertility patterns

Childlessness, 6, 153, 158–160, 161, 166

Class, 4, 15, 24, 31, 47–48; Weber on, 26, 28–29; scheme, Goldthorpe's, 26–27, 29, 34; system, as hierarchical, 27–28; continuity, intergenerational, 33

—mobility, 23–52; and the closure thesis, 27–28, 38, 41; and the structural dominance thesis, 28–29, 34, 41; and the structural dominance thesis, 28–29, 34, 38, 49; and the life-course thesis, 29–31, 39, 41, 49; and the counter-mobility thesis, 30, 33; and the rationalization thesis, 31–32, 47–48, 49; and the reproduction thesis, 32–33, 44, 47; gender differences and, 41, 46, 49; entry estimates of logistic response models for, 44, 45

Coale-McNeil (1972) model. *See* Hazard rate models, Coale-McNeil model (1972)

Cohabitation, 6, 10, 18, 204–225

Competition, 70n1, 100–101

Computer programs, 242, 244, 247, 249, 251; PHGLM procedure in SAS program, 60; FORTRAN subroutines, 192; BMPD program, 242, 247; GLIM program, 242, 247, 249; SPSS program, 250

Constant rate models. *See* Hazard rate models, constant rate models

Contract theory, 98

Covariates, variation of, 9, 11–12, 16, 167,